Criminal Justice
Recent Scholarship

Edited by
Marilyn McShane and Frank P. Williams III

A Series from LFB Scholarly

Capital Punishment and Latino Offenders
Racial and Ethnic Differences in Death Sentences

Martin G. Urbina

LFB Scholarly Publishing LLC
New York 2003

Library of Congress Cataloging-in-Publication Data

Urbina, Martin G. (Martin Guevara), 1972-
  Capital punishment and Latino offenders : racial and ethnic differences in death sentences / Martin G. Urbina.
      p. cm. -- (Criminal justice)
Includes bibliographical references and index.
  ISBN 1-931202-60-5 (alk. paper)
  1. Discrimination in capital punishment--United States. 2. Discrimination in criminal justice administration--United States. 3. United States--Race relations. 4. Hispanic American criminals--Civil rights. I. Title. II. Criminal justice (LFB Scholarly Publishing LLC)
  HV8699.U5U73 2003
  364.66'089'68073--dc22

2003016255

ISBN 1-931202-60-5

Printed on acid-free 250-year-life paper.

Manufactured in the United States of America.

DEDICATION

To:

the Forgotten Voices

the Neglected Voices

the Stranger

the Outsider

the Other

TABLE OF CONTENTS

LIST OF TABLES

PREFACE

A review of the existing literature on death sentence outcomes (i.e., executions, commutations) shows evidence of differential treatment against minority defendants (e.g., African Americans). However, in large part because data on Latinos is either non-existent or extremely difficult to locate, there is not much on the Latino experience. Most prior studies have followed an African American/Caucasian and/or commutation/execution approach. Latino defendants have either been excluded or treated as a monolithic group. Thus, little is known about death sentence outcomes for Latinos, whose experiences differ from those of African Americans and Caucasians. Additionally, little is known about the treatment of the various ethnic groups (e.g., Cubans, Mexicans) that constitute the largest minority group in the United States, Latinos. Additionally, since the focus has been on executions and/or commutations, there is not much about other possible death sentence outcomes: sentence declared unconstitutional, sentence overturned, and conviction overturned.

Therefore, the main objective of this study is to go beyond traditional approaches and to address these shortcomings empirically by analyzing death sentence outcomes data for California, Florida, and Texas between 1975 and 1995. In addition, this study will explore the effects of legal variables in death sentencing as well as race and ethnicity.

In an attempt to better understand why, how, and when racial and ethnic minorities are more likely to experience discrimination, a review of historical relationships between African Americans, Caucasians, Cubans, and Mexicans is provided. To enhance our understanding of race and ethnic differences in death sentencing, a theoretical typology will be proposed: a four-threat theory of death sentence outcomes.

Logistic regression, controlling for time under the sentence of death, prior felony convictions, age at the time of the offense, marital status, and education, shows that discrimination in death sentence outcomes is not a phenomenon of the past. The findings reveal that race/ethnicity and several legal variables still play a role in the legal decision-making process. Focusing primarily (but not exclusively) on race and ethnicity, the results are discussed in relation to the four-threat theory, which attempts to explain race and ethnic difference in death sentence outcomes.

Lastly, parts of Chapter 6 appear in *Social Justice* (v. 31, no. 95), and parts of Chapter 7 appear in *Journal of Ethnicity in Criminal Justice* (v. 1, no. 1).

ACKNOWLEDGMENTS

It would have been impossible to write this book without the advice and support of several dedicated individuals. In particular, my sincere gratitude goes out to Drs. Susan Carlson, Ashlyn Kuersten, Charles Crawford, and Douglas Davidson. This book would never have become a reality without their perseverance and sage advice during the early stages of the project.

My deep appreciation and many thanks go to Professors Marilyn McShane and Frank P. Williams III, series editors, for their valuable recommendations and support. I'd like to say a special thanks to Leo Balk, my publisher, for being so helpful, understanding, and patient throughout the entire process.

Lastly, I'd like to recognize the heroic efforts of all the individuals who contributed to this book in one way or another. I'm well aware that few people are privileged to work with individuals with such talent, vision, and good spirits.

Martin G. Urbina

CHAPTER 1

Introduction

Traditionally, capital punishment researchers have emphasized the unequal death sentencing of African American and Caucasian defendants (as well as deterrence, capital punishment states and crime rates v. non-capital punishment states, and capital punishment and crime rates over time, especially during the pre-*Furman*/post-*Furman* period). Data on Latinos (and Latinas) is either non-existent or extremely difficult to locate. Additionally, some of the existing information on Latinos contains various reliability and validity shortcomings (see Aguirre and Baker, 1988).[1] As a result, only a few studies have examined unequal death sentence outcomes (executions and/or commutations) by race and ethnicity. In particular, it is difficult to find studies that have examined: (1) a capital sentence of the individual when declared unconstitutional by State or U.S. Supreme Court, (2) a conviction affirmed, but sentence overturned by appellate court, or (3) a conviction and sentence overturned by appellate court, as three possible death sentence outcomes by race and ethnicity. Similarly, it is difficult to locate studies that have analyzed the experiences of inmates who still remain under the sentence of death, which by default means life imprisonment. Thus, since no action has taken place, this in and of itself constitutes a possible death sentence outcome.

There are two major limitations to these earlier approaches. First, researchers have been forced to either omit people of Spanish heritage, or treat them as a monolithic group, usually under the broad popular labels of "Hispanic," or "Latino." Consequently, important issues have received little attention (see Perea, 1997). For instance, people of Spanish heritage not only constitute the largest minority group in the United States, but they are also a very diverse population, whose experiences in the United States, and by extension, treatment by the criminal justice system, differs from those of African Americans.

Equally important, the fact that the experiences of the various ethnic groups (e.g., Mexicans (or Mejicanos), Mexican Americans, Cubans) that make up the Latino population vary widely has also received little attention. Furthermore, how the various ethnic groups view themselves and each other, how they are perceived by the Caucasian majority, and how they are treated in the criminal justice system varies in numerous fundamental ways.

Second, exclusive focus on executions and/or commutations yields a limited picture of death sentence outcomes. For instance, the conditions under which death sentence outcomes take place vary widely. While racial and ethnic differences might be relatively small at any particular stage of the decision-making process, cumulative effects of these differences on the overall outcomes could be significant.

Therefore, the primary goals of the current study are to: (1) analyze prior death sentence and death sentence outcomes studies that include race and/or ethnicity as a variable; (2) include a Latino category in the analysis; (3) disaggregate the Latino category; (4) provide a discussion of the Latinos who were executed during the time under study; (5) provide an examination of the history of U.S. race and ethnic (e.g., African Americans, Caucasians, Cubans, Mexicans) relations; (6) analyze and provide a sound theoretical framework that will account for the differential treatment of the various racial and ethnic groups who are sentenced to death; (7) develop a new typology of death sentences and death sentence outcomes; (8) analyze the legal decision-making process across multiple decision points (executions, commutations, and sentence and/or conviction overturns by the courts as well as those who still remain under the sentence of death); and (9) provide a discussion of death sentence outcomes.

The results of this study should further our knowledge of race and ethnic differences in death sentence outcomes of not only African Americans and Caucasians, but also of the Latino population and the various ethnic groups that make up the Latino category. Analyzing the latest "punitive trend" is warranted, because it reveals which convictions and/or sentences were overturned by an appellate court, which capital sentences were declared unconstitutional by a state or the U. S. Supreme Court, who was granted a commutation, who was executed, who still remained under the sentence of death as of 1995, and the frequency of these events.

In addition, by focusing on what is often considered the most severe form of criminal punishment, critical questions, especially concerning the magnitude of race and ethnic differences in death sentence outcomes, may be raised about the various issues (e.g., offender characteristics, legal variables) surrounding the capital punishment debate. These are important issues in terms of their economic and political implications, especially after entering the 21st with individuals in office arguing that the justice system is being soft on violent crime and that we need to become even more punitive.

In order to determine whether certain disparities exist in death sentence outcomes, the proposed study will include both tabular analysis and logistic regression analysis (selected based on the nature of the data and the level of measurement of the variables), to determine the influence/significance of factors such as the state where the sentencing occurred, sex, race, ethnicity, education, marital status, age when the capital offense was committed, and prior felony conviction(s) in death sentence outcomes.

This approach should clarify whether African Americans and Latinos have received more punitive sentence outcomes. In other words, I expect race and ethnicity to have independent effects on unequal death sentence outcomes after controlling for legal and sociodemographic factors. Given the history of race and ethnic relations and the complex environment in which the legal decision-making process operates, I predict that African Americans and Latinos, especially people of Mexican extraction/descent, have received more severe death sentence outcomes.

Before beginning our journey, it should be emphasized that understanding death sentence outcomes and their implications requires an appreciation of historical events, including the distribution of "justice," and the relationships between Caucasians (Caucasian, "white," Anglo- or Euro-American–categorical designations used interchangeably herein to signify the non-minority, dominant race in North America) and non-Caucasians (e.g., African Americans and people of Spanish heritage). While conflict in relations between Caucasians and African Americans has been traced by a number of scholars, documentation regarding the relationships between people of Spanish heritage (Hispanic or Latino–categorical designations used interchangeably herein to signify the minority ethnic group in the United States who is neither African American nor Caucasian) and Anglo-Americans is minimal and difficult to locate, especially valid and reliable information.

It is also important to point out that since people of Spanish heritage can be of any "color" (including "white") and not necessarily speak Spanish the terms of primary use will be Caucasian or Euro-American when referring to the non-minority population from this point forward. Similarly, since people of Spanish heritage may also be black, the term of primary use will be African American when referring to the black population who is not of Spanish heritage or Caucasian from this point forward. Also, since the term Latino carries less political baggage than the term Hispanic, the term of primary use from this point forward will be Latino/a when referring to people of Spanish heritage who are not Caucasians or African Americans.

Furthermore, the terms Mejicano/a, Mexican, Mexican American, Chicano/a, Tejano/a, and Californio will be used interchangeably when referring to a person who has roots in the Republic of Mexico, independent of his/her status (e.g., U.S. citizen, permanent resident, undocumented worker) in the United States. Also, the terms Cuban and Cuban-American will be used interchangeably when referring to a person who has roots in Cuba, independent of his/her immigration status.[2]

With this in mind, let us explore a few additional critical issues, while keeping death sentences and death sentence outcomes in mind. First, as it was mentioned above, in part due to data limitations, the few studies that have explored the historical relationship between Latinos and Euro-Americans have followed a dichotomous approach. The relationships have been treated as Caucasians versus Latinos giving little attention, if any, to the various ethnic groups that constitute the largest and one of the fastest-growing minority groups in the United States. Also, keep in mind that most studies have not equated the fact that the relationships between

Latino groups and Euro-Americans have not only varied widely, but the experiences of these various ethnic minority groups in the United States have been at times polar opposites.

While some scholars (e.g., Wilbanks, 1987) argue that race and ethnicity does not matter, history reveals a very different picture. Far from being color-blind, the United States has been extremely "color-conscious." As a consequence, the administration of justice has been informal, irregular, and subjective. As some observers have pointed out, historically, the justice system has demonstrated a clear tendency to take more punitive actions against African American offenders than Euro-American offenders (see Gibbons, 1994; Johnson and Secret, 1990; Pollock-Byrne, 1989). For Latinos, racially biased actions have also been witnessed at most, if not all, stages of the criminal justice system (see Aguirre and Baker, 2000). As Shorris (1992:157) observes, "in every Latino neighborhood in the United States, with the possible exception of some parts of Miami, police treat all children, especially adolescent boys, as if they are criminals."

In thinking about death sentences and death sentence outcomes, consider the following figures. In *Malign Neglect* (1995), Michael Tonry states that the prison population nearly tripled during the 1980s, and by 1990 a quarter of young African American males were in jail or prison, on probation or parole. The chance that an African American male was in jail or prison was seven times that of a Caucasian male. A 1990 analysis revealed that nationally 23% of African American males aged 20-29 were under the control of the criminal justice system (Tonry, 1995). In California, 33% of African American males aged 20 to 29 were under the control of the criminal justice system in 1990 (Tonry, 1995). And, as Levin (1999) points out, as a result of the so-called "War Against Drugs," almost 30% of all young African American men are presently under the control of the criminal justice system.

Although African Americans make up approximately 12.3% of the U.S. population, they comprise nearly half of the population of U.S. prisons and jails, and, in recent years, more than half of those sent to jails or prisons. The situation for Latinos does not look much better; in fact, it is getting worse. For instance, from 1980 to 1993 the percentage of Latinos in prison rose from 7.7 to 14.3%–not including Latinos incarcerated in facilities under the jurisdiction of the Immigration and Naturalization Service (INS). During this same period, the number of inmates tripled from 163 to 529 per 100,000 Latino residents. In contrast, Latinos make up approximately 12.5% of the U.S. population, and the U.S. Census has predicted that by the year 2020, the Latino prison population ages 18 to 34 will grow to 25.6% (see Garcia, 1994; Nixon, 1996).

Today's prison population tends to be young African American and Latino males who are uneducated, without jobs, or, at best, were marginally employed in low-paying jobs (Irwin and Austin, 1997). According to Irwin and Austin (1997:4), almost one in three (32.2%) African American men in the age group 20-29 is either in prison, jail, on probation, or parole on any given day. More than one in ten Latino men (12.3%) in the same age group is either in prison, jail, on probation, or parole on any given day. For Caucasian men, the ratio is considerably lower: one in 15 (6.7%). Sixty years ago, less than one-fourth of prison admissions were non-Caucasian. Today, nearly three-fourths are non-Caucasian. African Americans and Latinos constitute almost 90% of all offenders sentenced to state prison for drug possession. And finally, African American women have experienced the greatest incarceration increase, rising by 78% from 1989 through 1994.

An analysis of national trends on prison admissions reveals similar patterns. The majority of new admissions were young males (18-29), disproportionately African American (54%), and lacking a formal high school education (62%) (Irwin and Austin, 1997:22). And contrary to popular belief, the vast majority (73%) of these inmates were admitted for either nonviolent crimes or no crimes at all (Irwin and Austin, 1997:22). Most of the crimes for which offenders were sent to correctional institutions (52.6%) fall into the "petty category," and less than five percent of the individuals being sent to prison committed a crime that could be classified as very serious (Irwin and Austin, 1997:32).

The rising levels of African American (and Latino) incarceration did not just happen. According to Tonry (1995:4), "they were the foreseeable effects of deliberate policies spearheaded by the Reagan and Bush administrations and implemented by many states." Unfortunately, "crime controllers made no effort to minimize foreseeable racial disparities" (Tonry, 1995:5).

To obtain an in-depth perspective of the prejudice and discrimination that is deeply rooted in American society, as well as the differential treatment of various racial and ethnic U.S. minority groups by the criminal justice system and the general public, one needs to carefully examine historical facts. One needs to keep in mind the simultaneous interaction of both structure and ideological factors that ultimately shape and re-shape the experiences of minority groups (e.g., African Americans, Cubans, Mexicans) in the United States.

Chapter II explores a number of theoretical perspectives on the subject of racial and ethnic disparity in death sentence outcomes in the United States, and identifies a number of general hypotheses for the current study. Chapter III analyzes prior death sentence and death sentence outcomes studies, and explains the limitations of prior research as well as various remedies to deal with them. Chapter IV provides an historical analysis of race and ethnic relations in the United States, and sets forth specific hypotheses for the current study. Chapter V explains the methods for the current study in addition to looking into why the various possible death sentence outcomes constitute a complex and confusing phenomena. Chapter VI details the characteristics of executed Latinos between 1975 and 1995 in the United States. Chapter VII describes the results of the logistic regression analysis. Lastly, Chapter VIII discusses the conclusions of the current study and their implications.

CHAPTER 2

Theories of Race and Ethnic Differences in Punishment and Sentencing

While theorists have explored and provided a number of explanations on the subject of racial disparity in punishment, death sentences, and death sentence outcomes, they continue to disagree over the sources of disparities. This chapter provides a brief overview of five criminological/sociological theories that attempt to explain racial disparities. It include a detailed discussion of four additional perspectives, which will serve as the foundation to the development of a new approach to the explanation of death sentence outcomes in the United States. Such theories will also be part of the foundation utilized in the derivation of hypotheses for the current study.

NORMATIVE THEORIES

At the heart of normative theories is the presumption that penalties are applied by the criminal justice system primarily in relation to the seriousness of crimes committed, with the most serious legal sanctions imposed only on the most serious and violent offenders, especially recidivists. It is presumed that the administration of criminal justice treats most, if not all, offenders equally, without regard to their social standing or other personal characteristics (Blumstein, 1982; Bridges and

Crutchfield, 1988; Durkheim, 1964; 1973; Hindelang, 1978; Langan, 1985).

Normative theories attribute the variation in disparity to differences in criminal involvement between minorities, especially African Americans and Euro-Americans. Legal sanctions are imposed only in reaction to criminality and, thus, high minority imprisonment rates are attributed to disproportionate minority involvement in criminality, especially violent crimes and drugs.

Based on normative theories, racial differences in imprisonment take place mostly because minority males, especially African American, violate the law more often and commit a higher rate of serious crimes than members of other racial groups (Blumstein, 1982; Hindelang, 1978; Langan, 1985). The racial distribution of individuals imprisoned is approximately equal to the racial distribution of individuals arrested, because no significant racial differences exist in the treatment of the accused following arrest; that is, at prosecution, conviction, sentencing, or in actual time served in a correctional facility.[3]

STRATIFICATION THEORIES

Stratification theories explain legal sanctions as an institutional mechanism utilized by dominant social classes to control and regulate populations that threaten political and/or economic hegemony (Chambliss and Seidman, 1971; Christianson, 1980a; 1980b; Lizotte, 1978; Quinney, 1970a; 1974; Peterson and Hagan, 1984). These theories (Marxist/conflict) view racial disparity in imprisonment, and other differences in the disposition of criminal sentencing, in terms of racial biases in the legal process' treatment of Euro-American and minority defendants. While minorities may commit a large share of serious and violent acts, the system often complicates the problem by imposing more severe sanctions on minorities than on Caucasians committing similar acts (Chambliss and Seidman, 1971). Minorities are more often detected and detained, more likely to have a pretrial, more likely to plea guilty, and more likely to receive longer sentences upon conviction (Christianson, 1980a; 1980b; Lizotte, 1978; Quinney, 1970a; 1974).[4] Chambliss and Seidman (1971:468) observe that

The judge's role in Anglo-American law in sentencing allows for at least as great discretion as do the roles of the prosecutor and the police. . . . The demands for efficient and orderly performance of the court take priority and create a propensity on the part of the courts to dispose of cases in ways that ensure the continued smooth functioning of the system. The consequence of such a policy is to systematically select certain categories of offenders (especially the poor and the black) for the most severe treatment.

In addition, Richard Quinney (1970a:142) notes that

Obviously judicial decisions are not made uniformly. Decisions are made according to a host of extra-legal factors, including the age of the offender, his race, and social class. Perhaps the most obvious example of judicial discretion occurs in the handling of cases of persons from minority groups. Negroes in comparison to whites, are convicted with lesser evidence and sentenced to more severe punishment.

This suggests that discretion in sentencing and parole processes may penalize minority groups. In jurisdictions and areas of the country where legal processing is individualized and sanctions are discretionary, officials often set correctional terms according to the offender's background and living conditions. Individuals with ties to the local community and promises of future employment usually serve shorter jail and prison terms. Minorities, however, are often incapable of meeting such conditions (including access to jobs) of release and, therefore, serve longer terms than Euro-Americans and are less likely to obtain early release (Carroll and Mondrick, 1976; Petersilia, 1983; Pruitt and Wilson, 1983; Swigert and Farrel, 1977). A related question is whether the sentence is proportionate in its severity to the gravity of the offense.

DESSERT THEORIES

What "blueprint" should officials (e.g., governors, judges, prosecutors, parole boards, juries) rely on when deciding how much more or how much less punishment a given offender should receive? Based on the principle of proportionality ("just desserts" or "commensurate desserts"), penalties need to be proportionate in their severity to the gravity of offenses (von Hirsch, 1981; 1993).[5] In other words, penalties should be graded in severity to reflect the gravity of the charges involved. In von Hirsch's (1993:21) words, "punishment conveys censure or blame, and hence should be ordered according to the degree of blameworthiness of the conduct."

Ordinal proportionality asks that equally serious behavior be sanctioned with approximately equal severity, and that unequally serious criminal conduct be penalized as to reflect the differences in gravity involved.[6] Thus, a sentencing legal system can, to a greater or lesser degree, sanction comparably blameworthy behavior similarly, and if carefully worked out, can achieve proportionality to a reasonable degree (von Hirsch, 1993).

The criteria for dessert, claims von Hirsch (1993), rule out the horrifying and unjustifiable forms of penal utilitarianism (e.g., selective incapacitation). Dessert rejects a utilitarian approach, which calls for imposition of substantial lengthy sentences for "high risk" offenders, especially those deemed likely to recidivate, and "utilize indicia of risk which have little bearing on crime gravity–such as prior arrests, drug abuse, lack of schooling, and unemployment" (von Hirsch, 1993:95). Hence, a utilitarian perspective that calls for large disparity in the severity of sentences of offenders deemed dangerous, as compared with other offenders convicted of similar criminal acts, should not be considered in a proportionalist approach of sentencing (von Hirsch, 1993).

Under this approach, policy makers and implementors must support judgements that one kind of behavior is more serious than another.[7] The focus is on equal treatment of offenders convicted of equally reprehensible behavior, and thus, it is fair and just or "at least as little unjust as possible" (von Hirsch, 1993:103). According to von Hirsch (1981:250), "in the American criminal justice system . . . an offender's record of previous convictions considerably influences the severity with which he is punished. The first-time offender can expect more lenient punishment than a recidivist. But, why so?"[8] One theory is predictive and another is deterrence or recidivism.[9] However, von Hirsch's (1981) commensurate-desserts approach takes into consideration only the seriousness of the offender's prior criminal acts.[10] He argues that legal sanctions for first offenses should be kept on the low end, reflecting doubts about the offender's culpability, and more severe sentences should be reserved mainly for offenders who have offended and been formally punished before.

The commensurate-desserts approach, then, while taking prior crimes into account, would exclude irrelevant factors (e.g., lack of a fixed home, a steady job, or a high school diploma). It suggests that race and ethnicity are irrelevant factors, and thus there are no racial or ethnic disparities in sentencing. And if there are, this approach will eliminate differential treatment. These "factors would be ruled out: we would look only to the number and seriousness of prior convictions" (von Hirsch, 1981:252). This allows one to call for the maintenance of a balance between the seriousness of the behavior and the severity of the prison/jail sentence.

Thus, the proportionalist (or balance) principle looks retrospectively to the seriousness of the offender's prior record (von Hirsch, 1981). The seriousness of the crimes embraces the defendant's prior criminal record (both the number of convictions and the seriousness of the acts). If the offender has a prior record at the time of the conviction, the number and gravity of prior crimes should be taken into account in assessing seriousness (von Hirsch, 1981). The absence of a prior criminal record may be mitigating to an extent, but the current charge should bear primary weight in determining the punishment (von Hirsch, 1993).

In short, dessert theorists assert that their propositions might not remedy social disadvantage, but at least they do not disadvantage offenders who are worse off. The variables determining crime-seriousness (and hence the severity of the sanction) are the conduct's harm and the offender's degree of criminal intent. Social factors such as race, ethnicity, employment, and education generally carry little weight.

MARXIST THEORIES

According to Marxist theories, the application of criminal punishment and sentencing is closely related to economic stratification. These perspectives suggest that powerful economic elites use legal institutions (i.e., the criminal justice system) to control and manage society's "problem" populations, particularly the unemployed and individuals living in poverty. In communities characterized by economic stratification and in heavy urban concentrations of poverty, powerful elites are likely to utilize the criminal justice system as a weapon to maneuver and enforce laws that preserve the economic order (Chambliss and Seidman, 1971; Humphries and Greenberg, 1981; Jacobs, 1978; Rusche and Kirchheimer, 1968; Spitzer, 1975; Wallace and Humphries, 1981).

This theory implies that racial differences in sentencing and imprisonment would be expected in those areas of the country and historical periods where levels of African American/Caucasian economic inequality among the indigent and African American concentrations in the urban areas are striking. African Americans will be incarcerated at disproportionately higher rates than Euro-Americans in those areas where African Americans are more heavily represented among the poor and more heavily concentrated in urban areas than Euro-Americans (Bridges and Crutchfield, 1988). Given this, these theories are of utility in deriving hypotheses for the current study, which includes three states with a high concentration of minorities.

CONFLICT THEORIES

Conflict theories focus on the degree of minority threat to the political hegemony of Euro-Americans as a major cause of racial discrimination in the legal process. Minority threat is likely to vary in relation to the size of the minority community, with larger minority groups substantially more threatening to Caucasians than small minority groups (Barth and Noel, 1972; Blalock, 1967; Brown and Fuguitt, 1972; Frisbie and Neidert, 1976). Discrimination occurs mostly in areas where minority groups are largest and thus, present the most serious political threat. If sentencing and imprisonment disparities are a reflection of racial discrimination, this theory suggests that sentencing and imprisonment disparities will be highest in those areas where minority size is greatest.

To the extent that perceptions significantly and substantially shape the filtering of cases under "threatening" conditions, minorities may be harshly penalized. Thus, we will now examine four critical-oriented theories that will be used to explain capital punishment sentencing outcomes in the United States. Let us turn to the first explanation of disparities in sentencing outcomes in general, and then proceed to death sentence outcomes, particularly those directed toward minorities: "power-threat" hypothesis first introduced by Hubert Blalock (1967). Because other theorists discussed herein borrow from Blalock's work, the power-threat theory will be examined here in considerable detail.

POWER THREAT

Blalock (1967) identifies two different psychological mechanisms linking the size of the minority population and discriminatory behavior: (1) fear of competition and (2) a power threat based on the fear that the minority might gain political dominance.[11] Specifically, according to Blalock (1967:28),

> (1) exposure to large numbers of minority members is a forcing variable that threatens individual members of the dominant group; (2) these threats combine with personality variables to produce motivation to discriminate; (3) similarly motivated individuals interact with each other in such a way as to bring about concerted action leading to actual discrimination; and (4) the discriminatory behavior, when aggregated in some way, leads to lowered (aggregated) minority levels.

Blalock (1967) hypothesized that fear of competition (economic) should lead one to expect a nonlinear relationship with a decreasing slope, whereas fear of power threat (political) should produce a nonlinear relationship with an increasing slope.[12] In other words, economic and political threats posed by minorities lead to a positive relationship with a decreasing slope associated with economic threats and an increasing slope associated with political threats. And, as the percentage of minorities approximates 50%, minorities assume more positions of political power as well as positions in the criminal justice system–e.g., police department. Thus, minorities are no longer viewed as a significant threat by authorities.

Where race is defined as a continuous variable rather than a dichotomy, percentage of non-Caucasians may be only weakly related to the power-threat factor. For motivated behavior to occur, all three variables must take on values greater than zero. Asymmetrical relationships in the form of: "the greater the X, the greater the Y," which indicate that an increase in X will produce an increase in Y, even though the converse will not necessarily hold, will be formed.

According to Blalock (1967:110), "power is the actual overcoming of resistance in a standard period of time." He further argues that power is a multiplicative function of two very general types of variables, total resources (actual resources of power, or those properties of the individual or group that provide the power potential or ability to exercise power) and the degree to which these resources are mobilized in the services of those individuals or groups exercising the power, actually exercised or kinetic, rather than potential. The power-threat would be of greater significance during political instability, or in instances where the minority group could be expected to form a coalition with "outside enemies." The "threat," if any, claims Blalock (1967), may be conceived as being primarily to one's own status rather than to Euro-Americans as a group. Notice that both of his two major types of power variables–resources and mobilization–depend on motivation.

In short, Blalock (1967) maintains that there are three dimensions of Caucasian privilege that are jeopardized by the threatening minority group(s): economic, political, and status. While he chooses not to deal with status, he claims that political threats and economic competition should produce somewhat different relationships between non-Caucasian concentration and discriminatory efforts by the majority group.[13]

The core argument is that as each group struggles toward dominance or to maintain a favored position, its success depends on its level of resources (including size), its degree of cohesiveness, and the extent to which competing groups are fractionated. Resources (financial and political) are invoked as needed to prevent competing groups from moving forward, significantly. The majority's resistance to minority efforts to improve its position should increase exponentially with noticeable increases in minority size or resources until the minority group reaches numerical majority or has accumulated sufficient resources to assure its dominance. At that point, such protection efforts will decrease. (Please see the Appendix for more specific theoretical propositions.)

Blalock's (1967) power threat hypothesis provides a valuable direction in our search for the underlying causes of prejudice and discrimination in sentencing and sentencing outcomes by the powerful elite majority. It suggests that, as control agents, authorities are responsible for the problem populations, especially minorities, whose presence in society is often viewed as politically threatening. Following Blalock (1967), it is reasonable to argue that control agents are motivated to charge, convict and give longer and/or more severe sanctions to those individuals who pose a political threat, especially as the minority group gets larger. From Blalock's (1967) notion that the power-threat is of greater significance during political instability, and that it may be conceived as being primarily to one's own status, I would argue that decision-makers (e.g., legislators, governors, judges, prosecutors, and parole boards) are indeed individuals who perceive a threat to their own status not only during political instability but also during "punitive trends." They do not want to be viewed as being "soft" on crime, especially during election years, whether they are hoping to get into office, retain the post, or aspiring for higher office. And since race and ethnicity are not continuous categories in the United States, minorities, who more likely than not, have few, if any, resources, are likely to receive longer and/or harsher sentences.

SOCIAL THREAT

Liska (1992) focuses primarily on the threat hypothesis of the conflict theory of social control. He asserts that deviance and crime control are responses to social threats, such as criminal acts and riots, which are especially threatening to the interests of authorities, and individuals who are perceived as dangerous and out of control (e.g., minorities and the unemployed). Focusing on social control from the conflict perspective, particularly on the threat hypothesis of the perspective, Liska (1992) categorizes social control patterns along a scale ranging from the stick (deadly force) to the carrot (beneficent controls), and categorizes the macro causes of threat into actions (crimes and riots) and people (the proportion of minorities and the unemployed, and the degree of racial segregation and income inequality). He emphasizes the central role of "threat" in conceptually organizing and integrating the above macro-conditions and in linking them to various types of formal social control. According to Liska (1992), the perception of threat by authorities, though, may not necessarily lead to all forms of social control. Some forms of control may require substantial economic resources. And, "some types of threat may lead to specific forms of control" (Liska, 1992:29).

Liska (1992) further argues that there is a direct causal relationship between forms of social control where a decrease in one form directly increases another. To a high degree, this occurs through the allocation of infinite resources. Thus, resources expended on one form are not available for others. There is also an indirect causal relationship between forms of social control through social threat. Specifically, as one form of social control expands, it increases social threat, which increases other forms of social control. Forms of social control are also correlated, due to common causes. Forms of social control are caused by both unique and common factors. Unique effects occur when causes of one form are unrelated to the causes of others, so that alterations in the causes of one form yield variation in that form that is unrelated to variation in the other forms. Common causes that positively or negatively affect forms of social control yield a positive covariation between them, and common causes that positively affect one and negatively affect the other yield a negative covariation between them. The same is true of correlated causes. If they positively affect each form of social control and are themselves negatively correlated, then the two forms will negatively covary.

Liska (1992) also hypothesizes that the relative size of the minority community must reach a certain proportion of the population before it is perceived as threatening by the Caucasian majority. From that point, further increases generate increases in perceived threat, linearly or even at an increasing rate, until some upper level is reached, at which point further increases in the size of the minority group(s) yield no increase in the perceived threat of the majority.[14]

Lastly, social threat affects the expansion more than the concentration of social control. Specifically, "increases in social threat generate increases in social control but decreases in social threat do not generate decreases in social control, particularly in organizational forms of control" (Liska, 1992:187). Thus, once formal social controls are established, internal processes of organizations maintain them. They assume a life of their own; in their struggle to survive, they may create or manufacture additional threats.

Following the social threat hypothesis, I would argue that under threatening conditions (e.g., riots, criminality), control agents will charge, convict and implement longer and/or harsher sentences to threatening individuals in order to protect the majority's interest as well as their own. And, since minorities, who are for the most part poor and unemployed, are constantly being perceived as threatening (i.e., rioters and criminals), they receive harsher and longer sentences. Furthermore, based on the social threat hypothesis, I would argue that in places where there is a high concentration of unemployed poor minorities, the perceptions of threat by authorities will result in longer and/or harsher sentences for minorities if the jurisdiction has the necessary resources.

Notice that there are three critical caveats. First, some types of threat (e.g., drugs or homicide) may lead to specific forms of control (long mandatory sentences), and some forms of control may require economic resources, the best illustration being the death penalty. Second, as one form of control expands, it increases social threat, which increases other forms of social control. For instance, it is probable that the expansion of long mandatory sentences for drug offenses and homicide has increased the social threat, which in turn has increased application of the death penalty. Third, increases in social threat generate increases in social control, but decreases in social threat do not generate decreases in social control. Thus, decreases in social threat (as a result of decreases in drug offenses or homicides) will not necessarily generate a decrease in long mandatory sentences for drug offenses, nor will executions decline.

RACIAL THREAT

Crawford, Chiricos, and Kleck (1998) respond to the argument that minorities are frequently perceived as posing a criminal threat (Turk, 1969) by claiming that punitive trends have not been driven by criminality but instead by a racial threat.[15] Crawford et al. (1998) utilize the term racial threat to characterize what they call an evolving race- and crime-specific dimension of Blalock's (1967) "power threat" and Liska's (1992) "social threat" perspectives. To them, racial threat is crime specific and implies that the magnitude of race effects (situations in which African American defendants are significantly more likely to be sentenced to prison) vary from jurisdiction to jurisdiction. Additionally, following Sampson and Laub (1993), they claim that racial threat is understood as threatening to mainstream U.S. as well as political elites.

According to these authors, a racial threat interpretation of sentencing outcomes indicates that race effects, what remains after other variables are controlled, are more often significant in sentencing contexts that are low in terms of percent of African Americans, racial income inequality, drug arrest rates, and violent crime rates. They claim that when race effects are analyzed contextually, the results raise several critical questions. For instance, "is the pattern of findings consistent with a racial threat hypothesis" (Crawford et al., 1998:503)?

According to Crawford et al. (1998), originally cast in political and economic terms, the threat posed by minorities, especially African Americans, has been gradually recast in terms of crime. For instance, former FBI Director, J. (John) Edgar Hoover's, "paranoia had a special racist flavor, and he warned bureau agents to guard against the rise of a 'black messiah'" (Walker, 1980:239). In the 1980s such threat principally involved urban underclass African Americans and drugs, but in the 1990s it has grown to include the threat of violence (Sampson and Laub, 1993). Though an enduring element of U.S. culture (Hawkins, 1995), the caricature of the African American crime threat has achieved an especially media-saturated salience (Barak, 1994; Drummond, 1990) during the years of the imprisonment binge. Not surprisingly, media frenzies have portrayed both crack cocaine and juvenile violence as "ghetto pathologies" spreading to previously safe locations (Chiricos, 1996). According to

Anderson (1995a), the African American civil rights protester has been replaced by the young African American male criminal in the whirlpool of racial threat. The objective, then, is to assess whether race effects are amplified in racially "threatening contexts" (Crawford et al., 1998).

Based on the racial threat hypothesis, I would argue that the racial threat posed by race has a substantial and significant influence on sentencing decisions independent   of other factors (e.g., criminality, including drug arrest rates and violent crime rates). As the threat to Caucasians, especially political elites, increases, the relevance of race and racial threat in the social control equation increases and, thus, minorities are more likely to receive longer and more severe sentences.

Race effects might be more significant in the sentencing context, that are low in terms of minority percentages, but if the minority group has or is on the rise toward obtaining political clout, it could be perceived as a potential direct and/or indirect threat to the majority, which theoretically could lead to longer and/or harsher sentences. The minorities might not be so numerous as to constitute a major racial threat, but if the group is on the rise toward obtaining political power and/or if it is considered a social ill, it could very likely be perceived as constituting a potential racial threat. Also, race effects might be more significant in sentencing contexts that are low in terms of racial income inequality, but minority group(s), especially those being sentenced, have few, if any, resources. Lastly, while race effects vary from jurisdiction to jurisdiction, the outcome will be highly influenced by a number of perceived threats.

ECONOMIC THREAT

Just as minorities compete for power (politically), they compete for jobs (economically). In trying to understand this phenomenon, some theorists have developed a number of theoretical explanations. For instance, the conflict perspective assumes enlightened self-interests, especially on the part of economic elites, create a hostile environment. It assumes an uneven distribution of self-interests in crime control and an uneven distribution of power to implement self-interests into crime control legislation. The conflict theory asserts that the greater the number of deviant acts and people threatening the interests of the powerful, the greater the level of deviance and crime control, which is essentially the threat hypothesis. Two scholars who have attributed differential treatment to economic threat are Spitzer (1975) and Bonacich (1972; 1976; 1979).

In analyzing the creation and maintenance of "problem populations," Spitzer (1975) states that one must not only ask why specific members of the "underclass" are selected for official control, but also why they behave as they do. One must investigate where problematic groups originally come from, why their actions and characteristics are considered problematic, and how they are transformed in a developing capitalist political economy. To Spitzer (1975), one needs to understand why American capitalism produces both pattens of activity and types of people that are defined (and re-defined) and processed as deviant. The concept of deviance, claims Spitzer (1975), offers a starting point for the examination of both criminal activity and formal social control.

To Spitzer (1975:640), "deviance production involves all aspects of the process through which populations are structurally generated, as well as shaped, channeled into, and manipulated within social categories defined as deviant." This process includes the formation of and changes in three areas: (1) deviant definitions, (2) problem populations, and (3) control systems.

He further argues that if one assumes that class societies are based on fundamental conflicts between groups, and that harmony is achieved through the dominance of a specific social class, it makes sense to argue that deviants are filtered from groups who create specific problems for those who rule society. One must explain why a control system emerges under specific historical conditions and accounts for its size, primary focus, and working assumptions.

According to Spitzer (1975), problem populations tend to share a number of social characteristics. The most important among them is "the fact that their behavior, personal qualities and/or position threaten the social relations of production in capitalist societies" (Spitzer, 1975:642). Specifically, Spitzer (1975:642) argues that populations become generally eligible for management as deviant when they significantly disturb, hinder, or call into question any of the following:

(1) capitalist modes of approaching the product of human labor (e.g., when the poor "steal" from the rich); (2) the social conditions under which capitalist production takes place (e.g., those who refuse or are unable to perform wage labor); (3) patterns of distribution and consumption in capitalist society (e.g., those who use drugs for escape transcendence rather than sociability and adjustment); (4) the process of socialization for productive and non-productive roles (e.g., youth who refuse to be schooled or those who deny the validity of "family life"); (5) the ideology which supports the functioning of capitalist society (e.g., proponents of alternative forms of social organization).

Problem populations are created either directly through the expression of fundamental contradictions in the capitalist mode of production, or indirectly through disturbances in the system of class rule.[16] A surplus-population is a necessary product of, and condition for, the accumulation of wealth in terms of capitalism, "but it also creates a form of social expense which must be neutralized or controlled if production relations and conditions for increased accumulation are to remain unimpaired" (Spitzer, 1975:643).

According to Spitzer, the rate at which problematic populations are converted into criminals will reflect the relationship between these populations and the control system. A rate which, the author argues (1975:644-645), is likely to be impacted by the following seven factors:

(1) extensiveness and intensity of state controls; (2) size and level of threat presented by the problem population. (The larger and more threatening the problem population, the greater the likelihood that this population will have to be controlled through deviance processing rather than other methods. As the threat created by these populations exceeds the capacities of informal restraints, their management requires a broadening of the reaction system and an increasing centralization and coordination of control activities.); (3) level of organization of the problem population. (When and if problem populations are able to organize and develop limited amounts of political power,

deviance processing becomes increasingly less effective as a tool for social control. The attribution of deviant status is most likely to occur when a group is relatively impotent and atomized.); (4) effectiveness of control structures organized through civil society; (5) availability and effectiveness of alternative types of official processing; (6) availability and effectiveness of parallel control structures; and (7) utility of problem populations. While problem populations are defined in terms of their threat and cost to capitalist relations of production, they are not threatening in every respect. They can be supportive economically (as part of a surplus labor pool or dual labor market), politically (as evidence of the need for state intervention) and ideologically (as scapegoats for rising discontent).

Thus, the legal system helps to control problem populations–especially those whose portion is young, vocal, active, and potentially most economically threatening–by creating and applying formal sanctions when deemed necessary to secure the economic order.[17]

One caveat is that the factors that are described as economic (or political, social and/or racial) threats may actually be "class" or at least "income" effects.[18] For instance, Bonacich's split labor market theory (developed in the early 1970s) of ethnic antagonism reveals a somewhat different picture, while maintaining a conflict orientation. Her theory stresses the role of a certain kind of economic competition in the development of ethnic antagonism.[19]

The central tenet of Bonacich's class theory of race and ethnicity suggests that racial and ethnic conflict are rooted in differences in the price of labor. To her, the race question is really a class matter in that racially oppressed individuals typically constitute cheap labor. "Race, sex, and nationality become the symbolism in which the conflict is expressed, but they are not in themselves its cause" (Bonacich, 1972; 1976; 1979:34).[20] According to Bonacich (1979:35), "'Race' is important only so long as it is rooted in class processes." To Bonacich (1979:19), individuals do not hate one another because of the "color of their skin." Thus, the racism issue is one of a complex class struggle.

To be more specific, "ethnic antagonism has taken two major, seemingly antithetical forms: exclusion movements, and so-called caste systems" (Bonacich, 1972:548).[21] Apart from manifesting antagonism between ethnic elements, these two forms seem to have little in common. For instance, while an effort is made to prevent an ethnically different group from being part of the society, an ethnically different group is essential to the society: "it is an exploited class supporting the entire edifice" (Bonacich, 1972:548).

Bonacich challenges the Marxist and neo-Marxist assumption that racial and cultural differences in themselves prompt the development of ethnic antagonism by arguing that economic processes are more substantially more significant. To her (1972:549), "ethnic antagonism first germinates in a labor market split along ethnic lines" (her central hypothesis). To be split, though, a labor market must contain a least two groups of workers whose price of labor differs for the same job, or would differ if they did the same job.

Bonacich further argues that labor markets that are split by the entrance of a new group develop a dynamic that may in turn significantly influence the price of labor. Thus, one needs to distinguish initial from later price determinants. The initial factors can be divided into two broad categories: resources (e.g., level of living, information, and political resources) and motives (e.g., fixed or supplementary income goal and fortune seeking). Moreover, the weaker a group is politically, the more vulnerable it is to the use of force, hence to an unfavorable (wage) bargain or no bargain at all (e.g., slavery). The price of a labor group varies inversely with the amount of force that can be used against it, which in turn depends on its political resources. Also, one cannot overlook the fact that governments vary in the degree to which they protect their citizens in the United States.[22]

Given this, if several ethnic groups who are approximately equal in resources/goals enter the same economic system, then a split labor market will not be created. And, in a two-ethnic-group contact situation, if one group occupies the position of a business elite and has no members in the labor market or in a class that could easily be pushed into the labor force, then independent of the other group's price, the labor market will not be split. (However, a split labor force does not stem solely from ethnic differences.)

That the initial price discrepancies in labor should ever fall along ethnic lines is a function of the original wage agreement arrived at between business and new labor. This often takes place in the labor group's point of origin and nations or individuals that have lived relatively separately from one another and are likely to have developed different employment motives and levels of resources.

To Bonacich (1972), the prejudice of business does not determine the price of labor, darker skinned or culturally different individuals being paid much less because of them.[23] Instead, business tries to pay as little as possible for labor, regardless of ethnicity, and is held in check by the resources and motives of labor groups. However, since these often vary by ethnicity, it is common to find ethnically split labor markets.[24]

In split labor markets, conflict develops between business, higher paid labor, and cheaper labor. The business'/employers' goal is to have as cheap and docile a labor force as possible "to compete effectively" with other business (Bonacich, 1972:553). Higher paid labor is extremely threatened by the introduction of cheaper labor into the market, fearing that it will force them to leave the area or reduce their wages. And, if the labor market is split ethnically, the class antagonism takes the form of ethnic antagonism. To Bonacich (1972:553), then, "while much rhetoric of ethnic antagonism concentrates on ethnicity and race, it really in large measure . . . expresses this class conflict." And, finally, employers use cheaper labor partly to undermine the position of more expensive labor, through strikebreaking and undercutting.

In summary, ethnic antagonism is specifically produced by the competition that evolves from a price differential and varies considerably over time and place. An oversupply of equal-priced labor does not create such antagonism. But, it does threaten individuals with the loss of their jobs. Hiring practices, though, will not necessarily fall along ethnic lines, there being no advantage to the employer in hiring workers of one ethnicity over another. When one ethnic group is decidedly cheaper than another (labor market is split) the higher paid employee faces more than the loss of his/her job. S/he faces the possibility that the wage standard in all jobs will be undermined by cheaper labor. However, if an expensive labor group is strong enough, it may be able to resist being displaced. Lastly, Bonacich (1972:558) states that "a labor element that shares ethnicity with people who have sufficient resources to become the business elite is generally likely to come from a fairly wealthy country and have resources of its own." Under these conditions, such systems are likely to develop split labor markets.

Following these last two theories, it seems reasonable to argue that differential treatment in punishment and sentencing is attributed, to a high degree, to an economic threat posed by certain populations. Based on Spitzer's (1975) reasoning, I would argue that offenders, especially those who are young and active, are filtered from problem populations, most of whom are members of the underclass, who create specific problems (e.g., property crimes, drugs) for those who rule (e.g., economic elites).

In the case of minorities, the situation is even more critical, since their behavior, personal characteristics, and/or positions are perceived as threatening to the social relations of production. For instance, minorities are often associated with property crimes and/or drugs. Therefore, it is reasonable to argue that they would receive the longer and harsher sentences, especially since their relationship with the criminal justice system is not, and never has been, a peaceful one, or, as Spitzer (1975:643) would say, a population ". . . which must be neutralized or controlled. . . ." Because the size and level of threat posed by minorities has increased in recent years, Spitzer's (1975:644) first social control factor, "extensiveness and intensity of state controls," has increased (e.g., additional jails/prisons, longer and more severe sentences) in recent years for minority groups. This is clearly a reflection of minority groups' lack of political power.

Moreover, following Spitzer (1975), one needs to underscore the fact that social control of minorities varies from place to place, depending, for instance, on their level of utility. Depending on time and place, minorities will be viewed as an economic plus or surplus labor pool; as a political plus, as evidence of the need for state intervention; and as an ideological plus, as scapegoats for rising discontent. By focusing blame on "outsiders," the rulers of a society are able to preserve their privileged positions of power, even if their social control policies and social programs are, in fact, responsible for pervasive economic hardships. As Spitzer's (1975) theory indicates, the conditions of economic existence determine social existence, and help explain the creation of groups who become both threatening and vulnerable at the same time.[25]

From Bonacich's (1972) perspective, while an effort is made to prevent an ethnically different group from being part of the community, an ethnically different group is essential to the dominant society. It seems reasonable to predict sentencing disparities among the various ethnic groups. Furthermore, based on her observation that minority groups do not have the same amount of resources when they arrive in the United States, one would expect disparities in sentencing outcomes among the various ethnic and racial minority groups. Their experiences will also depend on the degree to which they are protected by their country of origin.[26] Because resources vary by ethnicity, a logical argument would be that sentencing outcomes will differ by ethnicity. If economic competition varies over time and place, then there will be disparities in sentencing outcomes depending on place and time.

Although Bonacich (1972; 1975) does not stress harsh social control by Caucasian laborers as a strategy for achieving their objectives under economically threatening conditions, it is a logical implication of her theory. Also, given the weaker a group is politically and economically, the more vulnerable it is, I would argue that formal sanctions are more likely to fall on minority groups to secure the perceived economic burdens. For instance, Bonacich (1972:554) observes that if a labor group is "strong enough," it may be able to resist being displaced. This implies that if a minority offender is "strong enough," s/he may be able to resist being sentenced, especially a long and/or severe sentence. Minority group members, however, are seldom "strong enough."

LIMITATIONS OF CURRENT THEORIES

Psychologist Kurt Lewin is quoted as saying, "nothing is as practical as a good theory" (Winfree and Abadinsky, 1996:360). Lewin's suggestion, without question, is of critical importance to theory development. Unfortunately, developing and implementing a "good" practical theory is anything but quick and easy, as one will notice in the following discussion. Since similar limitations apply to various theories, some of them will be analyzed together (traditional theories, threat theories). Though close attention will be given to individual theories when deemed necessary, some criticisms overlap between traditional and threat theories.

Traditional Theories

While traditional theories of race and ethnic differences in punishment and sentence outcomes have underscored the importance of history in their mode of analysis, they often lack sensitivity to the historical experiences of the various racial and ethnic groups, especially the Latino population and the various ethnic groups that make up Latino community. Threat theorists have tried to incorporate the historical component, they (including Bonacichs' split labor market theory) too, however, have fallen short. Furthermore, traditional theories, for the most part, attempt to understand punishment and sentence outcomes apart from historically specific events and/or organizations (e.g., political and economic). Both sets of theories have focused almost exclusively on the experiences of African Americans to develop models that are later applied to Latinos at different points in time, independent of whether they fit the Latino experience or even the African American experience. A reductionist approach (e.g., overlooking cultural values and practices and reducing everything to class), for instance, fails to account for the many factors, especially the more subtle ones, that might influence the decision-making process.

A sound theory of race and ethnic differences in punishment and sentencing outcomes must be able to account not only for the history of African Americans, but also of the Latino population. Additionally, it must recognize that the Latino population is an extremely diverse community. The various ethnic groups (e.g., Mexicans, Cubans, Puerto Ricans) that make up the Latino population, not only have distinct histories, but experiences within the same group vary, depending upon place and time. For instance, in terms of racial, political, and economic implications, theories of sentencing outcomes have not underscored that Mexicans, like African Americans, have traditionally been given the worst jobs (e.g., "hamburger and/or pick-and-shovel jobs") the community has to offer. Such theories (including Bonacich's theory) fail to emphasize that when labor is scarce, Mexicans and African Americans generally occupy the lower rungs of the job ladder; when economic conditions decline, Caucasians take over the jobs previously set aside as "Negro" or "Mexican" work (Acuna, 1988; Tabb, 1970:27). Additionally, these theories ignore that, as with African Americans, the negative stereotypes of Mexicans portrayed by the media often alarm residents over presumed "crime waves," increasing the fear of Mexicans. Nor have they adequately explained why the situation for Cubans, as will be explored in Chapter IV, has been quite different from Mexicans, or even African Americans.

Thus, it is evident that theories of race and ethnic differences in punishment and sentencing outcomes have not been sensitive enough to the structural basis of the behavioral characteristics, which come to official attention, as well as the process through which individuals, especially racial and ethnic minorities, are sentenced. Most theorists have failed to properly investigate where these groups come from, why their behaviors and characteristics are considered problematic and threatening, and how they are transformed in a developing political economy, class and color conscious society, contrary to the position of Bonacich (1972; 1976; 1979). Above all, in a capitalist and color conscious society, most theorists have failed to properly analyze the origins of stereotypes or their consequences, which vary, depending on time and place (e.g., state, region).

While conveying an image of neutrality, for instance, the implications of dessert theories are critical for minority groups, as a number of scholars have observed. Morris (1981:257) who has analyzed the question of equality of treatment, which lies at the heart of dessert-based theories of sentencing, observes that "equality in punishment is not an absolute principle; that equality in punishment is a value to be weighted and considered among other values, no more; and that there can be just sentences which like criminals are not treated alike, as to either who goes to prison or for how long." As Morris (1981:266) points out, there are plenty of "situations in which justice and the principle of equality are not coterminous."

Hudson (1987) notes that disadvantaged (e.g., indigent) defendants are more likely to be convicted on more serious charges than the more privileged who are charged with similar acts.   Inadequate legal representation places poor individuals, most of whom are minorities, at a relative disadvantage when sentences are given, because no effort is made on their behalf to create a more favorable attitude towards them than the evidence in the case alone warrants (see Aguirre, 1982; 1984; Briere, 1978; Chang and Araujo, 1975; Comment, 1978; Cronheim and Schwartz, 1976; Governor Young's Report, 1930; Mendoza Report, 1978; Perez, 1969; Safford, 1977; Vandiver, 1999). They are given harsher and longer sentences than others who commit similar acts, but whose resources permit a more hopeful and appealing scenario to be presented to the sentencing authorities (e.g., judges, prosecutors).   Additionally, some convicted individuals are sentenced according to their criminal behavior, while others are given sentences according to the judge's idiosyncratic notions that have little (or no) sound foundation in principle.[27]

Tonry (1992) argues that since the standards for proportionality rely on legal categories (lumping moral dissimilar cases together), no proportionalist sentencing scheme is capable of actually serving true justice. To Tonry (1992), the standards merely purport to be fair and just, but in fact are unfair. Not surprisingly, then, Morris (1981:263) refers to von Hirsch's (1981) recommendations as "short-cuts to rational sentencing."[28] Thus, as Hudson (1987) suggests, less reliance on dessert, and more on non-legal factors should be given.

The criminal record of an individual presents an especially difficult problem for a dessert-based theory of sentencing. It is expected that "habitual offender" or "career criminal" laws will result in longer and harsher prison terms for people with extensive histories of criminal behavior. To the extent that minority defendants are more likely than Caucasians to have criminal histories, they will tend to serve longer jail and prison terms in those states with habitual offender statutes.[29]

Threat Theories

Although threat theories have similar as well as additional limitations, discussion will be limited to a few specific issues. First, if discrimination toward minorities by means of mechanisms such as status consciousness is likely to be related to class discrimination, as Bonacich (1972) and others have argued, then an implication would be that racial discrimination in death sentence outcomes may very well be confounded with class prejudice in empirical research. Thus, disparity results in death sentence outcomes (executions and commutations) studies that have been interpreted as being the consequences of discrimination, are perhaps due to class discrimination instead.

One might ask if it is possible to explain death sentences and death sentence outcomes in the context of political, economic, social, and racial threats. Yes. First, one needs to underscore the fact that while race may be highly associated with class, thus making it difficult to separate the two empirically, few can deny that the United States has been defined along racial and/or ethnic lines to varying degrees, depending upon time and space. Liska (1992), for example, observes that the premier indicator of "status" within the southern community during the late 19th and early 20th centuries was one's race. While testing the racial hypothesis may be complicated, since it is often difficult to separate the unique effects of racial threats from those of social, economic, and political threats, I would argue that these four threats (referred to from this point on as "the four-threat theory of death sentence outcomes" or simply "the four-threat approach") need to be analyzed as a unitary concept while acknowledging that the four threats have, depending on time and space, a non-zero impact on death sentence outcomes, especially for minority offenders.

I believe that decision-makers and the general public (e.g., political and economic elites, authorities, politicians, majorities, middle class, bureaucrats) perceive minority threat primarily (or even exclusively) as one of political, social, racial or economic competition. Take into consideration, for instance, how a local politician with aspirations of higher office (or simply obtaining or retaining office) might feel threatened by minority candidates, especially if their agenda goes against the status quo.[30] In such a case, this creates a threat not only to the politician, but also to the rest of the dominant group.

At the same time, the politician might be presented with an economic threat: if members of minority groups are "competing" for jobs and perhaps securing a job that is not labeled, say, "Mexican," his/her children might be without a job in the local job market. And, of course, since the town needs to feel safe during election time, the politician is now confronted with a social threat as well. To be on the safe side, the politician will have to "get tough" on those who pose a threat to the social order, even if s/he needs to implement additional formal sanctions, especially against minority members within the community. Notice that, in each case, the situation carries racial implications. Also notice that it is probable that this same situation would yield different results during "hard times."

Thus, taken together, these perspectives indicate that the state's control agents (e.g., legislators, judges, governors, prosecutors, parole boards) respond to changes in the political and economic structure, as well as to the level of racial and social threat posed by minorities. During times of political, social, racial, and economic tension, death sentences and death sentence outcome decisions, particularly those that involve poor, young, and uneducated male minorities with a prior record carry considerable meaning. For instance, death sentences and death sentence outcome decisions can be influenced by the "economic threat" posed by young minority groups during the troughs of business cycles. As a consequence, the probability of minorities having a sentence and/or conviction overturned or commuted is reduced and the probability of execution increases. Along with additional executions, not granting a commutation, or overturning a sentence/conviction can be used to regulate the population that is considered threatening.

An advantage of such approach, then, is that it broadens the study of death sentences and death sentence outcomes. Keep in mind that the focus of all the above theories has been on sentencing, mostly on non-capital cases, and less on death sentences or death sentence outcomes. Little attention has been given to execution and commutation as death sentence outcomes, and three additional death sentence outcomes have received little academic attention: (1) sentence declared unconstitutional by State or U.S. Supreme Court, (2) sentence overturned by appellate court, and (3) conviction and sentence overturned by appellate court. The four-threat approach will enable us to develop hypotheses related to these outcomes.

Additionally, by bringing together different issues into a unified framework, one is able to show the significance of several historical factors and their impact on death sentences and death sentence outcomes, not only for Caucasians and African Americans, but also other minority groups such as the Latino population and the subgroups that constitute this diverse population.

Thus, originally cast in a political, social, racial and economic fashion, the threat posed by minorities can be reconstructed in terms of death sentence outcomes not only for Caucasians and African Americans, but also for other minority groups, such as the Latino community and its various subgroups. I will interpret Spitzer's and Bonacich's analyses primarily in economic terms (encompassing both race and ethnicity), Blalock's power threat factor as representing a fear of political power in the hands of minorities and/or anyone posing a threat or viewed as an "outsider," and Crawford and colleagues' racial threat will be extended to include other minorities: a "race and ethnicity threat." Thus, along with race effects, we will have race and ethnicity effects. And, Liska's social threat will be interpreted as any social threat posed by minorities and/or anyone posing a threat or viewed as an "outsider."

In sum, the four-threat approach might not provide a full explanation, but it will definitely enhance our understanding of what is beyond death sentence outcomes as punishment for criminal acts (e.g., homicide), especially for African Americans and Latinos. As Thomas Kuhn (1996:180) points out, a paradigm, a set of recurrent and quasi-standard illustrations of various theories in their conceptual, observational, and instrumental applications, may not give us the answers to our questions, but it tells us where to look by governing "not a subject matter but rather a group of practitioners."

In this study, the objective will be to explore the following five questions: (1) Are extralegal attributes (e.g., race, ethnicity, sex, age of the offender when s/he committed the act, education, marital status) of the defendant a basis of differential treatment in death sentence outcomes in the Unite States?; (2) If so, what is the magnitude of such differential treatment?; (3) Under what circumstances does the differential treatment in death sentence outcomes occur?; (4) Is the defendant's prior felony record a significant and substantial indicator in the decision process?; and, (5) Does number of years under a death sentence influence death sentence outcomes?

GENERAL PREDICTIONS

Based on the four threat (political, social, racial, economic) theories, discrimination in death sentencing and death sentencing outcomes can be conceptualized as an attempt by Caucasians, the ruling racial group, to control a threatening minority population (and any other outsider) who is perceived as a real threat.[31] Disparities in death sentence outcomes is simply part of this pattern. Having outlined the four threat theories, an explanation of race and ethnic differences in death sentence outcomes will be provided next. Following the various theories (normative, stratification, dessert, Marxist, conflict) discussed herein, several factors (prior felony convictions, sex, education, number of years under death sentence, age of offender when s/he committed the offense, marital status, state) will be included in the analysis as control variables.

Predictions Based on Threat Theories

Based on Blalock's (1967) power-threat theory, Liska's (1992) social threat hypothesis, Crawford's et al. (1998) racial threat hypothesis, and Spitzer and Bonacich's economic approach, we can derive two general expectations (predictions) concerning how, when, and why racial and ethnic minorities are more likely to receive harsher sentences than their

Caucasian counterparts. Specifically, minorities (African Americans and Latinos) are:

1. More likely to be executed than their Caucasian counterparts.
2. Less likely to be granted a commutation than their Caucasian counterparts.

Before stating three additional hypotheses, it is important to emphasize that threat theories often lead to competing hypotheses. One could reasonably predict that minorities are:

1. Less likely to have their sentence declared unconstitutional by State or U.S. Supreme Court than their Caucasian counterparts.
2. Less likely to have their sentence overturned by an appellate court than their Caucasian counterparts.
3. Less likely to have their conviction and sentence overturned by an appellate court than their Caucasian counterparts.

Given the nature of the decision-making process, however, the opposite may also be possible. Minorities may be more likely to receive these death sentence outcomes than their Caucasian counterparts due to the high possibility of "errors,"which set grounds for overturning the sentence and/or conviction by the courts, in capital trials involving minority defendants. As noted earlier, due to limited resources, minorities seldom hire competent private counsel or forensic experts. Consequently, minorities are often wrongly convicted. Thus, due to questionable "evidence," there could be a high possibility of sentences and/or convictions being overturned by the courts. It is reasonable, then, to make the additional predictions that minorities are:

1. More likely to have their sentence declared unconstitutional by State or U.S. Supreme Court than their Caucasian counterparts.
2. More likely to have their sentence overturned by an appellate court than their Caucasian counterparts.
3. More likely to have their conviction and sentence overturned by an appellate court than their Caucasian counterparts.

The type of relationships described above are most likely during/if the following 21 factors apply. Specifically, if:

1. The concentration of minorities is high (power, social, and racial threat).
2. The percentage of minorities in the population is small, but there is a perception that minorities are on the path to obtaining political dominance (racial threat).
3. The size and level of threat has reached a critical level, or is on the rise (economic threat).
4. The group lacks economic resources (power, social, economic and racial threat).
5. Minorities have little, or no, economic/political power (economic threat).
6. Minorities are unemployed (social threat).
7. Minority income inequality is high (racial threat).
8. If minority income inequality is low, but they lack the necessary resources (racial threat).
9. Minorities are extremely vulnerable in general (economic threat).
10. There is a punitive trend in society at large (power threat).
11. The jurisdiction has the necessary resources (social threat).
12. The jurisdiction has extensive and intense state controls, or if such mechanisms are on the rise (economic threat).
13. The relationship between them and the criminal justice system is not a peaceful one (economic threat).
14. The personal characteristics of minorities is viewed as unconventional (economic threat).
15. Minorities are viewed as an underclass (economic threat).
16. Minorities are considered outsiders (economic threat).
17. Minorities are young (economic threat).
18. Minorities are active/vocal (economic threat).
19. Their positions are perceived as threatening (economic threat).
20. The overall behavior of minorities is viewed as unconventional (economic threat).
21. Minorities are perceived as being of little or no utility (economic threat).

In addition, the type of relationships described in 1 through 5 will vary by time and space since economic competition varies depending on time and space (racial and economic threat).

It should be underscored that some types of threats (e.g., drugs or homicide) may lead to specific forms of social control (long mandatory sentences without the possibility of parole), and some forms of social control may require economic resources (e.g., death penalty). Also, as one form of social control expands, it increases social threat, which increases other forms of social control. It may be that the expansion of long mandatory sentences without the possibility of parole for drug offenses and homicide has increased the social threat, which in turn has increased application of the death penalty. It is important to recognize that increases in social threat generate increases in social control, but decreases in social threat do not generate decreases in social control. To this end, decreases in social threat (as a result of decreases in drug offenses or homicides) will not necessarily generate a decrease in long mandatory sentences for drug offenses, nor will executions decline. Similarly, commutations will not necessarily increase nor will the number of sentences and/or convictions being overturned increase.

While an effort is often made to prevent an ethnically different group from being part of the community, an ethnically different group is considered essential to dominant society. All minority groups do not have the same amount of resources when they arrive in the United States. Likewise, resources vary by ethnicity even after living in this country for several years. Lastly, their experiences will also depend on the degree to which they are protected by their country of origin.

The Four-Threat Theory of Death Sentence Outcomes

While each of the different threat perspectives has its own merits, incorporating similar issues, events, dimensions, and perspectives into a more holistic approach will yield stronger predictions. For instance, the four-threat approach provides stronger confidence that under various threatening conditions Caucasians in superordinate positions act in such a manner as to preserve their positions as well as the maintenance of the status quo. Since Euro-Americans are generally in superordinate positions vis-a-vis minorities, Caucasians will utilize whatever means necessary, including long and severe formal social control sanctions, against minorities in such a manner as to preserve their political and/or economic positions against racially and/or ethnically different individuals who might also be perceived as a social threat. Specifically, based on the four-threat theory of death sentence outcomes, it is reasonable to argue the following two points. Under politically, socially, economically, and/or racially threatening conditions, minorities are:

1. More likely to be executed than their Caucasian counterparts.
2. Less likely to be granted a commutation than their Caucasian counterparts.

In the next three hypotheses, we again see the potential for overlapping outcomes. One could reasonably predict that minorities are:

1. Less likely to have their sentence declared unconstitutional by State or U.S. Supreme Court than their Caucasian counterparts.
2. Less likely to have their sentence overturned by an appellate court than their Caucasian counterparts.
3. Less likely to have their conviction and sentence overturned by an appellate court than their Caucasian counterparts.

However, given the nature of the decision-making process, the opposite may also be possible. As mentioned above, minorities may be more likely to receive these death sentence outcomes than their Caucasian counterparts due to the high possibility of "errors" during the conviction/sentencing stages and/or lack of resources (e.g., financial, political), which set grounds for overturning the sentence and/or conviction by the courts, in capital trials involving minority defendants. Given this, it is reasonable to predict the following three factors, that minorities are:

1. More likely to have their sentence declared unconstitutional by State or U.S. Supreme Court than their Caucasian counterparts.

2. More likely to have their sentence overturned by an appellate court than their Caucasian counterparts.
3. More likely to have their conviction and sentence overturned by an appellate court than their Caucasian counterparts.

The type of relationships described above are most likely under the conditions previously described in "1" through "21," indicating specific aspects of each threat theory. In addition, the type of relationships described above will vary by minority group, time and location.

In sum, it should be underscored that as the four threat theories predict, the four-threat theory of death sentence outcomes contains competing hypotheses. Still, though, as with executions, not granting a commutation, or overturning a sentence and/or conviction to threatening individuals not only segregates them from society but identifies and reinforces the parameters of behaviors that social control agents find socially acceptable. The legal system provides the structural opportunity for control agents (e.g., legislators, governors, judges, parole boards) to operate interdependently to control individuals defined as threatening by the dominant group. In Chapter IV, the question of who and what are threatening, who and what are threatened, and the ramifications of these threats will be discussed further.

CHAPTER 3

Death Sentencing and Death Sentence Outcomes: Review of Prior Empirical Studies

The significance of the dynamics of the relationship between the state and racial and ethnic minorities is perhaps no more obvious than in death sentence outcomes. This is because, through racial and ethnic policies (whether explicit or implicit), state institutions organize and enforce the racial and ethnic politics of everyday life.

RACE AND ETHNICITY AND DEATH SENTENCING: PRIOR RESEARCH

While some early studies indicate that minority defendants have received harsher sanctions, others argue that minorities have not been discriminated against by decision-makers.

Table 1

Empirical Studies of Race and Ethnicity and Death Sentence*

Author(s) & (Year)	Jurisdiction [Time Period Covered]	Race/ Ethnicity [Gender]	Capital Offense	Dependent Variables	Independent Variables	Primary Sample	Main Type of Analysis	Race/ Ethnic Effect?
Brearley (1930)	South Carolina [1920-1926]	African American, Caucasian [male & female]	homicide	convicted	race and sex of victim and offender ...	407 capital cases	percentages	yes
Johnson (1941)	North Carolina, Virginia, Georgia [1930-1934]	African American, Caucasian [?]**	homicide	death sentence	race of offender & victim ...	122 death sentences	tabular analysis (no sig. tests or measure of association)	mix
Garfinkel (1949)	North Carolina (10 counties) [1930-1940]	African American, Caucasian [male & female]	homicide	charge/ conviction/ death sentence/	degree of homicide, race of offender & victim ...	821 capital cases	percentages (no sig. tests or measure of association)	mix
Ehrmann (1952)	Mass. (6 counties) [1925-1941]	African American, Caucasian, Chinese [?]	homicide	indictments, convicted	race, offense, county ...	113 capital cases	observation, descriptive statistics	N/A
Bensing & Schroeder (1960)	Cleveland, Ohio [1947-1953]	African American, Caucasian [male & female]	homicide	death sentence/ other	degree of homicide	662 capital cases	tabular analysis (no sig. tests or measure of association)	no

Author(s) & (Year)	Jurisdiction [Time Period Covered]	Race/ Ethnicity [Gender]	Capital Offense	Dependent Variables	Independent Variables	Primary Sample	Main Type of Analysis	Race/ Ethnic Effect?
Bensing & Schroeder (1960)	Cleveland, Ohio [1947-1953]	African American, Caucasian [male & female]	homicide	death sentence/ other	degree of homicide	662 capital cases	tabular analysis (no sig. tests or measure of association)	no
Bridge & Mosure (1961)	Ohio [1949-1959]	African American, Caucasian [male & female]	homicide	death sentence	race, age, marital status, weapon, education, prior record, birth place, occupation, type of crime, alcohol and narcotics, victim/ offender relationship, mental capacity ...	67 death sentences	tabular analysis (no sig. tests or measure of association)	no
Wolf (1964)	New Jersey [1937-1961]	African American, Caucasian [male]	homicide	death sentence/life in prison	felony/ non-felony, race, age	159 capital cases	test of significance	no
Florida Civil Liberties Union (1964)	Florida [1940-1964]	African American, Caucasian, Native American [male & female]	rape	death sentence/ other	race, sex ...	285 rape cases	tabular analysis (no sig. tests or measure of association)	yes

43

Author(s) & (Year)	Jurisdiction [Time Period Covered]	Race/ Ethnicity [Gender]	Capital Offense	Dependent Variables	Independent Variables	Primary Sample	Main Type of Analysis	Race/ Ethnic Effect?
Partington (1965)	Virginia [1908-1963]	African American, Caucasian [male]	rape	death sentence/ other	type of rape, race	2,798 rape cases	frequencies (no sig. tests or measure of association)	yes
Judson, Pandell, Owens, McIntosh & Matschull (1969)	California [1958-1966]	Mexican, African American, Caucasian, Native American, Oriental, other [male & female]	homicide	death sentence/ life sentence	race, age, sex, SES, prior record, occupation, characteristics of offense	238 first degree murder cases (Mexican: N=25)	test of sig., measure of association	no
Kalven (1969)	California [1958-1966]	? [?]	homicide	death penalty	?	238 death-eligible cases	?	N/A
Koeninger (1969)	Texas [1924-1968]	Latin, African American, Caucasian [male & female]ª	homicide, rape, armed robbery	life in prison/ prison term with possible parole	age, birth place, education, occupation, employment, prior record, weapon, drugs ...	460 death sentences (Latino/a: N=45)	percentages	yes

44

Author(s) & (Year)	Jurisdiction [Time Period Covered]	Race/ Ethnicity [Gender]	Capital Offense	Dependent Variables	Independent Variables	Primary Sample	Main Type of Analysis	Race/ Ethnic Effect?
Wolfgang & Reidel (1973; 1975)[b] Note: These results also appeared in Wolfgang (1974) and Wolfgang & Riedel (1976)	Alabama, Arkansas, Florida, Georgia, Louisiana, Mississippi, North Carolina, South Carolina, Tennessee, Texas, Virginia [1945-1965]	African American, Caucasian [male]	rape	death sentence/ other	race of defendant & victim, nature of offense, character of defendant & victim, relationship between victim & offender ...	3,000 rape cases; various sub-samples	null hypothesis & chi-square statistical test	yes
Kelly (1976)	Oklahoma [March 31, 1974]	Mexican, African American, Caucasian, Native American [?]	homicide	life-death sentence (combined)	age, marital status, education, prior record, type of crime, plea entered, type of attorney ...	356 capital cases (MexicanN= ?)	multiple regression	no Mex-ican: slight (-) effect

45

Author(s) & (Year)	Jurisdiction [Time Period Covered]	Race/ Ethnicity [Gender]	Capital Offense	Dependent Variables	Independent Variables	Primary Sample	Main Type of Analysis	Race/ Ethnic Effect?
Riedel (1976)	United States (28 states); region; Florida, Georgia, Texas, Louisiana, North Carolina, Oklahoma [December 31, 1971; June 29, 1972 to January 2, 1976; June 29, 1972 to August 1975]	Caucasian/non-Caucasian [?]	homicide	death sentence	race, age, employment, marital status, mental illness, prior record, victim characteristics, circumstances of offense & trial ...	493 pre-*Furman* cases & 376 post-*Furman* capital cases; 142 post-*Furman* capital cases	chi-square	yes
Zimring, Eigen & O'Malley (1976)	Philadelphia [1970]	African American, Caucasian [?]	homicide	life in prison, death sentence	race of offender & victim ...	204 capital cases	Fisher's Exact Test	yes
Lewis & Peoples (1978)	Florida [February to June 1977]	African American, Caucasian, other [male]	homicide	death row	multiple demographic, legal & extra legal variables	83 death row inmates	interviews	N/A
Boris (1979)	large northeastern industrial city [1972]	African American, Caucasian [?]	homicide	dismissed or prosecuted at preliminary hearing	race of offender & victim, occupation, education, age & # of arrests and convictions of offender & victim...	383 capital cases	multiple regression	no

Author(s) & (Year)	Jurisdiction [Time Period Covered]	Race/ Ethnicity [Gender]	Capital Offense	Dependent Variables	Independent Variables	Primary Sample	Main Type of Analysis	Race/ Ethnic Effect?
Arkin (1980)	Dade County, Florida [1973-1976]	African American, Caucasian [probably male & female]	homicide	conviction, sentence length, death sentence	race of offender & victim, type of felony …	350 capital cases	percentages	mix
Baldus, Pulaski, Woodworth & Kyle (1980)	California [pre-*Furman* period]	Mexican, African American, Caucasian, Native American [?]	homicide	life sentence, death sentence (violation of state law and/or 8th Amendment)	# of victims, criminal record, motive, mitigating factors, persons wounded, alcohol & drug use, weapon, employment …	239 death penalty cases (MexicanN= 26)	multiple regression analysis	no (Mex-ican: no effect)
Bowers & Pierce (1980)	Florida, Texas, Ohio, Georgia [1972-1977]	African American, Caucasian [male & female]	homicide	death sentence	race of offender & victim, jurisdiction, 7 aggravating & mitigating factors …	various sub-samples of capital cases	percentages, probabilities	yes
Radelet (1981)	Florida (20 counties) [1976-1977]	African American, Caucasian [?]	homicide	death sentence	victim/defendant relationship, race of victim & defendant	637 capital cases	chi-square, log-linear analysis	no
Thomson & Zimgraff (1981)	one southeastern state [1969, 1973, 1977]	Caucasian, non-Caucasian [male]	robbery	sentence length	race, class, education, occupation, previous incarcerations, total # of sentence received …	1,194 cases	multivariate analysis	yes

47

Author(s) & (Year)	Jurisdiction [Time Period Covered]	Race/ Ethnicity [Gender]	Capital Offense	Dependent Variables	Independent Variables	Primary Sample	Main Type of Analysis	Race/ Ethnic Effect?
Zeisel (1981)	Florida [1973-1980]	African American, Caucasian [probably male & female]	homicide	death sentence	race of offender & victim	228 capital cases	percentages	yes
Foley & Powell (1982)	Florida (21 counties) [1972-1978]	African American, Caucasian, other [male & female]	homicide	trial, jury re-commendation, judge's decision	age, sex, education, occupation, prior convictions ...	829 capital cases	linear analysis of covariance	yes
Jacoby & Paternoster (1982)	South Carolina [June 8, 1977 to November 30, 1979]	African American, Caucasian [?]	homicide	death sentence requests by prosecutor	race of victim ...	205 capital cases	proportions, ratios	yes
Baldus, Pulaski & Woodworth (1983)	Georgia [January 1, 1970 to September 29, 1972; March 28, 1973 to June 30, 1978]	African American, Caucasian [male & female]	homicide	assessment of the degree of comparative excessiveness in Georgia's death-sentencing system	aggravating & mitigating factors	130 pre-*Furman* capital cases; 594 post-*Furman* capital cases; focused on 68 death sentences	multiple regression analysis; logistic regression	yes
Bowers (1983)	Florida [1976-1977]	African American, Caucasian [?]	homicide	homicide indictment	race, region, type of attorney, aggravating factors ...	508 capital cases	multiple regression	yes

48

Author(s) & (Year)	Jurisdiction [Time Period Covered]	Race/ Ethnicity [Gender]	Capital Offense	Dependent Variables	Independent Variables	Primary Sample	Main Type of Analysis	Race/ Ethnic Effect?
Paternoster (1983)	South Carolina [June 8, 1977 to December 31, 1981]	African American, Caucasian [?]	homicide	death sentence requests by prosecutor	race of offender & victim, # of offenders & victims, victim/offender relationship, sex & age of victim, weapon ...	321 capital cases	ratios, logit analysis ...	yes
Radelet & Vandiver (1983)	Florida [January 1, 1973 to December 31, 1981]	African American, Caucasian [male]	homicide, rape	upholding death sentence by state Supreme Court (affirmed or non-affirmed)	race of defendant & victim, victim's sex, # of victims, type of attorney ...	145 direct appeal decisions	multiple regression	yes
Gross & Mauro (1984; 1989) Note: These results are part of the same study.	Arkansas, Florida, Georgia, Illinois, Mississippi, North Carolina, Oklahoma, Virginia [January 1, 1976 to December 31, 1980]	African American, Caucasian [male & female]	homicide	death sentence	race of offender & victim, nature of felony, relationship to victim, # of victims, weapon, location, aggravation ...	379 death sentences (various sub-samples)	tabulations, multiple logistic regression analysis	yes (race effect in all eight states)
Paternoster (1984)	South Carolina [June 8, 1977 to December 31, 1981]	African American, Caucasian [?]	homicide	death sentence requests by prosecutor	7 statutory aggravating circumstances ...	300 capital cases	descriptive statistics, probit analysis	yes

49

Author(s) & (Year)	Jurisdiction [Time Period Covered]	Race/ Ethnicity [Gender]	Capital Offense	Dependent Variables	Independent Variables	Primary Sample	Main Type of Analysis	Race/ Ethnic Effect?
Barnett (1985)	Georgia [between March 28, 1973 & June 30, 1978]	African American, Caucasian [probably male & female]	homicide	death sentence	region, prior record, nature of crime, race of victim & defendant ...	606 capital cases	descriptive statistics, s-values (using Barnett's scale)	no
Baldus, Woodworth & Pulaski (1985)	Georgia [between March 28, 1973 & June 30, 1978]	African American, Caucasian [male & female]	homicide	death sentence requests by prosecutor, death sentence	race of defendant & victim, mitigating & aggravating factors, status of defendant ...	606 capital cases	regression analysis (using Barnett's scale)	no
Liebman (1985)	Georgia [1973-1985]	? [?]	homicide	death sentence: dis-proportionate or excessive	aggravating & mitigating factors ...	133 capital cases	case comparison	N/A
Radelet & Pierce (1985)	Florida (32 counties) [1973-1977]	African American, Caucasian [male & female]	homicide	upgraded/ down graded: felony charges/non-felony charges	race, sex & age of victim, relationship to victim, age, # of victims, weapon ...	1,017 capital cases	chi-square, logistic regression	yes
Foley (1987)	Florida (21 counties) [1972-1978]	African American, Caucasian [male & female]	homicide	death sentence	race & sex of victim & defendant, age, education, prior record, relationship to victim, # of victims, accomplices, county, attorney, weapon, additional offenses ...	829 capital cases	chi-square, multiple analysis of covariance	yes

Author(s) & (Year)	Jurisdiction [Time Period Covered]	Race/ Ethnicity [Gender]	Capital Offense	Dependent Variables	Independent Variables	Primary Sample	Main Type of Analysis	Race/ Ethnic Effect?
Klein & colleagues (1987)	Los Angeles County [August 1977-January 1986]	? [?]	homicide	death sentence/life without possibility of parole	sex factors related to circumstances of crime & victim	874 death-eligible cases	logistic regression	mix
Smith (1987)	Louisiana [October 1, 1976 to December 31, 1982]	African American, Caucasian [male]	homicide	death sentence	race & sex of victim, # of victims, weapon, victim/offender relationship, location of offense	504 death-eligible cases	logistic regression	yes
Ekland-Olson (1988)	Texas [February 1974 to December 1983]	Latino/a, African American, Caucasian [male & female]	homicide	death sentence	race of victim & offender, sex of offender & victim, age, relationship to victim ...	1,148 capital cases (Latino/a:N= ~280)	multivariate analysis	mix
Paternoster & Kazyaka (1988)	South Carolina [June 8, 1977 to December 31, 1981]	African American, Caucasian [?]	homicide	death sentence requests by prosecutor/death sentences imposed (convictions)	race of offender and victim, prior record, # of victims, # of offenders, victim-offender relationship, # of mitigating & aggravating factors, weapon ...	302 death-eligible cases	logistic regression	yes

51

Author(s) & (Year)	Jurisdiction [Time Period Covered]	Race/ Ethnicity [Gender]	Capital Offense	Dependent Variables	Independent Variables	Primary Sample	Main Type of Analysis	Race/ Ethnic Effect?
Vito & Keil (1988)	Kentucky [December 22, 1976 to October 1, 1986]	African American, Caucasian [?]	homicide	death sentence requests by prosecutor	race of victim, 8 aggravating factors	458 capital cases	multivariate analysis	yes
Heilburn, Foster & Golden (1989)	Georgia [1974-1987]	African American, Caucasian [male]	homicide	life sentence/death sentence	age, education, school problems, running away from home, problems with police, employment, marital difficulties, fighting, vagrancy, lying ...	243 capital cases	ANOVA	no
Keil & Vito (1989)	Kentucky [December 22, 1976 to October 1, 1986]	African American, Caucasian [?]	homicide	death sentence requests by prosecutor/ death sentence	prior convictions, multiple victims, sex of victim, race of offender & victim ...	466 capital cases	logit regression	yes
Baldus, Woodworth & Pulaski (1990) Study 1: PRS[a]	Georgia [between 1973 & 1978]	African American, Caucasian [male & female]	homicide	death sentence requests by prosecutor/ life sentence/ death sentence	over 150 aggravating & mitigating factors	156 pre-*Furman* cases & 594 post-*Furman* capital cases	multivariate analysis	yes

Author(s) & (Year)	Jurisdiction [Time Period Covered]	Race/ Ethnicity [Gender]	Capital Offense	Dependent Variables	Independent Variables	Primary Sample	Main Type of Analysis	Race/ Ethnic Effect?
Baldus, Woodworth & Pulaski (1990) Study 2: CSS	Georgia [between 1973 & 1979]	African American, Caucasian [male & female]	homicide	grand-jury indictment, plea-bargaining by prosecutor, jury guilt-trial decisions, prosecutorial decision to seek death sentence after guilty trial, jury penalty-trial sentencing decisions	over 230 variables	1,066 capital cases	multivariate analysis	yes
Keil & Vito (1990)	Kentucky [between December 22, 1976 & October 1, 1986]	African American, Caucasian [probably male & female]	homicide	death sentence requests by prosecutor/ death sentence	nature of crime, prior record, relationship to victim ...	401 capital cases	cross-tabulation analysis, logit analysis	yes
Karns & Weinberg (1991)	Penn. [1978-1990]	Latino/a, African American, Caucasian, Asian, other [male & female]	homicide	death sentence requests by prosecutor, life imprisonment, death sentence	race of victim & offender, gender of offender & victim, aggravating factors ...	1,174 capital cases (Latino/a:N= 64)	Cramer's V	mix
Klein & Rolph (1991)	California [1977-1984]	Latino, African American, Caucasian [?]	homicide	death sentence	15 variables related to defendant, victim, & circumstances of offense	496 jury penalty cases (Latino: N=?)	cluster and CART analysis	no

Author(s) & (Year)	Jurisdiction [Time Period Covered]	Race/ Ethnicity [Gender]	Capital Offense	Dependent Variables	Independent Variables	Primary Sample	Main Type of Analysis	Race/ Ethnic Effect?
Radelet & Pierce (1991)	Florida [1976-1987]	African American, Caucasian [probably male & female][d]	homicide	death sentence	race, age, sex, county and date of crime, weapon	10,142 homicide cases & 368 death sentences	logistic regression	yes
Marquart, Ekland-Olson & Sorensen (1994)	Texas [various time frames between 1923-1988]	Latino/a, African American, Caucasian, other [male & female]	rape, homicide, arm robbery	death sentence/ life imprisonment	race, age, sex of victim & offender, education, occupation ...	various sub-samples of 900-plus death sentences (Latino/a: N= various sub-samples)	uncertainty coefficient, Somer's D², likelihood ratio chi-square	mix
Sorensen & Wallace (1995)	Missouri [1977-1991]	African American, Caucasian [male & female]	homicide	death sentence	offender & victim racial characteristics, aggravation ...	194 capital cases	logistic regression	no
Keil & Vito (1995)	Kentucky [1976-1991]	African American, Caucasian [?]	homicide	death sentence	6 characteristics of defendant & circumstances of offense	577 death-eligible cases	logistic regression	yes

54

Author(s) & (Year)	Jurisdiction [Time Period Covered]	Race/ Ethnicity [Gender]	Capital Offense	Dependent Variables	Independent Variables	Primary Sample	Main Type of Analysis	Race/ Ethnic Effect?
Rohrlich & Tulsky (1996)	Los Angeles [1990-1994]	Latino, African American, Caucasian, other [probably male & female]	homicide	death sentence	race of defendant & victim … (no controls for the death-eligibility of cases or through relative criminal culpability)	9,442 capital cases processed through L.A. courts (Latino/a: N=?)	logistic regression (not specifically stated, it appears that logistic regression was used)	no
Thomson (1997)	Arizona [1982-1991]	Latino, African American, Caucasian, Asian, Native American [?]	homicide	death sentence	race/ethnicity of victim & offender	2,028 capital cases (Latino: N=417)	tabular analysis (no sig. tests or measure of association)	mix
Baldus, Woodworth, Zucherman, Weiner & Broffitt (1998)	Philadelphia [1983-1993]	Latino, African American, Caucasian, Asian [?]	homicide	death sentence/life sentence	race & socio economic status of defendant & victim, statutory aggravating & mitigating circumstances, level of culpability	various sub-samples: 118 death sentence, 230 life sentence, 176 non-penalty trail cases[e]	logistic regression	yes

55

Author(s) & (Year)	Jurisdiction [Time Period Covered]	Race/ Ethnicity [Gender]	Capital Offense	Dependent Variables	Independent Variables	Primary Sample	Main Type of Analysis	Race/ Ethnic Effect?
Aguirre, Davin, Baker & Lee (1999)	California [1989-1994]	Latino, African American, Caucasian [probably only male]	homicide	life in prison with no parole/death sentence	race/ethnicity, age, sex, victim impact evidence, jury was "death qualified," murder in combination with various felonies & race of defendant & victim	151 capital cases (Latino: N=22)	cross-tabulation analysis	yes (Latino: moderate positive effect)

Overall Summary: Yes: 31   No: 14   Mixed: 8   NA: 4

* Some studies were included even though the data were not analyzed for processing points or outcomes but were relevant to ethnicity/race effects; each of these studies analyzed variables important to understanding potential sources of differential treatment, but they did not analyze data directly regarding decision-making outcomes.

** ? = unable to determine from text.

a According to Koeninger (1969, p.135), "most persons here classified as 'Latin' are white Texas of Mexican extraction."

b The 1975 study is an analysis of a subset of the data in the 1973 study. The two are treated as a single study.

c The authors present findings two studies: Procedural Reform Study (PRS) and Charging and Sentencing Study (CSS).

d Latinos were coded with Caucasians.

e Latinos: 70 (47%) of all death-eligible offenders; 34 (49%) of white offenders who advanced to jury penalty trial.

56

Based on the above studies, the death sentencing evidence is conflicting. A number of early studies found race and ethnicity to be influential factors in the death sentencing decision-making process, some found no race differences, and a few found mixed results.

Some early studies found that race was a significant factor in death sentencing (e.g., Florida Civil Liberties Union, 1964; Partington,1965; Wolfgang and Reidel, 1973; 1975). Wolfgang and Reidel (1973; 1975), for instance, discovered that race was found to be a significant factor in death sentencing in six Southern states between 1945 and 1965.

Some more recent studies have found similar findings (e.g., Baldus, Woodworth, Zuckerman, Weiner and Broffitt, 1998; Keil and Vito, 1995; Radelet and Pierce, 1991). Radelet and Pierce's (1991) multivariate Florida study, for example, showed that for Caucasian victims, the defendant was six times more likely to get the death penalty than in cases with African American victims. African American defendants who killed Euro-Americans were more than twice as likely to receive the death penalty than were Caucasian defendants who killed Caucasians. And, African American defendants who killed Caucasians were 15 times more likely to be sentenced to death than were African American defendants who killed African Americans. Baldus et al. (1998:1676) found that the race and ethnic differences in death sentencing in Philadelphia were substantial, consistent, and statistically significant, or nearly so; African American defendants were "treated more punitively than other defendants" on the average, especially in cases involving Caucasian victims, in death sentencing decisions.[32]

A number of other studies, though, have found race and ethnic differences in death sentencing. Among the studies that did not find race or ethnic differences in death sentencing are a number of early studies (e.g., Bensing and Schroeder,1960; Bridge and Mosure, 1961; Judson, Pandell, Owens, McIntosh, & Matschullat., 1969; Wolf, 1964). Judson et al. (1969), for instance, found that the race variable was statistically non-significant in death sentencing in California for the years 1958 to 1966.

Recent studies by Klein and Rolph (1991) and Rohrlich and Tulsky (1996) did not find race effects to be statistically significant. According to Sorensen and Wallace (1995), when one takes into consideration offender and victim racial characteristics, no overall statistically significant racial effects were found in the final stage of the capital process: death sentencing. For cases involving race of offender and victim and level of aggravation, cases were not significantly more likely to result in death sentences. Caucasian defendants were not significantly more likely to receive a death sentence than African American defendants. In cases involving Caucasian victims, cases were not significantly more likely to result in death sentencing.

A number of studies have reported mixed results. Among these studies are a number of early studies (e.g, Garfinkel, 1949; Johnson, 1941). Garfinkel (1949), for instance, found no race difference between African American killers as a group and Caucasian killers as a group, but when the defendant was African American and his victim was Caucasian, the defendant was sentenced to death in 43% of the cases. If the defendant was Caucasian and the victim was African American, the defendant ran no such risk of being sentenced to death.

More recently, Klein et al. (1987) did not find a statistically significant relationship for the race of the defendant, but the variable for the race of the victim did enter at the .01 level of significance. Thomson (1997) found that Caucasian offenders are about one and one-half times as likely to receive death sentences as minority offenders (4.7% versus 3.3%). Death sentencing rates were similar for African American and Latino offenders (3.7% and 3.6%). Overall, "white homicide offenders in Arizona are more likely to receive death sentences than minority homicide offenders" (Thomson, 1997:71-72), but Caucasian-victim homicides, especially involving minority offenders, were much more likely to result in death sentences than minority-victim homicides.

Marquart et al. (1994) did not find a statistically significant race difference between death sentences and life sentences between 1923 and 1971 in Texas, but found a statistically significant race of offender and race of victim difference between death sentences and life sentences between 1942 and 1971 for convicted murderers. In rape cases, the most powerful predictor of a death sentence was the combination of the racial or ethnic characteristics of the victim and the offender. "The probability that black offenders would be sentenced to death for rape remained between five and ten times the probability for white offenders" from 1925 to 1965 (Marquart et al., 1994:54). When an African American male raped a Caucasian female, the case was approximately 35 times more likely to result in a death sentence than a prison sentence. And, if a Latino male raped a Caucasian female, the comparative chances were about two to one.

Lastly, Marquart et al. (1994) found that between 1974 and 1988, 80% of the convicted Anglo defendants and 79% of the convicted African American defendants were sentenced to die. Latino offenders were sentenced to death at lower rates, 63%. Cases involving African American offenders and Caucasian victims were also associated with a higher likelihood of a death sentence, but the initially statistically significant effect disappeared once type of offense, presence of co-defendants, number of victims, and age and sex of the victim were controlled, the next topic of discussion.

First, while few researchers have included sex as a control variable in their analysis, in part due to the small number of females under the sentence of death in comparison to males, prior findings show that death sentencing is gendered. For instance, data for 1955 to 1958 show that there was a "greater reluctance to apply the death sentence to women than to men" (Bridge and Mosure, 1961:61). Marquart et al. (1994) found that while nearly 15% of the individuals charged with first-degree murder were women, no females were admitted under the sentence of death in Texas during the period under study. In addition, Marquart et al. (1994) found that between 1974 and 1988, males were more likely to be sentenced to death than females–77% compared with 55%, but the difference was not statistically significant.

Another variable of controversy is the age of the offender when the act was committed. An early study by Bridge and Mosure (1961) found that the highest percentage (22.4%) of those sentenced to death were the 25 to 29 year-old cohort. The average age of the 67 admitted under death sentences was 33 years. More recently, Marquart et al. (1994) found a statistically significant age difference between death sentences and life sentences between 1923 and 1971 for convicted murderers, but not between 1942 and 1971. Marquart et al. (1994) claim that, between 1974 and 1988, older offenders were sentenced to death in 80% of the cases, compared to 73% in the younger category, and the difference was statistically significant.

Marital status is also a variable in question. Bridge and Mosure (1961) found that 70% of the individuals under study were not married. Marquart et al. (1994) found that between 1923 and 1972 in approximately two-thirds of the cases, the defendant was single or divorced at the time of the offense.

Another variable that has been questioned and continues to create controversy in the criminal justice system is the level of education of the offender. Bridge and Mosure (1961) found that the average duration of formal education completed was seven and a half years. And, while all were declared legally sane at the time of their crimes, intelligence scores ranged from 49 to 120. Marquart et al.'s (1994) findings showed that between 1923 and 1972, most of the offenders were uneducated, and found a statistically significant education difference between death sentences and life sentences between 1941 and 1971 for convicted murderers. However, between 1974 and 1988, Marquart et al. (1994) found that the level of education made no statistically significant difference in the probability of a death sentence.[33]

Lastly, another factor of debate, especially between liberal and conservative legal scholars and policy-makers, is whether the defendant had a criminal history when the crime was committed and its future implications (e.g., stability, recidivism). Marquart et al.'s (1994) Texas study found that between 1923 and 1972, most of the offenders did not have a prior prison record. Specifically, Marquart et al. (1994) found a statistically significant criminal history (property convictions and prison) difference between death sentences and life sentences between 1941 and

1971 for convicted murderers. But, between 1974 and 1988 the number of prior arrests alone made little difference. Overall, when there was some evidence of past criminal activity, the probability of a death sentence increased. In fact, the authors claim that the variable most likely to increase this probability was offender's prior prison record, followed by cases involving multiple victims. In both cases, the effect was statistically significant.

In sum, while the death sentencing results are conflicting, there is an indication that early discrimination is not remedied at death sentencing.[34] As indicated in Table 1, young African American and Latino men remain heavily over-represented among those receiving death sentences. As the threat theory suggests, the implication could be that the results are due, in part, to the support of the rich and powerful. Thus, one could reasonably predict that the "get tough" movement has given some individuals the worst of both worlds: death sentencing without due process. With this in mind, an analysis of prior death sentencing outcomes studies follows.

DEATH SENTENCE OUTCOMES: PRIOR RESEARCH

While there is extensive literature on race differences in death sentencing, there are only a few empirical studies that have given close attention to the issue of death sentence outcomes. The studies that have been conducted have focused exclusively on commutations and/or executions. Given the fact that early studies rarely use statistical significance tests and contain various theoretical and statistical limitations, as indicated by a number of scholars, they will not be discussed in detail.

Table 2

Empirical Studies of Race and Ethnicity and Death Sentence Outcomes

Author(s) & (year)	Jurisdiction [Time Period Covered]	Race/ Ethnicity [Gender]	Capital Offense	Dependent Variables	Independent Variables	Primary Sample	Main Type of Analysis	Race/ Ethnic effect?
Mangum (1940)	Florida, Kentucky, Missouri, N. & S. Carolina, Oklahoma, Tennessee, Texas, Virginia [1909-1938]	African American, Caucasian [?]*	homicide	executed/ commuted	race and sex of victim & offender ...	1,272 death sentences	percentages, ratios (no sig. tests or measure of association)	yes
Johnson (1941)	North Carolina [1933-1939]	African American, Caucasian [?]	homicide	executed/ commuted	race of offender & victim ...	123 death sentences	(no test of sig. or measure of association)	mix
Ehrmann (1952)	Mass. (6 counties) [1925-1941]	African American, Caucasian, Chinese [?]	homicide	executed		113 capital cases	observation, descriptive statistics	N/A

Author(s) & (year)	Jurisdiction [Time Period Covered]	Race/ Ethnicity [Gender]	Capital Offense	Dependent Variables	Independent Variables	Primary Sample	Main Type of Analysis	Race/ Ethnic effect?
Giardini & Farrow (1952)	22 states [1924-1952]	Mexican, African American, Caucasian, Native American [probably male & female]	homicide, rape, robbery, other	executed/ commuted	type of offense, state, time lapses between dispositions	749 death sentences (Mexican: N=38)	percentages (no sig. tests or measure of association)	N/A (race/ ethnicity were not included in the analysis)
Johnson (1957)	North Carolina [1909-1954]	African American, Caucasian [male & female]	homicide, rape, burglary	% executed/ admissions to death row	race, education, occupation ...	650 death row admission	percentages, test of significance	yes
Sellin (1959)	various states [various time frames (e.g., 1926-1937)]	African American, Caucasian, Native American, Chinese, Filipino, Japanese [male & female]	various felonies	executed/ commuted	offense, race and sex of offender ...	various samples (e.g., 1473; 1872)	tabular analysis (no sig. tests or measure of association)	yes

63

Author(s) & (year)	Jurisdiction [Time Period Covered]	Race/ Ethnicity [Gender]	Capital Offense	Dependent Variables	Independent Variables	Primary Sample	Main Type of Analysis	Race/ Ethnic effect?
Bridge & Mosure (1961)	Ohio [various time frames between 1910-1959]	African American, Caucasian [male & female]	homicide	executed/ commuted	race & sex of offender, region, motive, drugs, weapon, age, place of birth marital status, occupation, education, mental health, family background, prior record...	67 death sentences	percentages, ratios (no sig. tests or measure of association)	yes
McCafferty (1962)	Maryland [1936-1961]	African American, Caucasian [male & female]	homicide, rape	executed/ commuted	race, age, education, marital status, prior record, elapsed time, victim/ defendant relationship, place of birth, occupation, motive, weapon, county of conviction ...	102 death sentences	percentages (no sig. tests or measure of association)	yes
Wolfgang, Kelly & Nolde (1962)	Penn. [1914-1958]	African American, Caucasian [male & female]	homicide	executed/ commuted	felony/non-felony, type of counsel, race, age, marital status, nativity, occupation	439 death sentences	test of significance, chi-square	mixed (felony, yes; non-felony, no)

Author(s) & (year)	Jurisdiction [Time Period Covered]	Race/ Ethnicity [Gender]	Capital Offense	Dependent Variables	Independent Variables	Primary Sample	Main Type of Analysis	Race/ Ethnic effect?
Bedau (1964)	New Jersey [1907-1960]	Caucasian/ non-Caucasian [male & female]	homicide	executed/ commuted	felony/non-felony, race, age, sex, prior record, time under death sentence, nativity, SES, occupation, appeals sought, appeals taken, stays, and reprieves & retrials granted ...	235 capital cases	test of significance, chi-square, Yates' correction for continuity	no
Bedau (1965)	Oregon [1903-1964]	Caucasian/ non-Caucasian [male & female]	homicide	executed/ commuted	race, age, sex, nativity, occupation, type of murder, victim/ defendant relationship, type of counsel, sentencing power of the trial jury, facility of appellate review, use of clemency power. ...	92 capital cases	percentages (no test of sig. or measure of association)	no

65

Author(s) & (year)	Jurisdiction [Time Period Covered]	Race/ Ethnicity [Gender]	Capital Offense	Dependent Variables	Independent Variables	Primary Sample	Main Type of Analysis	Race/ Ethnic effect?
Carter & Smith (1969)	California [December 2, 1938 to January 23, 1963]	Mexican, African American, Caucasian, Native American, Chinese, Filipino [male]	homicide, kidnaping & assault by life termer	executed	race, offense, victim-offender relationship, weapon, prior record, age, place of birth, education, intelligence, family & occupational background, marital status, psychiatric data ...	187 executions (Mexican: N=12)	percentages	yes
Koeninger (1969)	Texas [1924-1968]	Latin, African American, Caucasian [male & female]ª	homicide, rape, armed robbery	executed/ commuted	age, birth place, education, occupation, employment, prior record, weapon, drugs ...	460 death sentences (Latino/a: N=45)	percentages	yes
Johnson (1970)	Louisiana [1900-1950]	African American, Caucasian [male]	rape	executed/ commuted	race, type of execution ...	49 death sentences	percentages (no sig. tests or measure of association)	yes

66

Author(s) & (year)	Jurisdiction [Time Period Covered]	Race/ Ethnicity [Gender]	Capital Offense	Dependent Variables	Independent Variables	Primary Sample	Main Type of Analysis	Race/ Ethnic effect?
Bowers (1984)	United States (Ohio, Virginia, New Jersey, New York, Penn., North Carolina) [various time frames--e.g., 1920-1962]	Caucasian/ non-Caucasian, 'un-classified' [probably male & female]	homicide, rape ...	executed	age, appeal, region	5,743 capital cases	descriptive statistics	yes
Ekland-Olson (1988)	Texas [February 1974 to July 1987]	Latino, African American, Caucasian [?]	homicide	executed/ commuted	year of conviction, race of offender & victim ...	247 capital cases (Latino: N=31)	it appears that multivariate analysis was used	mix

67

Author(s) & (year)	Jurisdiction [Time Period Covered]	Race/ Ethnicity [Gender]	Capital Offense	Dependent Variables	Independent Variables	Primary Sample	Main Type of Analysis	Race/ Ethnic effect?
Aguirre & Baker (1989)	Arizona, California, Colorado, New Mexico, Texas [1977-1986]; Arizona [1910-1963]; California [1893-1967]; Colorado [1890-1901]; New Mexico [1933-1960]; Texas [1924-1986]	Mexican, African American, Caucasian, Chinese, Native American [probably male & female]	homicide	executed (compared with granted appeals)	appeal (yes/no)	Southwest: 5,708 (105 Mexicans); Arizona: 63 (21 Mexicans); California: 267 (52 Mexicans); Texas: 358 (23 Mexicans)	tabular analysis	N/A
Vandiver (1993)	Florida [1924-1966]	African American, Caucasian [male & female]	homicide, rape	executed/ commuted	race of defendant & victim, age, type of crime ...	255 death sentences	chi-square, phi-square, corrected contingency coefficient	mix
Marquart, Ekland-Olson & Sorensen (1994)	Texas [1923-1972]	Latino/a, African American, Caucasian, other [male & female]	homicide, rape, arm robbery, burglary	executed/ commuted	offender, victim, & offense variables	510 death sentences (Latino/a: N= 48)	percentages, ratios, & significance tests	yes

68

Author(s) & (year)	Jurisdiction [Time Period Covered]	Race/ Ethnicity [Gender]	Capital Offense	Dependent Variables	Independent Variables	Primary Sample	Main Type of Analysis	Race/ Ethnic effect?
Aguirre & Baker (1997)	Arizona, California, Colorado, New Mexico, Texas [1795-1987]	Mexican [male & female]	homicide, rape, robbery- murder, rape- murder, murder- burglary, rape-robbery, sodomy, buggery- bestiality, theft- steal …	executed	offense, age, occupation, (also includes method of execution)	14,570 (301 Latinos/as; 244 Mexicans) (These include state, federal, territorial & military executions)	tabular analysis	N/A
Pridemore (2000)	south states/ non-south states [1974-1995]	African American/non- African American [male & female]	not specified (but it appears that the sample contains various felonies)	executed/ commuted	race, age, sex, prior felony, marital status, region, education, election year, political party	414 death sentences	logistic regression	no

Overall Summary: Yes: 10   No: 3   Mixed: 4   NA: 4

* ? = unable to determine from text.

a To Koeninger (1969, p.135), "most persons here classified as 'Latin' are white Texas of Mexican extraction."

69

Race and Ethnicity

Beginning with race and ethnicity, the two variables of primary interest, a number of early studies have found race and ethnic differences in death sentence outcomes (e.g., Bridge and Mosure, 1961; Johnson, 1957; Johnson, 1970; Mangum,1940; McCafferty, 1962; Sellin, 1959). For instance, Mangum (1940) found that the ratio of executions was higher for African Africans (73.5%) than Caucasians (55.5%) in Florida between August 1928 and December 1938. In Texas, the percentage was 83.2% for African Americans and 79.4% for Caucasians between February 8, 1924 to December 1, 1938.

Johnson (1957) found that first degree murderers and rapists had the highest execution rates, especially if the victim was a Caucasian female. Specifically, for homicide, 43.8% of Caucasians were executed compared with 62% of African Americans; for rape, 42.9% of Caucasians were executed compared with 56.4% of African Americans; and for burglary, 26.3% of African Americans, but no Caucasians, were executed for burglary in North Carolina from 1909 to 1954.[35] Sellin (1959) found that the likelihood of commutation in Ohio, given only race of offender, likewise penalized African Americans. Less than half as many African Americans as Caucasians sentenced to death benefitted from commutation.

Similarly, Bridge and Mosure (1961) found that a greater percentage of Caucasians than African Americans sentenced to death received commutations in Ohio from 1949 to 1959. Forty-nine percent of Caucasians has their sentences commuted versus 22% of African Americans. Conversely, 51% of Caucasians were executed compared with 78% of African Americans. McCafferty's (1962) Maryland study showed that of the 20 Caucasian inmates who were disposed of between 1936 and 1961, ten were executed and eight were commuted. For the 72 African American inmates, 47 (65.3%) were executed and 26 (36.1%) had their sentences commuted.[36] Johnson's (1970) Louisiana study showed that of the 39 executions, all but two were African American. Of the convicted rapists sentenced to death, whose death sentence was commuted to life imprisonment, two Caucasian men–one-half of all the Caucasian rapists sentenced to death–had their death sentences commuted.

According to Johnson (1970:217), "it is very difficult to secure commutation for a Negro convicted of rape."[37]

Some early studies, however, did not find race differences in death sentence outcomes. Bedau (1964) found that after controlling for felony/non-felony cases, race was not a significant factor in executions or commutations in New Jersey between 1907 and 1960.[38] A year later, Bedau (1965) discovered no race differences in Oregon between 1903 and 1964. Of the 83 Caucasians sentenced to death, 52 were executed and 21 had their sentences commuted; of the nine non-Caucasians sentenced to death, six were executed and two had their sentences commuted.[39]

In studies that have shown mixed evidence, Johnson (1941) found that for African American killers of Caucasian victims, the chance of commutation of the death sentence (19.5% of sentences commuted) was considerably lower than for any other capital offenders sentenced to death (35.6% for African American killers of African Americans, and 31.7% for Caucasians who killed Caucasians) during the period under study in North Carolina. In intraracial homicides, the percentages of death sentences commuted were about the same for African Americans and Caucasians, but when the offender was African American and the victim was Euro-American, the chance of receiving a commutation was one in five, instead of one in three. Wolfgang, Kelly, and Nolde (1962) found a statistically significant association between race and type of disposition, but only in felony cases. Specifically, compared to Caucasians, a significantly higher proportion of African Americans were executed instead of having their sentences commuted. However, controlling for felony/non-felony cases, Wolfgang et al. (1962) found race to be a significant factor in executions and commutations that pertain to felony cases, but not non-felony cases in Pennsylvania between 1914 and 1958.[40]

Criminal History

The offender's prior criminal history is an influential factor in death sentence outcomes.[41] Bridge and Mosure (1961) found that of the 37 who were executed in Ohio during the period under study, five had no previous criminal record, 13 had minor offenses, and 19 had felony convictions. Of the 23 who had their sentences commuted, six had no previous criminal record, 11 had minor offenses, and six had felony convictions.[42] McCafferty's (1962) Maryland study found that for those executed, seven out of ten had prior convictions; for those whose sentences were commuted, 59.4% had prior convictions. For those disposed of during the time under analysis, one-half of those with no prior conviction record were executed. For those with records who were disposed of, 60.3% were executed. Bedau's (1964) New Jersey study found a statistically significant relationship between carrying out the death sentence and previous criminal record, and between commutation and no previous criminal record. Lastly, Bedau's (1965) data showed that of the 39 with a prior conviction, 27 were executed and eight had their sentences commuted; and of the 16 death sentences with no prior conviction, three were executed and nine were commuted.

Other Demographic Variables

Although few studies examine gender due to the small number of females under the sentence of death, available data suggest that death sentence outcomes are "gendered." Few females have been executed in the United States compared to males (Bowers, 1974; Johnson, 1957). Homicide statistics show that of the 3, 464 legal executions carried out in 16 different states between 1830 and 1967, 35 (1%) were females (Bowers, 1974; Sellin, 1980; see also Gillespie, 2000). Of the 35 females executed, seven of the 33 whose race was known were African American (Sellin, 1980). Lastly, Bedau (1964) found a statistically significant association between death sentence commutation and females, and between the carrying out of death sentences and males.

For the next variable, age, prior research findings are quite mixed, but there is an indication that this variable has been an influential factor in death sentence outcomes.[43] Wolfgang, Kelly, and Nolde (1962) found that the polar ends of the age groups (15-19 years, and those 55 years and older) had the lowest frequency of execution and consequently, the highest frequency of sentence commutation. The highest frequency (92%) of executions occurred in the age group 20 to 24 years. Bedau (1964) found no statistically significant relation between execution and age, but did find a statistically significant association between sentence commutation and extreme youth. Bedau's (1965) data showed that youth, especially those under 20, increased the likelihood of sentence commutation. For the next-youngest age group (20-24), only two of the 15 death sentences were commuted, one of the lowest percentages of commutations among all age groups. His data also showed that young males guilty of felony murder are, if sentenced to death, not likely to receive commutation, and thus end up being executed.

As far as educational level of capital offenders, prior research findings also show that this variable has been an influential factor in death sentence outcomes. McCafferty (1962) found that the median school grade completed for those executed was seventh grade. Murderers who were executed had a median grade completed of 7.5, whereas for those executed for rape, the median was 5.3.[44]

As far as marital status of the criminal offender, a symbol of stability, prior research findings are inconclusive. McCafferty (1962) found that six out of ten inmates executed were single. For those executed for homicide, seven out of ten were single; for those executed for rape, five out of ten were single. Single inmates had a somewhat greater probability of being executed than married offenders. Wolfgang et al. (1962: 308), however, found "no important differences appear between the executed and commuted when examined in terms of marital status."

Death Sentence Outcomes

A third set of factors include the time spent under the death sentence, and the state where the death sentence outcome decision was made. For the first factor, little empirical work has been done, but prior findings suggest that the length of time between the death sentence and final disposition could be a critical factor. Bedau (1965) found that, overall, the mean time served from imposition of the death sentence to final disposition was 16 months. McCafferty (1962) found that the average days of elapsed time between the death sentence and disposition was lowest for prisoners executed. For the 57 executed, the average number of days was 220; for the 36 executed for murder, the average number of days was 257; for those executed for rape, the average number of days was 158. Inmates who had their death sentences commuted averaged 388 days between sentence and commutation. Murderers whose sentences were commuted averaged 448 days and rapists 312 days. Giardini and Farrow (1952) found that the time between the sentence of death and commutation was, on average, 9.6 months in Pennsylvania and 15.2 months in Kentucky. Marquart et al. (1994) found that the time from admission to death row to execution lengthened from something close to a month and a half in the 1930s to a period closer to five months in the late 1950s. The mean time for the 58 who were executed was 14 months.

Statistics for state and death sentence outcomes show that executions and sentence commutations vary by state (Sellin, 1980). Giardini and Farrow (1952), for instance, found that Pennsylvania executed an average of 8.6 offenders per year compared to Texas' average of 10.1 cases. Furthermore, when considering only homicide cases for Texas, the average drops to 7.6 cases per year. And, if one considers only homicide, Texas commuted 20% of the cases, compared to Pennsylvania's 18%. The difference, according to the authors, was not significant.[45]

The next two scholars, who have conducted evaluations of early studies, have made some critical observations of not only the findings but also of methods used to arrive at such conclusions. Hagan's (1974) reevaluation of the data shows some racial bias in sentencing for capital offenses, but only in the context of southern jurisdictions. Kleck (1981) reported some racial bias in death sentencing for capital offenses in the context of capital offenses. According to Kleck (1981), reevaluation of data on execution rates by race from 1930 to 1967, and on death sentencing rates from 1967 to 1978 show, except in the South, African American homicide offenders have been less likely than Caucasians to receive a death sentence or be executed. For the 11% of executions applied for rape, discrimination against African American defendants who had raped Caucasian victims was substantial, but only in the South.

When considering early studies, as Hagan (1974) and Kleck (1981) point out, one needs to consider the various limitations of such studies. As Kleck (1981) observes, a major shortcoming of early studies is that they nearly all fail to control for factors that might be influential (e.g., prior criminal record). Most studies that included controls, did not control all relevant factors simultaneously. Several early studies rarely used significance tests or measures of association. And, when significance tests were used, the authors relied primarily on them, but a problem with conclusions developed "solely on the basis of significance tests is the tendency to confuse substantive and causal significance with statistical significance" (Hagan, 1974:379). As a consequence, "we can only conclude that . . . the 'racial hypothesis' remains open to some doubt" (Hagan, 1974:368; see also Aguirre and Baker, 1990). One, however, cannot neglect the fact that these early studies, while not employing advanced analytical techniques or relying on sophisticated theoretical frameworks, clearly indicate that race is an important factor that needs to be analyzed critically, using a sound theoretical framework, and more advanced analytical techniques, especially since prior results are mixed.

As the next three studies, especially the last one, are central to this inquiry, I will discuss them in some detail. The first study is important not only because it is a recent death sentence outcomes study, but also because it analyzes one of our most important variables, race. The Florida (one of the three states included in the current study) data analysis employs various analytical techniques including chi-square, phi-square, and the corrected contingency coefficient. Using State Pardon Board files, opinions of the Florida Supreme Court and newspaper accounts, Vandiver (1993) examined all commutations and all executions (N=255) in Florida death sentences between 1924 and 1966, focusing particularly on whether the race ("white"/"black") of the defendants and victims influenced the decision to commute the sentence.

First, based on her analysis, of the total 255 (including two females) death sentences, 89 (34.9%) were Caucasian and 166 (65.1%) were African American. Forty-nine men (19.2%) were given the death sentence for rape, and 206 (80.8%) for murder. Furthermore, 92.9% of the death sentences were imposed for a crime against only one victim. In 74.5% of the cases the victims were Caucasian; in 25.5% they were African American. Sixteen defendants were 18 years old or younger at the time of their convictions, and 14 of those young defendants were African Americans.

According to Vandiver (1993:324), commutations were granted in 59 (23.1%) of the death sentences, while 196 (76.9%) were executed, but the data "shows no evidence that a defendant's race influenced commutation decisions." However, the victim's race had a strong influence upon the decision to commute the sentence; 44.3% of the defendants whose victims were African American received commutations, while only 15.2% of defendants whose victims were Caucasian received commutations.

African American defendants had a 41.1% chance of receiving a commutation if their victims were African American, but only a 5.3% chance if their victims were Caucasian. Commutations were granted to three African American defendants out of 55 condemned for the murder of Caucasian victims. The author tested whether the relationship of defendants and victims can account for racial differences. Among the category of "primary crimes" (homicides in which the victim and offender knew each other), a significant relationship between offender and non-stranger is observed, but such a relationship does not hold for the category of "non-primary" (homicides which occur between strangers) crimes.

After introducing "contemporary felony" (a crime, homicide, accompanied by additional felonies) as a control variable, the results showed that for non-felony cases, there was a statistically significant relationship between race and death sentence outcome. But, for felony cases, the relationship did not attain significance at the .05 level, although the relationship is in the predicted direction. African Americans were less likely to have their sentences commuted and more likely to be executed. A homicide committed in the course of an armed robbery might receive a harsher sanction than a murder arising from an argument. Additionally, a contemporary robbery could aggravate the punishment imposed for a rape charge. The results "support the hypothesis that defendants with contemporary felonies were less likely to receive commutations than those defendants whose crimes were not accompanied by additional felonies" (Vandiver, 1993:327).

Vandiver (1993) found that defendants whose death sentences had been imposed for committing rape had a lower chance of receiving commutation than those condemned for murder. After exploring this relationship by examining the influence of racial combinations of defendants and victims, and controlling for crime of conviction, "race continues to significantly influence outcome" (Vandiver, 1993:330). Of the 40 African American men sentenced to die for rape, only two (5%) received a commutation.

In short, race of both defendants and victims influenced the decision to execute or commute condemned prisoners in Florida between 1924 and 1966. In the words of Vandiver (1993:343), "the statistical analysis used in this study supports the hypothesis that the race of both defendants and victims influenced decisions to grant clemency [commutation]."

Vandiver's (1993) study, provides insight into executions and commutations, but the findings need to be interpreted with extreme caution. As the author acknowledges, there are a number of shortcomings. First, given the fact that the commutation and execution process operates in a very complex and subtle manner, the study lacks a more holistic theoretical base. Second, because of the small sample size, the missing data, and very small numbers in some of the tables, confident "interpretation of these results is difficult . . ."(Vandiver, 1993:327). Third, because of the lack of additional and critical control variables (e.g., ethnicity, prior criminal record), it is difficult to draw solid conclusions. Fourth, "the statistical analysis . . . was limited to very simple cross-classifications" (Vandiver, 1993:324). Thus, based on these limitations, the results must be viewed as tentative.

The next study by Marquart et al. (1994) is central to the current study not only because it is a recent death sentence outcomes study, but also because it analyzes our two most important variables, race and ethnicity, in Texas (one of the three states included in the current study), employing various analytical techniques (e.g., percentages and/or ratios). Specifically, Marquart et al. (1994) analyzed 510 capital offense offenders (507 males and 3 females) sentenced to die in Texas between 1923 and 1972. They analyzed the distribution of commuted and executed capital offenders by offender variables (race, ethnicity, mean age in years, gender, prior criminal record), offense variables (murder, rape, robbery by firearms), and victim variables (relationship to offender, race of victim, gender of victim, number of victims).

The results showed that of the 510 individuals sentenced to die, 92 had their sentences commuted (75 for murder, ten for rape, and seven for armed robbery) and 361 were eventually executed (71% for murder, 27% for rape, and one percent for armed robbery). All three of the women sentenced to die for capital murder had their death sentences commuted.[46]

Of the 361 who were executed, 107 (30%) were Caucasian, 229 (63%) were African American, and 24 (7%) were Latino. According to Marquart et al. (1994:23),

> once sentenced to die, blacks were more likely to be executed, 61 percent of the condemned whites having been eventually executed, compared with 82 percent of the blacks. Among Hispanics, the comparable figure was 50 percent, whereas only 20 percent of the black offenders received clemency. Interestingly, 46 percent of the Hispanic inmates received a commutation.

Their analysis of the percentage of African Americans versus Caucasians convicted of homicide who were eventually executed between 1924 and 1971 shows that the average yearly proportion of African Americans sentenced to die who were eventually executed was 84%, while 68% of the Caucasians sentenced to death were eventually executed over the same period. Thus, in cases of homicide, while the ratio of death sentences of Caucasians was following a downward trend, the rate of execution for African Americans remained almost 20 percentage points higher than for Caucasians. Similarly, death sentences involving the additional charge of rape were more likely to result in an eventual execution than were death sentences involving any other type of additional felony charge (e.g., robbery, burglary).

Of the 92 who had their death sentences commuted, 38 were Caucasian, 37 African American, and 17 were Latino. Among capital cases in which Caucasian victims were killed, 73% resulted in executions. By contrast, 62% of the capital cases involving African American victims and 46% of those involving Latino victims eventually resulted in the execution of the offender.

Lastly, based on their distribution of commuted (100) and executed (361) capital offenders by offender, offense, and victim variables, "race in combination with the type of offense charged, was a dominating influence on the commutation process" (Marquart et al., 1994:116). The authors found that offense variables and race and ethnicity were statistically significant at the .01 level.

All in all, 29% of all those who arrived on death row between 1923 and 1972 were granted clemency. However, according Marquart et al. (1994:119), Caucasian and Latino offenders benefitted more than African American offenders, "whose ancestors could be traced to the shores of Africa." Among the three major ethnic/racial categories (African Americans, Latinos, and Caucasians), Latinos, who were the least likely to receive a death sentence for murder, were the most likely to have their death sentences commuted, partly due to the higher proportion of "acquaintance" killings.[47]

An extensive criminal history (three or more offenses) also influenced the chances of being granted a commutation; that is, those with an extensive criminal history were less likely to have their death sentences commuted. Also, cases that involved single victims were more than twice as likely to result in a commutation (23%), compared to crimes in which two or more persons were victimized (11%). Moreover, Latino-victim cases were the most likely to be commuted; 50% (11 of the 22 cases) resulted in commutation. African American victim cases were the second most likely to result in commutation, 33% of such cases being commuted, compared with 19% of cases involving Caucasian victims. When the victim and offender were acquaintances or family members, just over one-third of the death sentences were eventually commuted. But, about one in ten of the death sentences for crimes involving strangers (especially women in rape cases) resulted in commutation. In short, commutation was more likely to have been bestowed on Caucasians who killed other Caucasians. Those who crossed racial lines to kill, especially African Americans, were more likely to be dispatched to the electric chair. In rape cases, again African American defendants were the least likely to be granted a commutation.

While Marquart et al.'s (1994) study provides insight into execution and commutation, the findings need to be interpreted with caution, given the fact that the study contains a number of shortcomings. First, given the fact that the commutation and execution process operates in a very complex, subtle, and manipulative manner, especially in recent years, the study needs a more holistic theoretical base. Second, since the authors combined (with no rationale for doing so) commutations, death sentences that were "reversed or dismissed" and/or death sentences that were vacated by the Supreme Court's *Furman* decision, confident interpretation of these results is difficult. (Though, it appears that the authors' main concern was that the inmates were released and not why they are released. The authors were analyzing post-incarceration behavior–i.e., amount of post-release crime like homicide.) Third, since the authors used the terms "commutation" and "clemency" interchangeably without making reference as to what was being discussed, it is difficult to draw conclusions. Fourth, because of the lack of additional and critical control variables (e.g., education), it is difficult to draw solid conclusions. Fifth, the statistical analysis was limited to very simple techniques. Thus, based on these limitations, the findings of the analysis must be viewed as tentative.

A study by Pridemore (2000) is one of the most recent death sentence outcomes study which analyzes race in various states, including California, Florida, and Texas (our three states of interest), in post-*Furman* capital cases, employing a highly advanced analytical technique (logistic regression analysis). Pridemore (2000) sought to determine which extralegal factors were significant in the commutation and execution decision-making process, which has been "highly discretionary," (and with no oversight) in capital cases from 1974 to 1995 (Pridemore, 2000:601). "Rather than directly testing a fully specified theory," the author seeks to answer the following questions:

> Do factors found to influence the final disposition of capital cases before the *Furman* decision still play a role in final dispositions today? Second, do distinctly political elements influence a governor's decision? Finally, what other possible characteristics might affect this process (Pridemore, 2000:607)?

His first hypothesis was that factors such as offender's age, sex, race, and prior felony, which were significant factors in the past, will still be significant today. According to Pridemore (2000), the young and the old are more likely to be granted a commutation in lieu of death than are offenders age 25 to 55. Since a prior felony is likely to mark the offender as a continuing danger, inmates with at least one prior felony conviction are more likely to be executed than those without them. Females, as in the past, are more likely than males to have their death sentences commuted. And, as in the past, African Americans are less likely than Caucasians to be granted a commutation.

His second set of hypotheses deals with a governor's possible political motives (e.g., reelection, a perceived need to appear tough on crime). While Pridemore (2000:602) notes that "the decision to commute may be political, exercised by the governor . . . with an eye to groups in the community who may be able to leverage power in their favor," he predicts no significant differences between Democrat and Republican governors in office at the time of the execution or commutation, due to the current punitive trend. But, he predicts that, since "opinion polls continue to show strong public support for the death penalty," a significant relationship between the date of final disposition (execution) and election year will prevail as a symbol of their "get tough" approach. Thus, in the words of Pridemore (2000:608), "I expect that offenders whose execution date falls in an election year are less likely to receive a commutation than those who are scheduled for execution at another time."

Thirdly, he predicted that offenders with higher levels of education, are more likely to receive a commutation than those with lower levels of education, due to the offender's possible future productivity. Similarly, he predicted that married offenders are more likely than unmarried offenders to have their sentences commuted, due to the offender's possible future stability, and thus, are less likely to recidivate. And, since "both southern society and southern justice are thought to be more punitive [a large proportion of the executions taking place there] and more violent than elsewhere in the country," Pridemore (2000:609) predicted that "such a tradition still exists and that offenders in the south are more likely than those in other regions to be executed."

After weeding out 40 "irrelevant" commutations, the author sought to measure the significance of sex, race ("nonblack/black"), age at disposition (continuous), education (less than high school/high school diploma/GED), marital status (not married/married), region (non-south/south), party (Republican/Democrat), election (no/yes) and the presence of a prior felony (no/yes), on the dichotomous dependent variable (commuted/executed) using the Bureau of Justice Statistics (BJS) data set (1997), which originally contained 454 death sentences (141 commutations and 313 executions) between 1974 and 1995.

Based on his selected sample of 414 death sentences (313 executions and 101 commutations), an adequate sample for the analytic technique being used and appropriate for testing the hypotheses under study, there were 405 men, nine women; 166 Caucasians, 215 African Americans; 272 had prior felony convictions, 99 did not; the average age at the final disposition was 36 and one-half years; 96 executions and commutations took place during a gubernatorial election year, 318 did not; 136 of the final dispositions were decided by Republican governors, 278 by Democratic governors; 298 executions and commutations occurred in southern states, 116 occurred in non-southern states; 149 received a high school diploma, 226 never finished high school; and 261 were not married, but 141 were. Based on Pridemore's (2000) logistic regression analyses, the offender's race (p=.754) and the presence of a prior felony (p=.754) were not significant factors in the execution decision-making process. However, the offender's age at disposition was significant (p<.001). In the post-*Furman* era, older inmates were not likely to be granted a commutation, but inmates 15 to 24 at the time of the final disposition are much more likely than older inmates to be granted a commutation.[48] Females are more likely to have their death sentences commuted.

The study concludes that "neither Democratic nor Republican governors are significantly more likely than their counterparts to choose an execution over commutation (p=.361)," but governors are significantly more likely to select execution in an election year than in a non-election year (p=.009) (Pridemore, 2000:614). Also, neither education (p=.998) nor marital status (p=.221) were influential factors in the decision-making process, but region appeared to be a strong factor in the execution/commutation process. Southern governors are much more likely than non-southern governors to choose execution over commutation (p<.001).

In a separate model, Pridemore (2000:615) limited the analysis to cases (374) that occurred between 1978 and 1995 to control for the "*Furman* impact." While the findings for race, sex, age, prior felony convictions, and education remain relatively unaltered, the governor's political party was now significant (p=.02): Democratic governors were more likely to execute than their Republican counterparts. Also, the significance level of election year changed to .106 and married offenders appeared to be granted a commutation more so than the unmarried. Among individuals with an original 50% chance of execution, the probability of execution decreased by 15% if they were married. Pridemore (2000:616) also found a significant interaction effect between race and region which indicated that "race does not seem to be a factor in the overall model, but perhaps nonblacks are treated differently depending on the region of the country." In testing for interaction between race and region as well as race and prior felony conviction, two different models employing interaction terms for race and region and for race and prior felony conviction were used, but there were "no significant differences" (Pridemore, 2000:616). Lastly, according to the author, between 1978 and 1995, offenders with a 50% chance of being executed faced a 20% increase in the likelihood of execution if they were a southern death row inmate.

According to Pridemore (2000:613), "several factors are correlated" with the decision to commute or execute, and "some degree of support is shown for each of the three sets of hypotheses." Finally, and perhaps most significant, is a concluding statement by Pridemore (2000:617): "it is a relief to find that race is not a factor in the decision to execute or commute." As with the earlier works, this study provides a sophisticated execution and commutation analysis, but "the findings presented here must be interpreted cautiously," because the study contains a number of critical limitations (Pridemore, 2000:617:621). First, there is a probability that the aggregation of race led to no effects. For instance, a "black/nonblack" dichotomy indicates that Pridemore (2000) categorized a very distinct population, Latinos, with Caucasians and African

Americans without providing a rationale for doing so. (No reference was made as to how the Latino population, the third largest group, was handled in his analysis.) There is also the probability that race was not significant because of multicollinearity among the independent variables. Thus, confident interpretation of these results is difficult.

Second, since the data clearly indicate that race (and ethnicity) effects vary from place to place (e.g., state to state), the "South/non-South" dichotomy approach utilized by the author (with little rationale for doing so), runs into similar problems. Pridemore (2000:608) acknowledges that

> it is true that certain segments of the population, via their power in society, may be able to influence a governor's decision to execute or commute. Because most states contain much higher proportions of white than black vote . . . a governor may be less inclined to commute a black offender's sentence.

While the number of death sentences, executions, and commutations vary widely across states, "the models estimated . . . operate on the assumption that the decision-making process is uniform across the country and that each governor in each state from 1974 to 1995 faced similar circumstances in making his or her decisions" (Pridemore, 2000:620).[49] And, indeed, Texas and Florida, two of our three states of interest, accounted for more than two-fifths of the cases (118 and 55, respectively, or 42%). Also, California, Florida, and Texas, our three states of interest, in combination commuted 48 death sentences, representing more than 48% of all the granted commutations. This, though, is not to imply that these three states should be lumped together for the purpose of analysis, as will be discussed in Chapter V.

As a third point, it is probable that age at the time of the offense would be a more appropriate measure than age at disposition to determine the impact of the death sentence on final disposition. Historically, age at the time of the offense, which carries a moral and passionate connotation, has often been controversial in terms of policy.

Fourth, the author assumes that everyone executed applied for clemency. He does, however, acknowledges that "it is likely that a handful of condemned did not seek a commutation" (Pridemore,

2000:622). Interestingly enough, while I agree with Pridemore (2000:622) that "it seems reasonable that nearly everyone facing death (or attorneys or family members working on their behalf) would apply for clemency," it also seems reasonable that the majority of those who did not seek a commutation were probably foreign nationals, given the fact that often the respective consulate, who is supposed to notify the defendant's relatives, is not notified by authorities. This information, however, is not available in the data set.

Lastly, the rationale for the exclusion of "commutations for judicial expediency" (five in Virginia and 29 in Texas) and commutations granted by former New Mexico Governor Toney Anaya (five) is not, in my view, convincing. An additional case was "deleted because the jurisdiction of the disposition was the District of Columbia," not involving "state executives" (Pridemore, 2000:610). Actually, the mayor of the District of Columbia has commutation powers similar to state governors. For instance, while Pridemore (2000:610) excluded Anaya's commutations because the "circumstances surrounding the crime and the characteristics of the offender were not relevant to the decision to commute," he decided to keep Ohio Governor Richard Celeste's commutations (eight) because of the Governor's claim that the death sentences "had been imposed unfairly." However, in the "Statement by Toney Anaya on Capital Punishment" (1993), Anaya made a similar (and more appealing) argument.

Because on these shortcomings, it is difficult to draw valid and reliable conclusions from Pridemore's (2000) analysis. One needs not only to be cautious when examining the results, but also with the author's interpretations of the findings. Overall, it is obvious that the wide discretion that led to the *Furman* (1972) decision, which supposedly was reduced by *Gregg* (1976), has not been eliminated. Additionally, such decisions attempted to remedy the capricious element in processing capital cases at the sentencing stage, but not for later stages: death sentence outcomes, executions and commutations. In the next section, after providing a brief summary of the strengths and weaknesses as well as the gaps in prior studies, I will address what I see as the most critical concerns.

SUMMARY OF PRIOR DEATH SENTENCE AND DEATH SENTENCE OUTCOMES RESEARCH

Strengths of Prior Studies

Prior studies have provided insight into the death sentencing decision-making process, as well as death sentence outcomes phenomena. Researchers have not only gone to great lengths to identify influential factor(s) in the decision-making processes, but have paved the way for additional studies, using more advanced quantitative and qualitative techniques, and more sound theoretical perspectives. While there is considerable debate over the various issues surrounding the death sentence and death sentence outcomes, there are some conclusions that can be made based on prior studies.

First, a review of the literature, which includes various time frames, jurisdictions, and at times large samples, on capital punishment clearly indicates that in the past death sentences were imposed capriciously in the United States. Second, on most issues relative to executions and commutations in capital cases prior research is inconclusive. As the tables above indicate, the influence of race and ethnicity on death sentence outcomes is mixed. However, based on the findings, one cannot rule out the possibility that race plays a significant and substantial role in determining who should receive a death sentence and who should not, who should be executed and who should not, and who should receive a commutation and who should not. On all three levels, there is an indication that African Americans have received the least justice.

Weaknesses of Prior Studies

It should be emphasized that while prior studies have become more sophisticated over the years, they still contain a few shortcomings (see Klepper, Nagin and Tierney, 1983). First, most death sentences as well as death sentence outcomes (executions/commutations) analyses have been based on bivariate analytical techniques (e.g., cross tabular analysis, ratios, chi-square, and trends over time). Second, most studies have included a number of relevant independent variables, but the included variables were not controlled for simultaneously. Third, few attempts have been made to make a clear distinction between the various possible death sentence outcomes. For instance, on a number of occasions (e.g., Marquart et al., 1994), various possible death sentence outcomes were combined for the purpose of analysis without making reference to what was being analyzed or providing a rationale for a given combination. As will be discussed in Chapter V, the process leading to commutations, which are mostly granted by state governors, is extremely political and not necessarily focused on possible trial errors. The decisions to overturn sentences and/or convictions, which are issued by appellate courts, rely on processes that are more concerned with trial errors and less political, since federal judges are appointed and not elected. This is not to say that federal judges are not political. Additionally, at times, the various terms (e.g., "commutation," "executive clemency," "clemency") have been used interchangeably without making clear distinctions about what was being analyzed and/or discussed.

Fourth, a number of previous studies examined whether racial differences occur at a single point in the legal process (death sentencing stage), and often focus solely on whether death sentencing decisions favor African Americans or Caucasians, as will become evident in the next two subsections. However, while racial differences in legal processing might be relatively small at any particular stage of the lengthy legal process, cumulative effects on the overall patterns could be significant and substantial. Thus, the legal decision-making process needs to be analyzed by the totality of outcomes–i.e., across multiple decision points. Fifth, death sentencing and/or death sentence outcomes jurisdiction has usually been operationalized as "South/non-South," and thus neglects the fact that disparities in death sentence outcomes vary depending on time and space, state to state.

Lastly, as Liska (1992) points out, the exact perceived threats operating have remained largely unmeasured in prior studies. The "threats" typically have not been included in a sophisticated fashion in empirical tests of the threat perspectives. Inferences of the type of threat operating generally have been based solely on Blalock's (1967) expectations of certain types of nonlinearities in the relationship between non-Caucasian, usually African American "concentration" and "discrimination" without reference to other minority groups. In addition, since discrimination has usually meant sentencing of non-capital cases, the analyses of executions and/or commutations, as two possible death sentence outcomes, have not only been limited, but little has taken place beyond these two decisions-making points.

Gaps in Prior Studies

While prior research has definitely enhanced our understanding of the decision-making process, a number of significant issues need further examination. First of all, as Pridemore (2000:601) points out, "in the voluminous literature surrounding capital punishment . . . relatively little contemporary empirical work focuses directly on the characteristics of the final clemency decision to commute or execute, especially post-*Furman*." Not only have few empirical death sentence outcomes (executions and/or commutations) studies been conducted, but it is difficult to locate studies that have empirically explored the following three additional (possible) death sentence outcomes, which constitute a significant number of death sentence outcomes in the post-*Furman* era: (1) "capital sentence declared unconstitutional by State or U.S. Supreme Court," (2) "conviction affirmed, sentence overturned by appellate court," and (3) "conviction and sentence overturned by appellate court" (Pridemore, 2000:601). Little emphasis has been given to inmates remaining on death row (under the sentence of death), which constitutes an "outcome." Since no action has taken place for those remaining under the sentence of death, this is an indication, by default, of life imprisonment. Thus, there is certainly not only a need to go beyond executions and commutations, but also to include those remaining on death row in the analysis.

Second, due in large part to the un-availability of information (or limited data), death sentencing as well as death sentence outcomes research has traditionally taken a dichotomous African American/Caucasian approach and thus, little attention has been given to other minority groups, such as the Latino community (approximately

12.5% or 35.3 million of the total U.S. population), a group that is now larger than the African American community, which constitutes approximately 12.3% or 34.7 million of the total U.S. population.[50] Traditionally, studies have totally left this group out, or combined it with the Caucasian and African American groups, though one cannot be certain as often no reference has been made as to how this population was handled in the analysis.

Two studies of death penalty discrimination in Texas (Ekland-Olson, 1988 and Marquart et al., 1994) included the Latino group in their analysis, but no attempt was made to disaggregate the Latino population. Thomson's (1997:69) study of racial and ethnic discrimination in death sentencing in Arizona, which begins at the earliest stage of the capital punishment process, acknowledges the diversity of "three distinct minority groups: Mexican-Americans, African Americans, and Native Americans," yet makes no attempt to disaggregate the Latino group. As indicated in Tables 1 and 2, few studies have included Latinos (or other minority groups) in the analysis, and little attempt has been made to disaggregate the Latino population in both capital punishment studies and non-death penalty studies.[51]

Addressing the Weakness and Gaps of Prior Studies

Given the various limitations of prior death sentence outcomes research, there are a number of questions that remain unexplored. For instance, do similar disparate trends exist in the three additional possible death sentence outcomes (vis a vis executions, commutations, and those who are still under the sentence of death)? Do similar disparities exist for Latinos (vis a vis African Americans and Caucasians)? How severe is the death sentence outcomes disparity among these U. S. populations (including African Americans and Caucasians) once the Latino group is included in the equation? How severe is the death sentence outcomes disparity among these segments of society once the Latino category is disaggregated and included in the equation? Which ethnic Latino members are on death row? Lastly, which ethnic Latino members have been executed in the

United States? (One thing to keep in mind is the fact that Latinos/as recently became the country's largest minority group.) Given the nature of the data, it will not be possible to address each and every one of these concerns, but great efforts will be made to address most of them.

First, given the fact that prior theoretical and empirical work has focused primarily on the experiences of African Americans (vis a vis Caucasians), and has given the Latino history little emphasize, a detailed analysis of the history of U.S. race and ethnic relations–especially between African Americans, Caucasians, Cubans, and Mexicans–will be provided in the following chapter. I argue that not only does the Latino population have a distinct and unique history, but so do the various ethnic groups that make up the Latino population. Historical insight will allow a better understanding of inequality in death sentence outcomes.

Second, not only will the "Latino" category be included in the current tabular and logistic regression analyses, but an effort will be made to disaggregate the Latino category for descriptive purposes. Specifically, the ultimate goal is to disaggregate the entire Latino category. However, due to time and resources, only those "Latinos" who were executed between 1975 and 1995 in the United States (including the three states of primary interest and three death penalty states with a significant Latino population), will be disaggregated for this particular project. While this will provide insight into only one of the five selected dichotomous dependent variables, executed (versus those still on death row) Latinos, it will allow speculations to be made about the other four dependent variables in the analysis. (A more detailed discussion of these issues will be provided in Chapter V.)

Third, given the complexity and confusion–especially with the terminology and rationale for categorization–of death sentence outcomes, I extend the examination of executions and commutations to include three additional death sentence outcomes (dependent variables), as well as those who still remain under the sentence of death. A detailed discussion of the various possible death sentence outcomes in the United States will be provided in Chapter V.

Fourth, every relevant factor (state where the death sentencing occurred, sex, race, ethnicity, education, marital status, age of defendant when the capital offense was committed, number of years under death sentence, and prior felony convictions) in the data set will be included in the analysis, which will consist of tabular analysis and logistic regression analysis (considered by some observers as the most advanced and adequate analytic technique for this type of quantitative research). Also, in addition to making certain adjustments (e.g., more appropriate coding) to the independent variables, careful attention will be given to missing data, which, in the past, usually has been discarded.

Finally, these steps will allow the discourse on race and ethnic differences in death sentence outcomes to move beyond two traditional approaches: (1) the Caucasian and African American dichotomist approach, and (2) the sole execution and/or commutation approach, which has been mostly qualitative, or limited to tabular techniques. Because both approaches have at times lacked a sound theoretical framework, new perspectives will be provided in Chapter IV to build on those provided in Chapter II.

CHAPTER 4

History of U.S. Race and Ethnic Relations

When interpreting the social conditions of inequality and marginalization faced by minority groups, one needs to look beyond culture-based explanations, which tend to minimize the role of political and economic structures. Additionally, to break down barriers to historical understanding among the various groups that comprise the United States, one needs to analyze the relationships between minority groups and Caucasians. Thus, the analysis needs to expand upon Earl Shorris' (1992:xv) friendly advice to: "Just tell them who we are and that we are not all alike."

This chapter begins by exploring the historical relationships between African Americans, Caucasians, Cubans, and Mexicans, and their interactions with the American criminal justice system. This historical background will enhance our understanding of when, why, and how African Americans, Mexicans, and Cubans are more likely to be executed or less likely to have their sentences and/or convictions overturned. Then, after the examination of specific race and ethnic histories (and relying on prior empirical and theoretical research), a new typology of death sentence outcomes will be offered and specific hypotheses for each group within each state will be proposed.

AFRICAN AMERICANS IN THE LAND OF EQUALITY

The Early Days in the Americas

According to Feagin and Vera (1995), Europeans held extremely negative views of African people long before the founding of the European colonies, although these negative ideas did not develop into full-blown racist ideologies until the 1700s. Feagin and Vera (1995) propose that negative images of African Americans were accepted (and perhaps even welcomed) by the framers of the Declaration of Independence and the U.S. Constitution. As Gordon (1964:89) explains, "the founding fathers of the American nation were by no means men of unthinking prejudices." Foner (1998:86) argues that "blacks formed no part in the imagined community of Jefferson's republic." For instance, despite Jefferson's indictment of slavery, he himself was a slave owner with racist ideas. Feagin and Vera (1995:68) write that "Jefferson argued that what he saw as the ugly color, offensive odor, and ugly hair of African American slaves indicated their physical inferiority and that their alleged inability to create was a sign of mental inferiority." Others like "Andrew Jackson committed more than his share of 'crimes against humanity'" (Acuna, 1998:70).

For eighty years, only Euro American immigrants could become naturalized citizens. African Americans were added in 1870 (Foner, 1998). The 1849 California State Constitutional Convention initially relegated African Americans to second-class legal status. The first draft of the "Right to Suffrage" stated that only "white male citizens of the United States" would be entitled to vote (Almaguer, 1994:38). African Americans were not only denied the right to vote, but also to hold public office, to testify in court against Caucasian individuals, to serve on juries, to attend public schools, or to homestead public land. It was not until the ratification of the 14th Amendment in 1870 that African Americans were granted the same legal rights as Caucasian people in California and the rest of the United States (Almaguer, 1994; see also Acuna, 1988). Unquestionably, the subordinate status of African Americans in California created tremendous and devastating consequences for their "life chances" in the state.

Thus, on one level, ". . . the world of white and black are distinct" (Ezekiel, 1995:310). On another level, the history of African Americans in the United States has been very different from that of other minority groups, as will become clear later. According to Cooper (1988:194), the African American was ". . . brought into this country by force and compelled under the lash to lend his brawn and sturdy sinews to promote its material growth and prosperity . . .." Brought to this country as forced labor and in servitude rather than in mere poverty, kept in servitude until a century and a quarter ago, and in political, economic, and social subjugation since, African Americans have been treated by the ruling elite as threatening and unassimilable. As a result, the cultural gap between African Americans and Caucasians has remained wide and deep (Gates and West, 1997; Griffin, 1961; King, 1981). (See Griffin's *Black Life Me* for a vivid account of the African American experience.)

In the early days, as Almaguer (1994) documents, slavery economically subordinated the nation's African American population to Caucasians, and their second-class social/political status structurally ensured that African Americans could not compete effectively with Caucasians at any level of the social, political or economic structure. Furthermore, history reveals that in the case of African Americans, the law silently but definitely separated people into various groups. Among these groups, precisely because of their internal histories as well as their external treatment, significant cultural and social differences existed (Gates and West, 1997).

Defining a Black Race

African Americans, as seen through racist eyes, have been viewed as people who do not want to work, who would rather be on welfare (or simply unemployed), who gain money through bullying, cheating and/or selling drugs, who rob and kill and who are violent by nature. African Americans, racists believe, want to hurt Caucasians, to assault verbally and physically, to rob Caucasian people, and to rape Caucasian females (Ezekiel, 1995; Gans, 1995). "Pressed for detail, white racists will estimate that eighty percent of black people are this sort" (Ezekiel, 1995:311).

Again, as Feagin and Vera (1995:68) point out, "the white tendency to view people of African descent as deviant or criminal is centuries old. Since the 1400s, rather than seeing a common humanity uniting Europeans and Africans, Europeans and their American descendants have mostly seen difference." These anti-African images were imported by the colonies, where images born in European ignorance were used to justify the manipulation, subjugation and exploitation of Africans brought and sold as slaves (Feagin and Vera, 1995).[52] Feagin and Vera (1995) further add that the negative stereotype of African American men as uncivilized and fear-inspiring "savages" who are a sure threat to Caucasian women is not new in that it dates back several centuries.

Views That Never Die

While some individuals claim that racism is a phenomenon of the past, such attitudes are still alive and active at every level. For example, Presidents and presidential candidates continue to make (or make use of) remarks and/or images reflecting racial and ethnic stereotypes. On this end, it is well known that while in office, President Richard M. Nixon had negative views of African Americans. And, Nancy Reagan reminded Caucasian Americans of the color line during her husband's presidential campaign. Speaking to Ronald Reagan in a telephone call being carried by a loudspeaker during the campaign, Ms. Reagan said that she would like for him to be with her in Illinois with "all these beautiful white people," an indication of how "white" that Republican campaign was (Simon, 1990:7).

The history of the African American race in America, including slavery since 1619, raises many critical questions about the construction of difference. How can one group of individuals treat another as if they were not human? Hess, Markson, and Stein (1998:258) argue that it can be accomplished, "only by defining 'the other' as so very different as to be 'non-human.'" An old proverb says that, "The devil is always painted black [or brown or red]–by white painters." It is also evident that this process is easiest when the "other," the "stranger," and/or the "outsider" has little resemblance to us, as in the case of black African tribal peoples compared to the European Christians on this continent who bought and sold them.[53]

In modern times, racists have found a new wave of influential supporters. For example, as King (1981) points out, in 1974 at Oxford University, John R. Baker concluded his study by rating human races on their innate capacity for originating civilization and ethical standards, and finds the African blacks in last place. It should come as no surprise that in addition to giving inferior positions on biological and cultural scales to living in "primitive" communities, Westerners have also rated minorities very low in morality, thus allowing the Western Caucasian to define and re-define him/herself as "the better person" (King, 1981). Such an image is further given life by best selling and award winning books claiming to have "proved anew that blacks and poor people are more stupid than everyone else . . . Or, 'generally inferior' to the rest of humanity . . ." (Williams, 1997:47).

Recently, *The Bell Curve* by Herrnstein and Murray (1994), *Why Race Matters* by Michael Levin (1997), *The g Factor* by Arthur Jensen (1998) and *Race, Evolution, and Behavior* by J. Philippe Rushton (1999) have shown that stereotypes persist and even offer the intellectual rationalization for modern racists. To Herrnstein and Murray (1994), the source of inferior test scores, higher unemployment and other inequalities among African Americans is genetic.[54] Along these same lines, Gans (1995:60) made the observation that

> an underclass of young people becomes considerably more threatening when it is called 'feral,' and even worse is the idea of a biological underclass, which implies a genetic and thus permanent inferiority of a group whom public policy can render harmless only by sterilizing, imprisoning, or killing them.

Ideologically satisfactory "answers" are frequently easier and cheaper to find in already available statistics from which "undeserving" behavior and "undesirable" motives can be inferred (Gans, 1995). It is even cheaper, more convenient, and more satisfying for some to argue that personal beliefs are more accurate and convincing than empirical data, or as Representative William McCollum of Florida once said in a discussion of the death penalty, "While statistics might not indicate that it deters crime, it's common sense that it does" (Gans, 1995:128). Additionally, racial images and myths (e.g., "welfare queen," "Willie" Horton, "ghetto pathology") have served as convenient weapons, especially during election time. For example, a Republican gubernatorial candidate in Massachusetts once demanded the reinstatement of the death penalty, and the Democratic candidate went so far as to say that he would like to pull the electric switch (Feagin and Vera, 1995).

Controlling a Black Population

In *A Voice From the South* Anna Julia Cooper (1988:92), notes that from the beginning of time, humanity has had its

> vultures and sharks . . . That this virulence breaks out most readily and commonly against colored persons in this country, is due of course to the fact that they are, generally speaking, weak and can be imposed upon with impunity.

In her analysis of America's race problem, Cooper (1988:163) documents a historical trend: "America for Americans! . . . Lynch, suppress, drive out, kill out! America for Americans!"

Franklin and Moss (1988:436) claim that dismissals from jobs, denials of loans, and foreclosures of mortgages were among the several manipulating tactics used to decimate the ranks of active and vocal African Americans. As if this was not enough, Anglos most threatened were often ready to use other means necessary. For example, in analyzing the life of African Americans, well known and respected scholars Henry Louis Gates and Cornel West (1997:56) characterize the end of the 20th century as "a ghastly century whose levels of barbarity, bestiality, and brutality are unparalleled in human history."

Thus, African Americans were not only viewed as an inferior caste, widely disfranchised, and usually segregated in areas ranging from public restrooms to universities, but were frequently lynched and mobbed (Gates and West, 1997). For instance, Caucasian racial violence in the South after

Reconstruction was a means of social controlling what latter would be viewed as a threatening surplus population. Caucasians in positions of power preserved Caucasian domination, through the threat of violence, and actual violence (e.g, lynching). Case in point: In the century after Reconstruction, it has been estimated that somewhere between 3,000 and 5,000 African Americans were lynched by Caucasians. Aguirre and Baker (1999) and Mann (1993) document the fact that executions and lynchings of African Americans, were a major factor as late as the early 20th century. From 1882 to 1899 there were 1,043 lynchings for homicide, from 1900 to 1929 there were 750 lynchings, and 44 lynchings took place between 1930 and 1977. Over this 85-year time frame, 73% of these illegal murders were African Americans. Many of the victims were burned alive, chained to iron stakes that had been driven into the ground; others were hanged. The "lucky" ones were shot soon after the burning or the hanging began. There are many horrendous accounts of desperate individuals crawling from the flames and being pushed back in. Bodies were slashed; fingers were cut off. Often the victim's genitals were cut off (Dike, 1982; Ezekiel, 1995; Johnson, 1990; McGehee and Hildebrand, 1964; Reggio, 1997; Sellin, 1980).[55] One case that will forever be remember, I would hope, is the case of legendary U.S. Supreme Justice Thurgood Marshall. In 1946, while in Columbia, Tennessee, on NAACP business, Marshall was stopped on a lonely road by sheriff's deputies and highway patrol officers while clansmen waited nearby at the Duck River. The future Justice of the U.S. Supreme Court was rescued from the lynch mob by an armed escort of local African Americans who grabbed him from police custody. The following day they returned to the scene and found a lynch rope and noose still hanging from a tree by the river. They cut it down and gave it to young Marshall for a souvenir (Marshall joined the Supreme Court in 1967). An investigation was requested, but no officers were ever prosecuted and, even more strangely, no charges were ever brought against Marshall's African American rescuers, who were well known to the local law enforcement officials (Rowan, 1993).

A vivid illustration of modern brutality and discrimination are the well documented attacks on the Philadelphia-based MOVE organization by law enforcement officials. In fact, some observers document that members of the organization have been subjected to some of the worst forms of injustices seen in 20th century America. More specifically, founded in 1972 by Vincent Leaphart, MOVE spoke out vehemently against all forms of government, and on August 8, 1978 MOVE members and law enforcement officers were engaged in a deadly confrontation. Since, one officer was killed, allegedly by MOVE members, nine MOVE members were convicted on third degree murder charges and received 30 to 100 year sentences. Then, on May 13, 1985, there was a second major controversial confrontation. The police (including snipers) destroyed the compound using M-16 assault rifles, M-60 machine guns, 50-caliber machine guns, and a bomb. By the time the tragedy was over, the fire had destroyed the MOVE compound as well as 61 other houses, leaving 260 people homeless. The bodies of six adults and five children were pulled from the burned house. There were only two survivors, and one of the two was convicted on riot and conspiracy charges. Criticisms for the aftermath of 10,000 rounds of ammunition, tear gas, and explosives were not delayed, but it took a long time before the city had to take responsibility for what had happened. After a long struggle, a jury found the city guilty of using excessive force and of violating MOVE's constitutional right to protection against unreasonable search and seizure (see Anderson and Hevenor, 1987; Goldberg, 1996; Nelson and Maddox, 1996; Wagner-Pacifici, 1994).

According to Cooper (1988), there are two perspectives that turned many southern Caucasians against African Americans. "The one is personal and present, the fear of Negro political domination. The other is for his posterity–the future horror of being lost as a race in this virile and vigorous black race" (Cooper, 1988:219). Ezekiel (1995) adds that such cruelties can be seen simply as the furthest extent of the cry of superiority and control, the mob's ultimate proclamation of the degradation of the African American community, especially the young. The cruelty may also be fueled by the aggressor's fear of his/her own sexuality. To King (1981), cultural history not phenotype or biology is the defining factor. In other words, culture plays the major role in determining how society judges its members and how individuals react to one another. It is culture, not genotype, that leads one segment of society to attempt, often with great success, to cripple or kill off another that it considers racially different. This in part is affirmation of the charge of genocide against "white" America.

Modern Times

The formal end of slavery in 1865 brought one kind of freedom but left former slaves under the control of a range of "Jim Crow" laws designed to limit their choices of jobs, residential location, right to vote, education, and so forth. It was these limitations, written into law, that created the system of de jure segregation that was dismantled with the civil rights acts of the 1960s (Feagin and Vera, 1995; Hess et al., 1998). Yet, many Anglos continue to view African Americans in very negative ways. Not surprisingly, while some changes were taking place, Myrdal (1944) was writing about the "American dilemma": the tension that exists in the United States between the widely proclaimed ethic of equality and the reality of everyday and everynight prejudice, racism and inequality. A few years later, the Kerner Commission found America to be racist. In the words of the Commission, "Our nation is moving toward two societies, one black, one white–separate and unequal" (Tabb, 1970:134).

Today, African Americans comprise about 12.3% of the total U.S. population, but remain disadvantaged along many dimensions of social stratification. African Americans are over-represented at the lower end of the income and occupation hierarchies, and under-represented in positions of political and economic power. In addition, the employment and income gaps that had been narrowing between 1965 and 1980 began to widen once again, as the Reagan and Bush administrations cut programs that assisted racial minorities and failed to enforce regulations designed to reduce discrimination in housing and jobs. The result has been labeled American apartheid, in reference to the systematic residential segregation of African Americans in areas where employment opportunities are almost nonexistent.

To place the current situation of African Americans into perspective, consider the following figures. The proportion of African Americans living in poverty (over 30%, triple that of Caucasians) is no lower now than in the early 1970s. African American males are unemployed at twice the rate of the national average and, in the state of California, African

American youth have an unemployment rate of approximately 50 percent. Furthermore, African Americans are only 4% of all college professors; 3% of physicians; 2% of lawyers; and only slightly more than one percent of teachers in elementary grades are African American males. On this end, notice that during last three decays, some observers argued that the situation was getting better. However, in terms of education and social control, the situation remains relatively the same, if not worse. The 1990 Sentencing Project found that "the number of young Black men under the control of the criminal justice system–609,690–is greater than the total number of Black men of all ages enrolled in college–436,000 as of 1986. For white males, the comparable figures are 4,600,000 total in higher education and 1,054,508 ages 20-29 in the criminal justice system" (Mauer, 1990:1). And, based on the latest statistics (e.g, disproportionate minority confinement data), the situation is not significantly better. In particular, the government is using anti-drug legislation (e.g.,sentence enhancement laws, Racketeer Influenced and Corrupt Organizations Act, better known as RICO) to warehouse African Americans, especially those who are defined as "gangsters," in jails and prisons. It should be emphasized that traditionally the majority of people under the control of the criminal justice system have been men. However, the rates of women, especially African American women, under the control of the system have increased during the last few years (see Currie, 1993; Irwin and Austin, 1997; Tonry, 1995). Case in pont: In large part attributed to the introduction of crack cocaine into the ghetto and the war on drugs, the government has implemented very punitive measures against "crack mothers" (see Humphries, 1999). Unfortunately, as Humphries (1999) documents, little effort was made to access the special needs of trouble women before the criminalization of crack mothers became a media spectacle.[56] Furthermore, the 1989 median African American family income was 59.4% of Caucasian family income, and was lower than it had been in 1970. Additionally, African American babies are twice as likely to die as Caucasians, and over 40% of African American children lived below the poverty level in 1989. Almost 50% of the homeless are African Americans, and over 40% are functionally illiterate (Brigham, 1996; Gans, 1995).

The homicide rate for African American men between the ages of 15 to 44 is 10 times that of Caucasians.[57] It has been estimated that ". . . in California, African-American males are three times more likely to be murdered than to be admitted to the University of California" (Brigham, 1996:102). In part, this is the result of U.S. historical racism. For example, in September 1974, Bostonians rioted when authorities attempted to integrate the school system. An Anglo demonstrator summed up the mood of the "Archie Bunkers" (a term now synonymous with bigot) when he yelled: "The real issue is nigger" (Acuna, 1988:365)! Indeed, 45 years after the *Brown* case (1954), many schools remain separate and unequal (see Baldus and Cole, 1980).

Brigham's (1996) analysis of the 1992 Los Angeles riots reveal that over two-thirds of the African Americans arrested were unemployed; of all looters, 60% were high school drop outs; and 87% reported income of less than $1,000 per month. Thus, if one is seeking a realistic snap shot of the "underclass" in the United States, one need only explore for a moment the profile of those involved in the looting and burning of Los Angeles, a profile that is virtually unaltered since the Watts riot of 1965.

In Case You Are Not Dead

One of the more recent assaults on the African American community is the termination of affirmative action in some universities. A new piece of propaganda has been advanced that discrimination no longer exists. In fact, some go as far as saying that Caucasians are now the victims of discrimination. For instance, Anglos often claim that unqualified African Americans are now entering the privileged world of universities because of affirmative action. The truth is, though, that far more Caucasians have entered the gates of the ten most elite institutions through 'alumni preference' than the combined numbers of all African Americans and Chicanos entering through affirmative action (Stein, 1995). Ironically, in 2002, the University of Michigan's affirmative action admissions policies are being contested in two cases before the U.S. Supreme Court.

Even worse, some politicians apparently see nothing strange in the fact that just in the last few years the U.S. government has spent billions of dollars fighting or preparing for wars (not to mention the millions of dollars spent on space exploration). Yet, many of these same politicians throw up their hands before they will consider overhauling our schools, cleaning the slums, and really abolishing poverty, especially among the young (Tabb, 1970).

Harrington (1971:5) once made the observation that "clothes make the poor invisible too: America has the best-dressed poverty the world has ever known." In fact, Congress allocated only $1.6 billion annually to eliminate the so-called "discovery of poverty. " Perhaps $1.6 billion may seem like a large sum, however, considering that there are some 30 to 40 million poor in the United States, this amount did not go very far (Acuna, 1988). Actually, from its beginning the war on poverty was in trouble; it lacked resources, motivation, and honesty–beyond good intentions. Money that could have been allocated was syphoned off for space, missile, and armament programs, taking precedence over people.

As illustrated by the following cases, this pattern has been active since the Republicans began dismantling social services. President Nixon's advisor Arthur Burns, defined poverty as an "intellectual concept" in 1969. Soon afterward, President Nixon appointed Burns to the Federal Reserve Board. In addition, the new Burger Court was less interested in improving access for minorities (Mowry and Brownell, 1981). Even President Reagan's second Attorney General Edwin Meese III once stated that there was no authoritative evidence that hunger existed in America. Reagan himself firmly believed that hunger and poverty did not exist and blamed hunger on a "lack of knowledge."[58]

As the Road Comes to an End

Gans (1995) claims that although the long and turbulent fight against racial prejudice and discrimination cannot be said to have been won, and sometimes has actually driven anti-African American and anti-Caucasian attitudes underground, its net effect has been mostly positive. For him, the country is better off for that long and difficult fight. Others, however, argue that "institutionalized racism remains a powerful determinant of the life chances of African Americans" (Hess et al., 1998:261; Anderson, 1995b).

The frustration of African Americans is perhaps best illustrated in the case of W.E.B. Du Bois. As Gates and West (1997:111) point out, after 95 years of the most courageous and unflagging devotion to African American freedom and progress witnessed in the 20th century, Du Bois not only left America for Africa but concluded, "I just cannot take any more of this country's treatment. We leave for Ghana October 5th and I set no date for return. . . . Chin up, and fight on, but realize that American Negroes can't win." Nation of Islam leader Don Muhammad remarked: "Blacks have been in America 437 years, and people who have been here 437 days have walked past us" (Levin and McDevitt, 1993:148).

Some years later, Tabb (1970) pointed out that prejudice and racism pervaded every institution in the United States from churches to universities. Cooper (1988) asserts that African Americans in the United States have suffered and continue to experience many injustices. More recently, constitutional scholar Derrick Bell (1992) has argued that racism is so fundamental to this nation that African Americans will probably never gain equality with Caucasian Americans. Frequently, many Caucasians support the cause of equality and "equal" justice for African Americans, only when it is in their interest to do so (Bell, 1980). Today, however, racism is sometimes more subtle. For instance, many racists wear suits, not sheets. And, of course, we cannot neglect the fact that some are probably sitting in honorable positions. To African American nationalists, American "democracy" is a modern form of tyranny and manipulation on the part of the ruling Caucasian majority over the African American minority (Gates and West, 1997).

What Are the Choices?

To Cooper (1988:173), the United States needs African Americans for "ballast if for nothing else." Following Andrew Hacker, Gans (1995:92-93) says that

> whites need the 'nigger,' because it is the 'nigger' within themselves that they cannot tolerate. . . . Whatever it is that whites feel 'nigger' signifies about blacks–lust and laziness, stupidity or squalor–in fact exists within themselves. . . By

creating such a creature, whites are able to say that because only members of the black race can carry that taint, it follows that none of its attributes will be found in white people.

At the end of the Tunnel

At least in Texas, two sets of relations existed side by side: pre-capitalism and slavery. Racial prejudice and ideologies still undergird and rationalize widespread Caucasian prejudice and discrimination against African Americans. All in all, modern racial discrimination is, as the late U.S. Supreme Court Justice William O. Douglas put it in the late 1960s, a "spectacle of slavery unwilling to die" (Feagin and Vera, 1995:168). Well known and respected legal scholar Richard Delgado (1995) articulates a Law of Racial Thermodynamics: racism is never eliminated but always comes back in new forms in more appropriate times. And, indeed, slavery-era arguments are very much alive, though often translated into modern political and media jargon. It is also evident that the character of racial action is influenced by the social, economic, and political resources at the discriminator's command.

While legislation has made several forms of discriminatory acts illegal, it has not been able to end the broad array of blatant, subtle, and covert racism in the criminal justice system, in jobs, in housing, in education, and in political campaigns. Not surprisingly, rationalized prejudice/racism has become the soup of the day. Race and ethnicity is said to determine IQ, and IQ is supposed to determine economic status. "Black men are still considered likely to be criminals" (Feagin and Vera, 1995:69). In fact, today the obsessive fear of the mythical African American rapist monster continues unabated. And, as in the early days, the fear of the African American rapist is used to rationalize or legitimate Caucasians' continued bad faith toward African Americans in the United States.

As Park (1950) points out, though Caucasians and Africa Americans have lived and worked together in the U.S. for over 300 years, the two races were still in a certain sense strangers to one another, a phenomenon that has not improved much in 2002. Gordon (1964:165) also made the valid observation that African Americans "and whites generally remain apart." To Brigham (1996:91), ". . . little if anything has changed for the better in relations between African-Americans and whites." A few decades ago, Adrian Dick Gregory remarked, "In the South, whites don't care how close Negroes get, just as long as they don't get too big. In the North, whites don't care how big Negroes get, just as long as they don't get to close." This mentality, I would argue, has not changed significantly, it at all.

Lastly, more than ever before in our history, African Americans are succumbing to and internalizing the racial assumptions that there can be no meaningful bonds of intimacy between African Americans and Caucasians (hooks, 1995). But, still, as Shorris (1992:159) points out, "the truth of racism is that the power to define belongs to the racist."

In the next section, the experiences of two Latino groups (Mexicans and Cubans) will be explored. As will discussed, in many ways the experiences of Latinos, especially Mexicans, are similar to those of African Americans, but in many ways the experiences of African Americans and Latinos, especially Cubans, are very different. Similarly, just as the experiences of the country's two largest minority groups (African Americans and Latinos) differ, the experiences of Latinos (e.g., Mexicans and Cubans) are very different.

LATINOS IN THE LAND OF OPPORTUNITY

According to Hess et al. (1998), the five major subgroups of Latino Americans (Cuban, Central American, Mexican, Puerto Rican, and South American) are often categorized, as mentioned earlier, under the broad labels of "Hispanic," "Spanish Origin," or "Latinos."[59] These groups, however, are "very different from one another in racial/ethnic ancestry, immigrant history, and current status" (Hess et al., 1998:266). In the words of Earl Shorris (1992:444),

> Latinos are the first immigrants and the last, indivisible families of individuals, brown when they are white, poor when they are rich, racist victims of racism, always on the rise while dying in a fall; they are required to forget even as they learn.

Latinos are a diverse community, multinational in origin, multiethnic, and by extension, hold diffuse ideologies. These various ethnic groups need to be analyzed as such in order to obtain a more complete picture of their experiences in the United States and their relationships with Caucasians. For this particular project, however, the focus will be on people of Mexican and Cuban heritage for two reasons: (1) based on 2000 census figures, Mexican Americans constitute the largest (approximately 7.3%) Latino group in the United States; and (2) Cubans constitute the third largest (approximately 0.4%) Latino group in the United States (see also Garcia, 1994; *San Diego Union-Tribune*, 1993).[60]

Mexicans

In the United States, it rarely occurs to scholars to ask how the experiences and perceptions of Mexicans differ from those of the dominant group. As one of the foremost Mexican historians, Rodolfo F. Acuna (1998), has pointed out, for the most part, many scholars isolate people of Mexican extraction and the "other" from the social relationships that created them. In the words of Acuna (1998:60),

> it is logical to conclude that the experiences of Third World nations is not like the experiences of colonizers. Similarly, the experiences of workers is not that of their *patron* (boss), and the experience of Mexicans in the U.S. is not those of other ethnic and mainstream groups.

As we will see, Mejicanos (Mexican nationals) and Mexican Americans differ from other Latinos by duration and number, as well as by character. Thus, the challenge of the serious ethnic scholar is to reclaim these historical experiences and views.

As the largest Latino subgroup (approximately 58%), some individuals of Mexican extraction are descendants of people who settled in the Southwest territories before that area was annexed by the United States in 1848 under the Treaty of Guadalupe Hidalgo. Others have lived in the United States for several generations, and still others have entered more recently in response to employment "opportunities" in North

American factories and in the agriculture industry.[61] Thus, unlike Cubans and other Latinos, most of whom arrived in the second half of the 20th century, Mexicans live in the light of their own history in the United States.

The Conquest: Quick, Swift, and Certain

Chicano playwright and film-maker Luis Valdez has succinctly summarized the disastrous outcome of the 1848 Treaty of Guadalupe Hidalgo, which transformed Northen Mexico into the U.S. Southwest, in his now famous philosophical phrase: "We did not come to the United States at all. The United States came to us." Or, "we never crossed a border. The border crossed us." At a practical level, the treaty ended the war, and the United States grabbed over half (this includes California, Texas, Nevada, Utah, and parts of Arizona, Colorado, Kansas, New Mexico, Oklahoma, and Wyoming) of Mexico's soil (Acuna, 1988; Shorris, 1992). As we will see shortly, the war turned out to be extremely costly to Mexico and to Mejicanos left behind.

The treaty did not stop the bitterness or the brutal and vicious violence between these two communities. In fact, according to Acuna (1988:9), "it gave birth to a legacy of hate." For instance, the conquest set a pattern for racial antagonism, viciousness, and violence, justified by the now popular slogans such as "Remember the Alamo!" and myths about the Mejicanos'/Chicano's treachery. To this day, as Shorris (1992) points out, the Alamo has been a shrine to anti-Mexican sentiment, the ultimate symbol of the glorious victory of the moral character of "white" over "brown." However, the only Texans who died defending the Alamo were eight Mexican nationals who opposed Santa Anna's highhanded politics. The government, then, had a justification to institutionalize racism and discrimination toward people of Mexican extraction. Lastly, as it will become evident in the following section, the "Anglo conquest was also a capitalist conquest" (Gonzalez and Fernandez, 1998:84).

Mexicans as "Half Civilized"

In the minds of some Americans, the Spanish conquest clearly demonstrated the inferiority of the Mexican Indian. A stronger race would not have been defeated (Reisler, 1997). Additionally, the *Manifest Destiny* (U.S. policy of expansionism) and the "free labor ideology" contributed to a general sense among Caucasians that Mexicans represented a degenerate "race" and culture and, by extension, that the region's natural resources were theirs to grab and exploit exclusively (Gutierrez, 1997). In the words of Almaguer (1994:33), "the notion of manifest destiny implied the domination of civilization over nature, Christianity over heathenism, progress over backwardness, and, most importantly, of white Americans over the Mexican and Indian populations that stood in their path."

According to historian George Fredrickson (1981:5),

Land hunger and territorial ambition gave whites a practical incentive to differentiate between the basic rights and privileges they claimed for themselves and what they considered to be just treatment for the 'savages' [Indians and Mexicans] who stood in their path, and in the end they mustered the power to impose their will.

Acuna (1988) asserts that the United States forged its present borders through expansionist wars, and, except in Hollywood movies, no such thing as the "Winning of the West" ever took place. Over and over, however, the myth of the "bloodless conquest of Mexico" has been repeated by the majority of historians and is believed by most people.

After the conquest, Anglos were convinced that "'there never was a more docile animal in the world than the Mexican'" and proceeded to treat him/her as such (Reisler, 1997: 25). Then, to reassure themselves of their "new victory" and, above all, to maintain and further their will, they made wide use of old and new manipulation labels. For instance, Caucasian antipathy toward Mexicans is illustrated by the bag of stereotypes which included labels/phrases such as "birth of laziness," "backward," "indolent," "submissive," "unproductive," "prodigal," "illiterate," "nomadic," "unable to rise in occupational status and contribute to community stability," "lazy peon," "irrigation equals Mexicans" (Acuna, 1988; Almaguer, 1994; Gonzalez and Fernandez, 1998; Reisler, 1997). In short, "The Mexican . . . was ambiguously deemed 'half civilized' and ambivalently integrated into an intermediate status within the new society" (Almaguer, 1994:4).

As mentioned above, "the concept that people of color are less than equal has been ingrained since the outset of U.S. constitutional experience" (Acuna, 1998:23). In later years, such labels have not only been accepted, but given new life by a number of individuals. Even Jean-Baptiste Lamy, a conservative French priest, was ambitious and openly racist. In 1851, he argued that Mexicans were poor, childlike creatures, given to gluttony, thievery, and wild sexuality (Shorris, 1992). These stereotypes have been supported by scholars such as Dr. Roy L. Garis of Vanderbilt University who claimed, sometime during the depression, that "their [the Mexicans'] minds run to nothing higher than animal functions . . . Yet there are Americans clamoring for more of this human swine to be brought over from Mexico" (Shorris, 1992:153).

Oppression and Suppression

Along with stereotypes, Anglos were able to use the law very effectively to suppress and control Mexicans. Acuna (1988) argues that Anglos gained control of the land by manipulating the law. In fact, even when legislation has been passed, purportedly to help Mexicans, the end result has often been devastating. For example, while the California State Constitutional Convention of 1849 formally granted Mexicans the same citizenship rights as "free white persons" in the state of California, Mexicans in California have never been seriously defined or viewed as "white" (Acuna, 1988; 1998; Almaguer, 1994).

In other instances, law has served as a "cover-up" as well as a convenient and useful weapon against Mexicans. For instance, while it has been noted by a number of individuals that unlike African Americans, Native Americans, or Asian immigrants, Mexicans were the only ethnic population in California during the 19th century that Anglos deemed worthy to formally marry, few are willing to acknowledge that the marriages, especially those between the old Mexican ruling elite and prominent Anglos, "made the Yankee conquest smoother than it might otherwise have been" (Pitt, 1970:124-125).[62]

Another powerful and convenient weapon has been the media. As Almaguer (1994:34) points out, on March 15, 1848, *The Californian* effectively summarized the negative feelings toward non-Caucasians by saying, "We desire only a White population in California." Such view is well illustrated by some of the California delegates who argued against the "introduction into this country of negroes, peons of Mexico, or any class of that kind" (Almaguer, 1994:37).

Thus, with numerous justifications, a racist media, and, above all, access to the law, Anglo settlers were in a powerful position to treat the Chicano population as people without rights who were merely obstacles to the acquisition and exploitation of natural resources and land (Gonzalez and Fernandez, 1998). According to Albert Camarillo (1984:25):

> once the subdivision of rancho and public lands had begun, the dominance of the emerging economic system of American capitalism in the once-Mexican region was a foregone conclusion. The process of land loss and displacement of the Mexican pastoral economy was fairly complete throughout the Southwest by the 1880s.

At this point, perhaps more than ever, the significance of economics becomes extremely obvious. As Mexicans lost more and more of their resources, they became weaker and weaker. The exploitation was absolute, for they had no allies, neither in the unions, nor in the churches, nor in the government. To the Anglos, the Mejicanos were the surplus labor that kept wages low. Case in point: In South Texas, the now famous King Ranch was pieced together out of the bad luck and lack of capital of many Mexicans.

Anglo victory was quick and cruel. In fact, Anglo domination was so ruthless and so thorough that any response would have been futile (see Acuna, 1988). The Mexicans not only lost in war, and by extension, their land, but their language, and their culture. They were socially, politically, and economically disenfranchised and forced to turn on each other. Their income per capita fell, and their infant mortality rate rose (Shorris, 1992).

As illustrated by the writings of authors like Jovita Idar (1885-1946), the life of the Mexican became a nightmare under Anglo control. It was a turbulent time for Mexicans in places like Texas during the late 1800s and early 1900s. The famous Texas Rangers, or "Los Rinches," were routinely lynching Mexican men, women, and children. Writing for *La Cronica*, Idar documented the lynching and hangings of a Mexican child in Thorndale, Texas by the Texas Rangers and the brutal and vicious burning at the stake of 20-year old Antonio Rodriguez in Rocksprings, Texas. (Note: As a young man, I lived and attended school in the small community of Rocksprings for one year. While my stay was brief, I noticed many incidents of hatred and hypocrisy.) Of Rodriguez, Idar wrote:

> The crowd cheered when the flames engulfed his contorted body. They did not even turn away at the smell of his burning flesh and I wondered if they even know his name. There are so many dead that sometimes I can't remember all their names.

The racism and brutality against Mexicans in Texas made Idar take more radical actions. In 1913, she started writing articles in favor of the famous revolutionary forces of General Francisco Villa, and she went to Mexico to serve as a nurse in la Cruz Blanca on the side of General Villa. As one would expect, this attracted the attention of the federal government and the Texas Rangers, who were having a difficult time apprehending Villa.

When Idar returned to Laredo in 1914 and wrote an article critical of President Woodrow Wilson's deployment of troops to the border, the infamous Texas Rangers went to Laredo to destroy her printing presses. Texas Rangers Hicks, Ramsey, Chamberlain, and another, who's name is not know, went up to the door and found Jovita blocking the entrance with her hands firmly grasping the frame and feet planted on the threshold. The Rangers asked her to move out of the way, but Jovita stood her ground. A crowd gathered to witness the spectacle. In one of the greatest historical moments of bravery by a young Mexican women, the Rangers backed down and left town. The news paper, the voice of La Raza, was safe for a while, but, as expected, only for a short time because the Texas Rangers came back in the stealth of the night and completely destroyed the newspaper. The Rangers had silenced a strong, effective, and vital voice for political and social justice for Mexicans in Texas (see La Voz de Aztlan, 2000).

Another mechanism of oppression was the peonage system. According to Gonzalez and Fernandez (1998), the peonage system amounted to slavery. Peons who ran away were hunted down, prosecuted, and sanctioned. For example, N.B. Appel owned a mercantile store in Tubac. His servant, indebted to him for $82.68, ran away and allegedly stole a rifle and other materials of worth. Authorities returned the peon to Appel and prosecuted him. Found guilty, he publicly received 15 lashes (*Weekly Arizonian*, 1859). In Riverton Ranch, seven peons escaped but were returned and charged with debt and theft. The overseer, George Mercer, whipped them and cut off their hair as punishment. Mercer's shears got out of control and he took some skin with the hair. Stories of the "scalping" spread as far as San Francisco (*Weekly Alta Californian*, 1859).

The cruelties of the peonage system were not only long lasting, but also served as a symbol of insult to all Mexicans. To this end, American employers were able to manipulate existing stereotypes about Mexicans to rationalize their use in the labor market (Acuna, 1988; Almaguer, 1994; Gutierrez, 1997). As a consequence, Mexicans, assigned the dirtiest, back-breaking jobs (often labeled as "Mexican work") received lower wages for the same jobs and were the first fired during difficult times (Acuna, 1988; Pumpelly, 1870; see also Darder and Torres, 1998). Additionally, while language and culture set the Chicano community apart from the world of European Americans, appearance also has a major impact on their employment and earnings. Mexican American people with dark skin and/or Native American features find it difficult to obtain employment, and if employed, receive significantly lower earnings than their more Anglo-looking peers, all other characteristics being equal (Hess et al., 1998; Ruiz, 1997).

Lastly, Mexicans, also referred to as "greasers" were often viewed as "gente sin razon (people without reason) by the "gente de razon" (people with reason). They were viewed with utter disdain; as people who could be tolerated only as long as they kept to themselves. "Whites Only" or "No Mexicans Allowed" signs served as bitter reminders of their second-class citizenship. In fact, all through the 1940s, signs that said, "No Mexicans Allowed" or "We don't serve dogs or Mexicans" were common in the United States.

Immigration: Wetbacks or Exiles?

In recent years, immigration issues have dominated political and media arenas, which have been highlighted by scandals, name calling, and accusations of stereotyping. And, although immigrants enter the United States from virtually every country, Mexico has long been identified as one of the primary sources of the economic, social, and political problems associated with mass migration, especially "illegal" immigrants, a powerful term used to negatively describe undocumented workers in the United States.

While arguing that race and ethnicity makes no difference, politicians and the media talk about "illegal aliens" to dehumanize and demonize undocumented persons, often targeting people of Mexican descent (Silko, 1994). Case in point: Legendary former FBI director J. Edgar Hoover once remarked: "You never have to bother about a President being shot by Puerto Ricans or Mexicans. They don't shoot very straight. But if they come at you with a knife, beware" (*Time*, 1970:16). A few years later, former CIA director William Colby stated in 1978 that Mexican migration represented a greater threat to the United States than does the Soviet Union. More recently (1985), Dallas Mayor Pro Tem Jim Hart warned voters that "aliens" had "no moral values" and were destroying the city's neighborhoods and threatening the security of Dallas. According Hart, Dallas women could be "robbed, raped or killed" (Cockcroft, 1982:58; *Los Angeles Times*, 1985c; Maxon, 1985).

The truth is that, at one level, "immigration" is a political euphemism that refers to people of color, especially people of Spanish heritage (Mexican in this case). Case in point: The Immigration and Naturalization Service's (INS) infamous witch hunt of 1954, referred to as "Operation Wetback," was a product of nativist/racist tradition of blaming the victim for inequality. This all-out assault was directed by retired generals (in some ways similar to the witch hunt of the 1930s), and resulted in the apprehension and repatriation of a reported 1,075,168 Mexicans (see Gutierrez, 1997). Vicki Ruiz (1997:138) documents that Mexicans, many of whom were native U.S. citizens, "were the only immigrants targeted for removal." Like those who favored the return of African Americans to Africa, nativists wished to preserve both their ideological and racial purity (Reisler, 1997). Furthermore, as if Myrdal's theory of the economic basis of racism needed additional proof, the most explicitly racist statements about Mexicans surfaced during the 1930's Depression years.

Over the years, arguments have been made that constitutional guarantees do not apply to undocumented workers in the United States. For instance, racially discriminatory legislation (Alien Land Laws of 1913 and 1920) declared it unlawful for "aliens ineligible for citizenship" to own private property in the state and further stipulated that they were not allowed to lease land for terms longer than three years (Almaguer, 1994). Further, during the 1994 earthquake in California, "many of the cheerleaders of the 1978 *Regents of the University of California v. Bakke* case angrily demanded that undocumented Mexicans be denied 'disaster relief'" (Acuna, 1998:24).

In the 1980s, some Anglos believed that an "immigration crisis" existed and had to be controlled using whatever means necessary. Hence, the conservative Reagan administration blamed undocumented workers for high unemployment, especially in the Southwest. Legislation such as the Simpson-Rodino law was the politicians' solution to this manufactured panic that carried a moral twist. And, in an election year and conservative era, it was extremely important for Americans to feel safe and secure. In the 1990s, as Acosta-Belen and Santiago (1998) have pointed out, immigrants became the scapegoat and target for many U.S. social ills.

On another level, as historian David Gutierrez (1997) documents, Anglos have used the rationale that Mexican workers are both culturally and biologically suited to perform the back-breaking jobs that are "beneath" American workers. While the majority of Chicanos now live in urban areas where the men typically find work as laborers and machine operators and the women as domestic servants (e.g., cocinera and/or costurera) or office cleaners, a segment still work in the dangerous agriculture industry, affirming the stereotype of the Mexican farmhand. It is important to point out that while the immigrant topic is widely debated, the danger issue is seldom mentioned or at least discussed in a meaningful manner. According to Farrell (1993), with the exception of mining, the agricultural industry has the highest death rate of any industry. According to statistics released on June 26, 2002 at the League of United Latin American Citizens (LULAC) national convention, workplace fatalities among Latinos rose by 53% between 1992 and 2000 (estimated by the U.S. Department of Labor). At least 815 Latinos died on the job in 2000. Could it be that "too many Mexicans" are employed in this industry and thus few care to improve the existing working conditions? (According to the U.S. Census Bureau, only 14% of Latino/a workers were employed in managerial or professional occupations in 2000.)

The problems of workplace fatalities and injuries are magnified by the probabilities that workers and their families are uninsured. In 2002, the U.S. Census Bureau released new data confirming that Latinos are the most likely of all people to lack access to health insurance (see also University of California, Office of the President, 2003). A third of Latinos (33.2%) have no health insurance, compared with just 10.0% of Caucasians and 19% of African Americans. Latino children continue to have the highest un-insurance rates among U.S. children.

Among the issues not covered in the media or by racially motivated right-wing individuals is the fact that the largest populations of undocumented people in the United States today are not Mexicans (or Haitians) but Canadians, Irish, Poles, and Russians. And, these individuals are seldom hunted by the INS (Silko, 1994). Indeed, after living for some time just south of the Canadian border, I realized that the citizen patrol is not out looking for "illegal" Canadians as it is on the Mexican border. Furthermore, despite the fact that the majority of Mexicans are legal U.S. residents, the social construction of "illegal alien" is often applied to all Chicanos (Garcia, 1994; Hess et al., 1998). Actually, the label often applies to anyone who looks brown or speaks Spanish, especially if s/he has an accent (Acuna, 1998; Shorris, 1992).[63]

To this day, few are willing to accept the statistics that point to the fact that undocumented workers are not the burden that some want us to believe, nor are they willing to recognize the contribution of these individuals. According to a 1985 Rand study, less than five percent of all Mexican immigrants received any form of public assistance (Becklund, 1985). Additionally, Sanchez (1998:104) points out that

> those decrying the social costs of undocumented immigration fail, of course, to recognize the $29 billion paid by Latinos in taxes in 1990 . . . as well as the contributions of this labor force in the face of extreme exploitation and oppression.[64]

Another historical fact that is seldom mentioned is that few are willing to accept and confront the brutal reality that over 300 Mexicans die annually in the process of trying to cross El Rio Bravo and/or the barbed-wire fences into the hostile "paradise" of "el norte" (Shorris, 1992). More recent figures, though, show that starting in 2000 one person dies daily (on average) trying to enter the U.S. along the 2000-mile border. The Mexican authorities and news agencies like Notimex, however, claim that U.S. figures are grossly under-estimated because U.S. statistics only include people who die in the U.S. to the exclusion of those who die in the Mexican side of the border. The U. S. Police and "La Migra" (the Border Patrol), the failed police arm of the Immigration and Naturalization Service (INS), kill some of them; others die trying to cross the freeways and the dangerous Rio Grande under the protection of the night; others are killed by bandits and "cholos" (Shorris, 1992). Between July 31 and August 14, 1989, seven murders, shootings, and stabbings of migrant workers were reported to police in the tiny cluster of farm towns in San Diego county (Shorris, 1992).

A report released by the Mexican consul in El Paso, Texas stated that over 2,000 abuses of human rights occurred in Texas in 1988 alone. Interestingly enough, all of the victims were Mejicanos or Mexican Americans. The majority of the abuses took place along the border (Shorris, 1992). In San Ysidro, California, a 23-year old Mexican man was shot by a Border Patrol agent, who claimed that the man had thrown a rock at him. However, a jury in U.S. District Court found the wounded

Mexican not guilty of throwing rocks. In another incident, Border Patrol agents shot a boy who they claimed was throwing rocks at them. Like many of the individuals shot by the border police, the bullet entered his body from the back. In fact, everywhere along the California border the response to brutal violence has been to create more vicious violence. Case in point: A Border Crime Prevention Unit organized jointly by the San Diego police and the Border Patrol shot 31 individuals (19 died), all Mexican citizens, in five years (Shorris, 1992). One witness described how INS agents sat him in a chair, handcuffed him from behind and pushed his face down toward some dog feces on the floor, saying, "That's what you are" (Shorris, 1992:273). From whatever angle the situation is analyzed, it is evident that "'. . . serious violations of the rights of Mexican nationals were found to be the norm rather than the exception'" (Garcia y Griego, 1997:69). The Border Patrol has become a universal nightmare for many Mexicans, some of whom are U.S. citizens (see Gutierrez, 1997). In fact, due to the terrorists attacks of September 11, 2001, the situation may be getting worse as more and more barriers are being implemented under the rationale of "national security." As noted by Mexican authorities and news agencies like Notimex, while national security should be a primary concern, the government is trying to save lives on one end, while increasing the danger for innocent people on the other end.

As a last resort, undocumented workers have relied on appellate courts. During the month of September 2002, the U.S. Department of Justice decided to reduce the power and number of INS appellate judges. Reducing the authority and number from 23 to 11, Secretary John Ashcroft argued that such drastic changes were necessary (Univision, 2002). There is a possibility, though, that these changes will worsen the existing situation–i.e., injustices.

In reality, as Shorris (1992) points out, no one really knows how many are killed.[65] The unknown dead lie somewhere in the hot desert and the rough mountains. No one counts the useless cruelties, the physical, emotional, and psychological beatings of the 2,933-mile border that has ended the dreams of many Mejicanos. Those who manage to cross into the "land of opportunity," quickly begin to feel the "after-shock" of their conquest. They immediately learn that in order to survive, they often need to alter their way of life, a situation that also has "side-effects." Shortly after, they encounter a world of prejudice, exploitation and discrimination (Garcia, 1997). For instance, notice that when an undocumented Mexican national enters the United States, s/he is branded with the now famous label "wetback," and often treated like a war criminal. As in the past, Mexicans often look to Mexico City, not Washington or the state capital, for protection and redress of grievances (Garcia, 1997).

At a more profound level, the life of "el mojado" (the wetback) resembles the life of the "pocho" (pocho now means a Mexican American who has traded his language and culture for the illusory blandishments of life in the United States). According to Shorris (1992:170), the pocho lives on the cultural and racial/ethnic fault line. The pocho is a profoundly homeless individual, utterly unprotected, despised on every side at all times. Too Mexican for the Anglos and too "agringado" [white] for the Mexicans. In Mexico, the pocho is the butt of a million jokes:

> "My name is John Sanchez," the pocho tells the border guard on his way in to Mexico.
> "And what is your occupation?" the border guard asks.
> "I am a Latin Lover."
> The border guard laughs, "A Latin Lover?"
> "Yes, when I walk down the street in my *patria chica* [literly, small country], Phoenix, Arizona, the gringos all say, 'Here comes that fucking Mexican.'"

Of course, the purpose of the joke is to reassure the Mejicanos who remain in Mexico that perhaps they have made the right choice.

Despite numerous studies that show otherwise, the propaganda promoted is that immigrants from Mexico are stealing jobs, undermining wage rates, committing crimes, threatening public health, and straining the already overburdened social welfare and public education system. The historical record, however, clearly indicates that the experiences of Mexicans during the 20th century was the history of adaptation to U.S. labor market needs. Most Mexicans migrated to perform the pick and shovel work, and generally occupied space "where only the weeds grew"

(Acuna, 1988:136). History also reveals Mexicans struggling to obtain not only equal justice but basic human rights as well. Hence, it is heartbreaking to see resolutions being passed across the country proclaiming that English be the sole official language. For instance, during the summer of 2002, Brown County (Green Bay), Wisconsin's all white board of supervisors passed a proposal for "English only" (see Phelps, 2002; Saldana, 2002; Thorsen, 2002; Toosi, 2002). Ironically, many area immigrants will be picking up the fruits and vegetables that the local citizens will be eating for dinner. With this type of legislation, we might as well have a display at all points of entry to the country stating, "We do not want you, if you cannot speak English."[66] And, while the United States is "tearing down walls" in other countries, it is building sophisticated walls along the 1,933-mile U.S.-Mexican border. How much of these actions is attributed to national security? How much of these actions is a result of Anglo disdain toward Mejicanos? Perhaps it is a little of both.

<u>Access to Opportunities</u>

The argument has been made that time is the best "healer." In the case of Chicanos, however, this has been more of an illusion than a reality. Contrary to the expectation of some Mexicans, World War II did little for Chicanos (Acuna, 1988). Even during the War, Mexicans continued to be viewed as second and third class citizens (see Acuna, 1988; Morin, 1966). The fact that 25% of the U.S. military personnel on the infamous Bataan "Death March" were Mexicans, and the fact that Mexicans earned more medals of honor during World War II than any other ethnic or racial group, did little to improve the tensions back home (Morin, 1966). (According to the Veterans Affairs, as of 2002, Latinos have been awarded the medal of honor 40 times, and most of them have been awarded to Mexicans.) For example, Sergeant Macario Garcia, from Sugarland, Texas, a recipient of the Congressional Medal of Honor, could not buy a cup of coffee in a restaurant in Richmond, California. "An Anglo-American chased him out with a baseball bat" (Perales, 1974:79). While some observers like to think so, the Garcia incident was not an isolated event. In Three Rivers, Texas, a funeral parlor refused to bury

Felix Longoria, a Mexican soldier who had been decorated for heroism in World War II (Acuna, 1988).

Tom Brokaw's widely acclaimed recent book (1998), *The Greatest Generation*, particularly irritated Mario T. Garcia, a University of California–Santa Barbara Chicano studies professor. The book, which told the vivid stories of Americans who weathered the Great Depression and World War II, did not include a single Latino. "It's unconscionable," said Garcia, "for Brokaw, plus his publisher, to have marginalized the Latino experiences in World War II" (Cardenas, 2002:2). Garcia's (and many others) discontent is not new in the since that Hollywood has failed to portray Latino/a heros (see Barrios, 2001; Gray, 2001). Instead, Hollywood has done an excellent job propagating the image that Mexicans (and Latinos in general) are violent, criminal, and unfaithful.

In the world of education, things were not any better. In the mid-1940s few Mexican children were enrolled in school. This was, in part, a deliberate policy to bar the sons and daughters of a conquered people, especially migrant workers, from enrolling in school (Gonzalez and Fernandez, 1998). For instance, one school board stated that "to admit the Mexicans into white schools would be to demoralize the entire system and they will not under any pressure consider such a thing" (Acuna, 1988:157). To top it off, Stanford psychologist, Lewis Madison Terman, placed the academic imprimatur on prejudice and racism in the early 1930s, giving life to the stereotype that Mexicans could not compete intellectually with Caucasians. What was Terman (1906), who is responsible for instituting the IQ test in America, thinking when he wrote, "Theory that does not in some way effect life has no value?"

The confusion of ethnicity, race, culture, class, geography, and capability is more subtle now, but there are still psychologists offering racist views on intelligence. For instance, in 1987, Lloyd Dunn published that "While many people are willing to blame the low scores of . . . Mexican-Americans on their poor environmental conditions, few are prepared to face the probability that inherited genetic material is a contributing factor" (Shorris, 1992:156). Yet, like Terman, he is the author of psychological tests used to determine how children should be educated.

Racism also impacts Mexican students experiences, limiting educational opportunities and ultimately, chances to succeed. According to Shorris (1992:104), "in 1968 there was no city or town in the United States in which Latino students were educated according to constitutional guarantees of equality of treatment under the law." For the poor Latino child, the situation is even worse. To finish high school s/he needs to overcome additional barriers: "money, history, psychology, prophecy, language, and the wall" (Shorris, 1992:217).

According to Sanchez (1998), Latinos have the lowest ratios of completed education. Statistics released in June 2002 at the League of United Latin American Citizens (LULAC) national convention revealed that the high school dropout rate for Latino children is estimated (by the U.S. Department of Education) to be about 33.5% (see also Greene and Winters, 2002; Levine, 2003). For the migrant child, the situation is even worse. As Shorris (1992) documents, the high-school dropout rate for migrant children is 80%. In fact, statistics indicate that "today's entering Latino kindergartner is as likely to go to jail as meet the admission standards of the state universities" (Acuna, 1990:B7). According to the law of probability in El Barrio, "twelve years after the class picture was taken, more of the children will have died or been killed than graduated from a four-year college" (Shorris, 1992:212). Based on 2000 census figures, of the nation's 35.3 million Latinos/as, only 11% have received a post-secondary education. Only 573,000 Latinos/as hold an advanced degree (e.g., master's, doctorate, medical or law) in 2000. For those who do succeed, the educational attainment rates, as Sanchez (1998) indicates, differ substantially by Latino origin. Only 6.2% of those of Mexican extraction will complete four years of college or more, compared with 18.5 percent of those of Cuban origin.

Contrary to popular belief, the Mexican community actually benefitted little from the civil rights movement of the 1950s. This, of course, was partly attributed to a series of historical events. For instance, not until the *Cisneros* case in 1970 did "a Federal district court . . . [rule] that Mexican Americans constitute an identifiable ethnic minority with a past pattern of discrimination in Corpus Christi, Texas." It was not until the 1970s that the courts stated: "we see no reason to believe that ethnic segregation is no less detrimental than racial segregation" (Acuna, 1988; Weinberg, 1977: 287). Three years later, the U.S. Supreme Court said that "Negros and Hispanos" suffered identical patterns of prejudice and discrimination. Even the United Civil Rights Committee, formed in Los Angeles in 1963, refused to admit Mexicans.

Ironically, little has changed since then. Cases such as the infamous 1978 *Regents of the University of California v. Bakke* decision have had a far-reaching impact on the relationships between Caucasians and people of color in the United States. Additionally, with the passage of Proposition 209, the product of the gradual promotion of a racist intent on the part of a right-wing elite, marks the termination of affirmative action in some places. Hence, a remedy for discrimination is buried. In addition to Proposition 209, Proposition 187, prohibiting school enrollment to undocumented students and eliminating the provision of all health services to immigrants who were not in the country "legally," has had a dramatic impact not only on Chicanos, but on other Latinos as well as African Americans. On a related vein, on July 2002, the government announced that the INS would be adding additional restrictions on commuter students who study on American Universities, hurting thousands of Mexican students.

Again, the consequences of such actions are often detrimental. Case in point: Federal court-imposed ban on affirmative action at the University of Texas Law School has resulted in a 92% decline in African American admissions and a 74% decline in Latino admissions. Also, as a result of the University of California Regents' 1995 decision to do away with racial preferences, African American admissions at Berkeley's law school dropped from 75 in 1996 to 14 in 1997, while at UCLA's law school, African American admissions fell from 104 to 21 (Acuna, 1998).[67] Thus, to avoid further deprivation of education, a group of national Latino/a leaders recently (January 2003) asked Republican President George W. Bush to officially support–i.e., to file an amicus brief–the University of Michigan's affirmative action admissions policies, which are being contested in two cases before the U.S. Supreme Court, as noted earlier (the decision could impact both private and public universities). However, following the footsteps of his brother (Jeb Bush, Republican governor of Florida), President Bush openly refused to support affirmative action policies in a televised conference on January 15, 2003.

On this end, as if there was not enough support for the claims of differential treatment, neglect, and hardship, an additional book recently came out in defense of those who claim that discrimination is a thing of the past. In *Increasing Faculty Diversity: The Occupational Choices of High-Achieving Minority Students*, Stephen Cole and Elinor Barber (2003) claim to have discovered that discrimination plays a small, if any, role in limiting the number of minority professors in academe. To them, the crux of the problem is simple: (1) affirmative action; (2) minority students' poor grades, and (3) short supply of minority professors. Such conclusions sound wonderful to many opponents of affirmative action and those who wish to maintain the status quo, who are taking the book as confirmation of what they've argued all along. Meanwhile, in 2001, according to the National Science Foundation, Latinos/as earned only 4.4% of the 40,744 doctorates nationwide. Within the ranks of full-time faculty members, the minority proportion is even lower. Latinos/as represent less than 3% of all full-time professors. The conclusions directly contradict those in *The Shape of the River: Long-Term Consequences of Considering Race in College and University Admissions* by former Harvard president, Derek Bok, and William Bowen (1998), who strongly endorse affirmative action.

In short, this century has seen cyclical media blitzkriegs against Mexicans, especially undocumented workers, beginning with reports promoting violence against the "zoot-suiters" of the 1940s; the deportation of "wetbacks" in the 1930s and 1950s; and the constant raids and border violence against Mexicans, especially undocumented workers, during the 1970s, 1980s, and 1990s. To top it off, cases like *Bakke*, as Acuna (1998) points out in *Sometimes There is No Other Side*, signaled a return to the fiction of separate but equal doctrine. Political forces were trying furiously to "turn back the clock of racial history" (*San Francisco Chronicle*, 1985). One significant observation that one cannot and should not overlook is the fact that, in part, the recent assault on issues like affirmative action has more to do with the political ideology of the culture warriors than with pure scholarship. In addition, such cases point to the fact that the often hostile reaction and consternation of Caucasians to the entry of Mexicans into the privileged world of the academy is but a modern-day expression of the same historical patterns of social closures. As Richard Delgado would say, some issues just keep coming back in one form or another.

Social Change: How Far Have We Come?

A historical analysis clearly indicates that the history of Chicano-Anglo relations goes beyond the story of cultural conflict and racism. Influential factors, such as economics, are crucial in shaping and re-shaping social and cultural forms. More important is the distribution of justice. There is also evidence of a complex interplay between class, race, and ethnicity, which has shaped contemporary racial and ethnic politics. For example, as a consequence of economic discrimination and social isolation, upward mobility has been severely limited. According to historian Mario Garcia (1997), although this capitalist country claims that we are all equal under the law, Chicanos are actually in inferior positions.

Hence, as historian Rodolfo F. Acuna (1998:10) points out, while

injustice and inequalities are rationalized as mutations, as anomalies, which will disappear in time because American society provides opportunity for those who want to better themselves . . . a study of history shows quite a different reality, one of exploitation, racism, and in recent years, a closing of opportunity.

Given North America's racial history, today we are faced with continuing political repression, and the repression of human rights is ongoing, not only against African Americans, but certainly against Chicanos/Mexicans (as well as other Latinos).

The Eurocentric cultural arrogance continues to stigmatize and racialize the nation's diverse ethnic populations on the basis of national origin, language, religion, or other cultural identifiers. Moreover, while few observers are willing to acknowledge it, dominance over Mexicans continues to be partially based on physical characteristics and ancestry. By extension, inequalities in the hiring, promotion, and retention of racialized groups in employment continue. As Almaguer (1994:211) points out, "California remains a contested racial frontier and the site of continued political struggle over the extension of this society's most cherished civil rights and equal opportunities to all cultural groups." In a few words, America continues to be a social world fundamentally structured along class, ethnic, and racial lines, determining where one lives, works, social status, and, above all, the distribution of (in)justice. Unfortunately, national leaders like former President Bill Clinton have only recently acknowledged that "white racism remains the nation's chief destructive edge" (Acuna, 1998:225).

For instance, isn't it ironic that Los Angeles, the city with the highest majority of Mexicans, is considered by some observers as the most permanently and brutally segregated city in the country (Shorris, 1992). (The 2000 census figures show that 97% of East Los Angeles residents in 2000 were Latino/a, highest of any place with 100,000 or more population outside Puerto Rico.) In fact, Acuna (1998) notes that in some ways, cities like Los Angeles are now more segregated than 40 years ago. Acuna (1998) further adds that a rich/poor gap exists in Los Angeles that ranks third behind those of Calcutta and Rio de Janeiro.[68] This, of course, is not limited to L.A. For example, according to Acuna (1998), Latinos in public schools across the United States are more segregated than they were in 1945. Family income and educational attainment for Latinos remain below the U.S. average, while family size is higher. Mexicans Americans earn far less than Caucasians even after three generations because they receive less school than almost all other racial and ethnic groups in the United States, according to a report issued May 22, 2002 by the Public Policy Institute of California. Grogger and Trejo, authors of the study, noted that this is especially true in California, where more than 20% of the population is Mexican. Some observes have noted that the percentage of young Latinos living in poverty in the United States has increased drastically during the last 30 years. The Bureau of census (2000), however, claims that the 2000 rate (21.2) of individual Latinos living in poverty matches the record lows reached in the 1970. The Bureau also places the real median of Latino/a "household" in 2000 at $33,455, the highest ever recorded. Yet, a total of 7.2 million Latinos/as were poor in 2000, not statistically different from 1999. In particular,

Latino males in 1997 earned just 66% as much as Caucasian men, down from 74% in 1980. Similarly, according to a list released on June 26, 2002 at the League of United Latin American Citizens (LULAC) national convention, between 1990 and 1996, Latino women saw their median wage decline by 3%, from $330 to $320 per week (according to the National Council of La Raza). In 1996, Latinas earned 72% as much as Caucasian women and 89% as much as African American women. Of the Latino elderly, 66% earn less than $16,700, and 30% earn less than $8,350 annually. LULAC also announced that since 1994, Latino homeowner ship has lagged Caucasians by 29% (estimated by the U.S. Department of Housing and Urban Development). African American homeowner ship lagged Caucasians by 27.5% during the same period. The widening wage gap, according to Acuna (1998), has been driven by discrimination against people of color. In *The Rich Get Richer* (1991:x), Braun notes that "despite the false appearance of economic growth, the pillars of the American economy have become rotten with neglect." Given these figures, it appears that a Mexican usually does not get paid what s/he is worth compared to an Anglo. Evidently, "segregation creates the structural niche within which a self-perpetuating cycle of minority poverty and deprivation can survive and flourish" (Massey, 1990:350).

In short, the evidence does not support the old adage that "they all look alike," and the belief that one can "pull oneself up by one's own bootstraps." The status of Chicanos has not changed significantly over the past several decades. In fact, there is evidence that the marginal gains made during the 1960s and 1970s are not only evaporating, but in some areas the situation is actually worse. For instance, in the 1970s, people of Mexican descent again became bandits, blamed for stealing jobs from Americans. Once again, Mexicans were made outlaws, stereotyped, criminalized, and paid lower wages, all in an effort to demonstrate the pseudo-necessity for greater funding to agencies like the INS. For the poor, as well as for the industrial working community, the first half of the 1980s became a nightmare. Then, when things appeared to be getting a little better, a number of events (e.g., attacks on affirmative action, attacks on bilingual education, attacks on undocumented workers, especially after the September 11, 2001 incident, attacks on the welfare state) started to take place, leading to what I see as the first universal nightmare of the 21st century for Mexicans (as well as other Latinos). Of course, as some observers have pointed out, for some Mexicans (and other Latinos), the nightmare has gotten worse and worse during the last 30 odd years. As with African Americans, the criminal justice system has relied on strict social control to incapacitate what it sees as a threatening surplus population–at times, for good reason; at times, for bad reason; and at times, for no reason. As an example I will mention two events that I utilized earlier to illustrate the treatment of African Americans: the incapacitation of gangsters and the criminalization of crack mothers. First, perhaps more than ever the government is now making use of whatever social control legislation is in existence to warehouse African Americans and Latinos, especially those who are defined as "gangsters," in jails and prisons (see Mann, 1993; Reiman, 1995; Zatz and Portillos, 2000). Second, as noted earlier, traditionally the majority of people under the control of the criminal justice system have been men. However, as with African American women, the rates of Latinas, especially Mexican, under the control of the criminal justice system have increased during the last few years (Diaz-Cotto, 1996; see also Zatz and Portillos, 2000). Like African American women, Latinas were not immune from the evils of crack cocaine in the Barrio or the punitive measures of the war on drugs (see Bourgois, 1995; Humphries, 1999).

Also, for Latino youth, the situation is getting worse. Just recently, Congressman Ciro D. Rodriguez expressed his disappointment about the treatment of young Latinos in light of a report released on July 18, 2002. The report, "Donde Esta la Justica? A Call to Action on Behalf of Latino and Latina Youth in the U.S. Justice System," reveals growing disparities in the treatment of Latino youth in the American criminal justice system. For instance, in Los Angles, where the majority of the Latino population is Mexican, between 1996 and 1998, Latino youth were not only arrested 2.3 times as often as non-Latino Caucasian youth, they were also prosecuted 2.4 times as often as non-Latino Caucasian youth, and imprisoned 7.3 times as often. (Los Angles is the second largest Mexican city in the world.) According to the report, they are disadvantaged by the lack of a culturally sensitive environment. In addition, inadequate data collection efforts and the lack of bilingual resources complicate the situation even more.

Thus, after experiencing the initial consequences of the Anglo-American conquest involving the loss of lands, racial and ethnic oppression, labor exploitation, and second-class citizenship, people of Mexican extraction continue to face historical barriers as we entered the 21st century. Mexicans continue to be strangers in their own land. The Mejicanos, once among the great cultures of the world, now find themselves among the poorest and the most despised in a *gabacho* world (Colon, 1999).

Cuban Americans

According to Hess et al. (1998), the first wave of Cuban immigrants consisted of relatively well-educated and affluent individuals fleeing the revolution that brought Fidel Castro to power in the mid-1950s. This cultural and social elite, many of whom were "descendants" of European Spaniards, settled in Miami, Florida, where a very successful ethnic enclave was established. In fact to this day, the nation's population of Cuban heritage is heavily concentrated in a single place. Based on 2000 census figures, more than half of the population of Cuban background (52%) lived in Miami (Dade County), Florida in 2000.

Over the years, the first wave of Cuban immigrants gradually accumulated great political influence. According to Hess et al. (1998:267), contrary to other Latino groups (and African Americans), "Cuban Americans are better educated, wealthier, and more assimilated than the other subgroups."[69] For instance, as noted earlier, only 6.2% of those of Mexican heritage complete four years of college or more, compared with 18.5 percent of those of Cuban origin. Additionally, based on 2000 census figures, Cubans (and Spaniards) had the highest home ownership among the Latino/a groups (58% each).

It should not come as a surprise, then, that their world views, especially toward the United States and, in retrospect, the views of Anglo citizens toward them, and their experiences in the United States have been very different from those of other Latino groups. For example, Cubans often describe themselves as "aggressive, assertive, and sometimes appallingly arrogant" (Shorris, 1992:63). While several illustrations may be provided, the following scenarios should suffice to illustrate not only the difference in ideologies, but also how Cubans have been viewed and treated by U.S. government agents, in comparison with other Latino groups and African Americans. Andrea Camps, who earned a Ph.D. in Cuba once said, "We Cubans are aggressive, progressive. We make the opportunity; it is not given to us" (Shorris, 1992:66). This view is not an isolated one. To Cuban writer, Ariel Remos, "people who want to work here can work. People who want to accept welfare are destroyed" (Shorris, 1992:237). It is as simple as that in the mind of the individual who covers international politics and economics for the most powerful right-wing newspaper in Miami, perhaps in the United States.

For the most part, Cuban immigrants do not define themselves as Latinos, but citizens of the world, often identifying themselves with the brutal, notorious, and vicious conquistadors. As Shorris (1992) points out, Cubans identify with the conquerors, not the conquered, the subject, not the object. And, indeed, some have argued that the Cubans who came in the first wave of exiles are more Spanish than Caribbean. According to Shorris (1992:55), ". . . Cubans and Spaniards are brothers in the Anglo mind . . .." Additionally, they view themselves (and are viewed) as exiles/refugees rather than immigrants (or "wetbacks"); they view the United States as a useful place, more like rental property than a home. But, for economic and ideological purposes, Cubans immigrants are generally pleased to be described as the Jews of the Caribbean.

According to Shorris (1992:74), Cuban sociologist Lisandro Perez, a professor at Florida International University, describes the differences between Cubans and other Latino groups, which are greater than the differences among all other groups, as follows: "There is an absence of minority-group orientation. Cubans have a very high self-concept–at times there is a certain arrogance–that's very different from the self-concept of Mexican Americans . . .." Perez's perspective is further revealed when he pointed out that once, at a meeting, he heard a Chicano complain of being unable to secure a bank loan because he was Mexican. To the contrary, a Cuban businessman replied that when he started his business he could not obtain bank loans because he was poor, not because he was Cuban. According to the Cuban businessman, "Now, I own twenty stores and everybody wants to lend me money, and I'm still Cuban."

In addition, Perez claimed that "I'm not sure that Cubans feel a brotherhood with other Latin Americans. The Cuban connection was more with Spain and the U.S." (Shorris, 1992:74). Notice that Perez' last statement is of particular importance, not only in terms of one's ideologies and experiences, but also possible implications (including one's chances of success and survival). For instance, economic and political outcomes often depend on how one identifies him/herself and how s/he is identified by others.

Shorris (1992:160) further notes that with so many complicated variables to choose from, almost every Latino can find a way to use racismo to his/her benefit, "but the most finely honed racismo belongs to the Cubans." Case in point: Cuban novelist Roberto Fernandez, whose novel *Raining Backwards* is full of personal and murderous wit, recalls the Cuban saying, "The black will never be brave and the tamarind will never be sweet." Then, to set peace within himself, Fernandez recites a poem about the deaths of legendary Cuban poet Jose Marti and the mulatto Antonio Maceo, which ends by asking, "what difference does it make if a black is lost?"

Ironically, not only do many light-skinned Cubans feel superior to blacks, but they also treated the arrival of Cental American refugees in Miami as "the Indian invasion." And, to further show the power of their privileged position, "Cuban teachers taunt the Mejicano farm-workers and their children by using common Cuban words that are considered obscene by Mexicans" in the schools of Homestead, Florida (Shorris, 1992:161). Mejicano parents complained, but the practice continued. Exasperated, the farm-workers took their children out of school. These are the acts that have led to the claim that "no one suffers racismo so much as the Mexicans and Mexican-Americans" (Shorris, 1992:165; see also Bourgois, 1995). Again, this is not an isolated case. It has also been well documented that Cuban doctors in Florida were charging Mexican farm workers exorbitant rates to provide them with the medical examinations required by the INS when applying for amnesty. Yet, to some Cubans, "they [Mexicans] don't get anywhere in the world" (Shorris, 1992:161).[70]

At any rate, the power structure of the Cubans is reflected in the fact that Miami became the first municipal government in the United States to provide services in both Spanish and English. In Houston, as in Los

Angeles, the Cubans rose quickly to become an elite group among the Latino community. For example, most Latino physicians are Cuban. In Houston almost all of the Latino physicians are Cuban refugees. For this same reason, Cuban and other refugees with medical degrees have swelled the ranks of Latino physicians in the United States. Furthermore, although they account for only a small part (approximately 1.2 million of 35.3 million) of the Latino community in the United States, Cubans dominate the economic realm. They are the investors in real and intellectual resources, and they have chosen Miami to build an economic fortress, which they utilize as a base, spreading throughout Florida and other parts of the country. For instance, figures show that by the mid-1980s, Miami ranked first in terms of the number of Latino/a-owned business relative to the size of the Latino/a population. The Cuban population was more than twice as likely to start their own businesses as other Latinos/as. Additionally, Cubans have also been successful in the founding of larger corporations. By the late 1980s, 31 of the top 100 Latino/a businesses in the U.S. were located in Dade County. For instance, Bacardi Imports of Miami was the nations most profitable Latino owned business with total sales in excess of $500 million in 1987 (see de la Garza and DeSipio, 1992). Even the Hispanic Cultural Organization is run by Cubans. When they host an annual ball, Cubans invite one of the more social Anglo families to reign over the ball, because they wish to move into Anglo society as quickly as possible (Shorris, 1992).[71]

The economic and political power of Cubans is also reflected by the various attempts by Anglos to impose "English only" legislation on the city government (*Migration News*, 1994; *Naples Daily News*, 1999; Partington, 1999). So far, these attempts have failed in the courts. In fact, some claim that the primary opposition to Cuban-American power today comes from local African Americans who feel that authorities favor Cuban refugees over native-born blacks (Hess et al., 1998).

Notice that in contrast; Mexicans, like African Americans, have not been able to gain a strong economic power base, which has kept both groups confined within the ghetto and El Barrio. Unable to secure bank loans to establish businesses and strengthen communities, these groups often times cannot get beyond the loan-sharking that has drained their communities almost from the beginning. Redlining by U.S. banks has taken the economic life out of Mexican and African American communities.

It should be underscored, though, that in Miami, Anglos remain mistrustful of their Spanish-speaking neighbors, especially after Castro expelled another wave of immigrants, some of whom were former prisoners, much poorer and less educated than the first wave of Cuban immigrants. And indeed, there is a significant difference between the first wave of anti-Castro, pro-capitalist immigrants and those who came later. It is worth pointing out that, according to Shorris (1992), some people have tried to draw distinctions between the early Cuban refugees and the Marielitos, who arrived much later and were said to have been undesirables, criminals and lunatics that Castro wanted to discard from Cuba. A close analysis, however, reveals that the real distinction between the two waves of Cuban "emigrants" was mainly in their level of education and the color of their skin. Many of the Marielitos were black, while almost all of the first wave of emigrants were white. According to Shorris (1992), since the native Cuban population was destroyed very early in the conquest, the Cubans were left with only two factors (black and white) from which to fashion a hierarchy.

Case in point: The figures are not consistent, but it is estimated that there were 2,500 Cuban immigrants detained by the INS in federal, state, and county detention facilities in the late 1990s, most of them having come to the U.S. in the Mariel boatlift (often referred to as the Mariel "Freedom Flotilla") in 1980. Most of the Marielitos have been held at the U.S. Federal Detention Center in Oakdale, Louisiana, the Federal Penitentiary in Atlanta, Georgia, the Krome Detention Center in Florida, and a few other locations. Originally, approximately 1,800 of the 125,000 Marielitos who left Cuba in 1980 found themselves detained in American correctional facilities, arguably because of their prior criminal acts committed in Cuba and/or the U.S. Apparently, more than 23,000 of the arriving Marielitos revealed to INS officials previous criminal convictions, and many suffered from serious medical and/or psychiatric problems. Some observers have noted that once the Cuban detainees convicted of crimes serve out their sentence, they remain incarcerated indefinitely because Los Marielitos cannot be returned to the island because Cuba has refused to take those who were excluded by the U.S. government and thus held in detention facilities. Hence, since they have been officially excluded from the U.S., they can remain in federal prisons until death without legal repercussions (based on a 1987 ruling by the Supreme Court). On this end, in 1991, the 9th Circuit in *Alvarez-Mendez vs. Stock* ruled that the detention is not an excessive means for protecting society from potentially dangerous aliens. Some observers claim that since their arrival, Los Marielitos have been denied several basic human rights (e.g., medical care), in part because they were classified as "excludable aliens." For instance, according to a 1986 Congressional Report on a riot in the U.S. penitentiary in Atlanta in 1984, the living conditions of Los Marielitos at the federal prison were intolerable even under the most minimal correctional standards. In addition, as administrative detainees, Los Marielitos are not entitled to the benefits of rehabilitation programs, such as continuing education and work experience, that characterize the criminal incarceration process. Meanwhile, another group of indefinite detainees is threatening to outnumber the 2,000-plus Marielitos who remain in INS custody. A significant number of Cubans have arrived in subsequent years. For instance, between January and August 1994, approximately 5,163 "balseros" arrived and were classified as excludable (see Inter-American Commission on Human Rights, 2001; Randall, 1999). In the *Abandoned Ones: The Imprisonment and Uprising of the Mariel Boat People*, Mark Hamm (1995) argues that the criminalization of Los Marielitos was orchestrated through the perceptions and actions of over-eager warriors, agents of the government, the media, and some segments of society.[72]

Thus, Cubans suffer less or more, depending on their skin color, and whether they left Cuba as angry exiles or the people Castro rejected. Keep in mind that for the most part, "whites do not open the door to dark-skinned people for any reason other than to use them" (Shorris, 1992:79). With few exceptions (mostly in California, New Mexico, and Texas), dark-skinned people rarely get elected or appointed to political posts. In fact, overall, Latinos/as constitute approximately 12.5% of the U.S. population, but comprised less than 4% in the judiciary in 2002. Some figures show that Latinos in the judiciary comprised only 3.8% of federal judges in 2003. According to the National Association of Latino Elected and Appointed Officials, nationally Latinos only hold 5,205 elected office in 2002. Often, though, the most complicated individual factor is one's country of origin, which is related to the individual's sense of a beginning. In fact, Shorris (1992) claims that in the case of the Cubans, history and culture determined success.

One cannot overlook the fact that outside Miami, much of Florida has little regard for Mexicans. For instance, the Homestead newspaper, the *South Dade News Leader*, is so racist that it does not even report athletic successes by local Latinos, especially Mexicans. When a float built by Mexicans won first prize in a parade held in 1987, the following day the *News Leader* published photographs of only the second, third, and fourth prize winners (Shorris, 1992).

In trying to better understand how Latino groups define themselves, how Anglo America perceives them, as well as their experiences in the United States, one needs to go beyond the "aggressive and progressive" view that is often used to identify Cuban Americans, especially if we are to make any kind of realistic comparison with other minority groups. The question should be: what has been the primary variable that actually describes the success of Cubans in the United States? Based on historical analysis, one of the primary factors is "differential treatment."

Even though Cuban Americans have the unique distinction of being identified as "model minorities" and plagued by the phenomenon of the "Glass Ceiling," one cannot and should not ignore the fact that "in general, the success of the Cuban immigrants was largely due to the resources with which they entered, and later to the degree to which their conservative political politics fit the spirit of the 1980s" (Darder and Torres, 1998; Hess et al., 1998:267). In contrast to other ethnic groups of Spanish heritage, Cubans, as reflected by their political ideologies, have been an extremely conservative population, highly favored under the Bush and Reagan administrations.[73] In 2003, the situation is not much different.

Case in point: While the Cuban community is small, several of the few posts occupied by Latinos are occupied by Cubans, as evidenced by the 2002 appointment of Raoul Cantero to the Florida Supreme Court by Republication Governor Jeb Bush. For women the situation is not much different. For instance, keep in mind that Cubans constitute 1.2 million out of 35.3 million Latinos/as in the United States, and then consider the ethnicity of the nine highest ranking Latinas currently working in the administration of President George W. Bush (former governor of Texas and son of a former U.S. president): 4 Cubans (Elsa Murano, Josefina Carbonell, Cari M. Dominguez, Cristina Beato), 3 Mexicans (Rosario Marin, Diane K. Morales, Theresa Alvillar-Speake), 1 Ecuadorian (Rebecca Campoverde), and 1 Honduran (Suzanne Biermann). Thus, the special treatment of Cuban exiles is worth careful consideration.

Interestingly, the Bush family has referenced its Mexican family members during campaigns. And, to further their diversity and understanding of the Latino/a community, they have on occasions nominated or appointed a number of ultra-conservative Latinos/as such as Chicana Linda Chavez to office. In other cases, Latinos/as who have little or no connections with the Latino/a community are selected, as evidenced by the September 2002 Senate Judiciary Committee confirmation of el Hondureno Miguel Estrada (who was nominated by Republican President George W. Bush) for a seat on the U.S. Court of Appeals for the District of Columbia. Or, consider the case of the new INS Commissioner, Michael J. Garcia. Garcia was designated Acting Commissioner by President Bush in November 2002; and he took office on December 1, 2002. Ironically, a New York native and career federal prosecutor, Mr. Garcia has little knowledge of the complex relations between the INS and the Latino/a community. The son of a Spanish father (i.e., Spain) and Puerto Rican mother, Commissioner Garcia has revealed almost nothing about his strategies for the implementation of a secure, safe, and just environment for both documented and undocumented workers in his televised "English speeches" to Latino/a audiences.

According to Torres (1998), after the 1959 Cuban revolution, U.S. policies politicized the process of immigration, establishing an unprecedented program of allowing private individuals to issue visa waivers to Cubans on the island. Based on her analysis, over 600,000 visa waivers were issued from 1960 to 1962 alone. In fact, "Operation Peter Pan" was designed to bring the children of the underground to the United States. She further points out that established immigration and security legislation was circumvented and eventually over 14,000 Cuban children were transported to the United States. Upon arrival, "aid packages and special privileges were also extended to Cuban exiles" (Torres, 1998:44).

Earl Shorris (1992:333-334) observes that the Cubans had the "impetus of the Cuban loan, one of many programs that provided direct assistance for medical care, education of Cuban children, social security for the elderly, and so on between 1962 and 1976." Cubans had access to various opportunities like job-training programs and placement services, housing subsidies, English-language programs, and business loans (Moore and Pinderhughes, 1995). T.D. Allman (1987) estimates that the total amount of aid to Cubans from all sources during that period came to $4 billion. To put the figure into perspective, Allman (1987) notes that even if only direct federal expenditures are counted, the $2.1 billion in aid for Cuban immigrants was greater than the entire budget for the Alliance for Progress, a program designed to finance what President Kennedy called a 'true revolution of progress and freedom' throughout Latin America. Federal and state economic assistance contributed significantly to the growth of a vigorous enclave economy and also to the development of Miami as an important center for international business, politics, literature, and art. This governmental financial aid allowed Cubans to own their own businesses, which in turn enabled them to hire fellow Cubans (Moore and Pinderhughes, 1993; 1995).

Figures show that as of 1986, the median income for Cubans living in the U.S. was $26,770, as opposed to $14,584 for Puerto Ricans, and $19,326 for Mexicans (see de la Garza and DeSipio, 1992). Even the "undesirable Cubans" benefitted (indirectly) from American aid. President Carter used his authority under the Migration and Refugee Assistance Act of 1962 to make $10 million available for transporting, processing, and caring for the arriving Marielitos. In the words of Shorris (1992:334), "no other group of immigrants or exiles in the United States has ever been treated so generously." Even during the turbulent 1980s, the political and economic climate was in favor of Cuban immigrants.

Even though President Carter did not welcome the entire new wave ("The Marielitos") with open arms, as he had promised in 1980, his support was vital. The Mariel group was visibly more racially and economically diverse, and thus, created a more fluid identity at the margins of the established exile community. Also, in the early 1990s, Miami became the home for a new wave of Cuban exiles: the babies of the Cuban revolution. However, in 1994, "President Bill Clinton changed a long-standing policy of accepting all Cubans who entered the United States" (Torres, 1998:54). Still, Miami and Cuba have been tied together culturally and economically since the little island of Cuba dominated the western hemisphere in the 16th century (Shorris, 1992).[74]

The city of Miami was transformed after the refugees began to arrive in the early 1960s. Although they were poor at first, they were given asylum, the right to work, moral support, and financial assistance from the federal government. More than anything, the right to work legally enabled Cuban immigrants to use their skills. It took some time for Cuban professionals to get licensed to practice, and Cuban businesspeople had to work "day and night" at difficult jobs to get the necessary capital to establish their own businesses, but they managed (Shorris, 1992). In short, combining the huge welcoming gift from the United States with their own vast resources, the new Cuban immigrants began to produce a strong economic and political base in Miami.

Interestingly enough, "the extraordinary treatment of Cuban exiles fostered a distinct exile formation" (Torres, 1998:44). In general, "the relationship of Cuban exiles to their host and home countries acquired a political significance not normally ascribed to immigrant communities" (Torres, 1998:44).[75]

The effect of class upon U.S. immigration policies is apparent at various levels. For instance, the success of the children of the first wave of Cuban exiles proved that an economic and intellectual class reproduces itself. "This, perhaps, led one individual to conclude that because Cubans were relatively well treated here, 'they kind of overestimate the benevolence of the system and may not be sufficiently critical of the way [it] treats other minorities . . .'" (Conciatore and Rodriguez, 1998:318).

QUE COMPARACION?

The data indicate that variables such as language, culture, race, ethnicity, class, geographical changes, and political and economic forces are strategies for struggle because they are often weapons used by hegemonic forces to oppress, exploit, manipulate, and divide communities. At every class level, for instance, European Americans sought to create, maintain, or extend their privileged access to racial and ethnic entitlements.

Additionally, along with African Americans, Latinos are still low on the social scale, not because of their genes, but because of a combination of these same historical factors that have functioned as a barrier and have been defined and redefined over the years. For example, as Almaguer (1994) makes clear, racialized relations in states like California reverberated along a number of racial fault lines and not a simple binary form or along one principal fault. Furthermore, it is evident that the allocation of group position in the social hierarchy is often the outcome of both cultural and material considerations.

The data also point to the fact that African Americans and Latinos have had different experiences with the dominate male U.S. culture. The Mejicanos' "conquered" legacy distinguishes them from other minorities and parallels the involuntary origins of African Americans, who were subjected to racial slavery for many years. Thus, just as African American ghettos reflect a history of slavery, Jim Crow legislation, and struggle for civil and economic equality, so the nation's Latino barrios reflect a history of conquest, immigration, and a continuous struggle to maintain cultural identity. One also needs to acknowledge that, although each ethnic group has been racialized differently, none were ever seen as the equal of Caucasians; none ever posed a serious threat to the superordinate racial status or privileged class position of Euro-American male immigrants. This is not to deny that there have been some significant changes. Yet, I would argue that, by and large, we continue to live the history of Euro-American male supremacy and hate. For instance, recent incidents between the police and the Mexican community indicate that prejudice and discrimination against Chicanos/as continues, and it is not restricted to a given time or place (American Civil Liberties Union, 2002; Bourgois,

1995; Kertscher, 2002). Furthermore, prejudice and discrimination against Mexicans is not restricted to the criminal justice system. Case in point: On July 5, 2000 seven Caucasian juveniles (maybe more) and one Cuban went "Mexican hunting" in the Carmel Valley of the City of San Diego, California. The juveniles, apparently a neo-Nazi group, brutalized elderly Mexicans for four hours (La Voz de Aztlan, 2000; see also Clair, 2000; Contreras, 2001). In New York, "in addition to the material fact of tolerating lower standards of living and of accepting more exploitative working conditions, new-immigrant Mexicans experience racism and subordination at work ..." (Bourgois, 1995:169).

While Latinos currently comprise approximately 12.5% (35.3 million) of the total U.S. population, their political influence, with "the exception of the strongly conservative and financially sound Cuban community in Florida," is diluted by the many divisions within this population, which is also stratified by socioeconomic status, skin color, and national origin (Darder and Torres, 1998; Gutierrez, 1997; Hess et al., 1998; *San Diego Union-Tribune*, 1993:1). Interestingly enough, according to a list released on June 26, 2002 at the League of United Latin American Citizens (LULAC) national convention, the top ten concerns for the Latino/a community are: (1) education, (2) civil rights and justice, (3) political access, (4) economic power, (5) immigrant rights, (6) environment, (7) housing, (8) health, (9) learning English, and (10) women's issues.

Lastly, we are not and should not be fighting to see who has been the most oppressed, nor who deserves more or less. We all have seen the hypocrisy. We all have felt the agony, humiliation, bitterness, and vindictiveness. We all have suffered, including the public at large. The objective should be to critically analyze this sad and humiliating historical situation and start taking steps to improve existing conditions. If African Americans, as this country's second largest historical minority and Latinos, the largest minority in 2000, work together, our climb may be a little less painful, perhaps even a little faster.

The history of U.S. race and ethnic relations now will be used in combination with the four-threat theory of race and ethnic differences in punishment and death sentence outcomes discussed in Chapter II to develop a new typology of death sentence outcomes in the United States.

As we will see, differences in historical relations between the Anglo majority and each racial and ethnic minority group leads to varying expectations in death sentence outcomes across groups.

DEATH SENTENCE OUTCOMES: A NEW TYPOLOGY

Working from the four-threat perspective analyzed in Chapter II and the historical analyses of race and ethnic relations discussed above, one can gain insight into how the distribution of death sentence outcomes in the United States are influenced by a number of intertwining historical factors, such as race, ethnicity, class, country of origin, ideologies, power, economic production (both ideologically and economically), among others, at different points in time and space. And, indeed, given the various historical facts, events, figures, and illustrations discussed herein, it is evident that these and other factors lead to expected disparities in death sentence outcomes. Before providing additional hypotheses, though, it would be wise to explore a few more issues that are central to our analysis. Keep in mind that in Chapter II, general hypotheses were provided. Here, specific hypotheses for each group within each state will be given.

First, power has proven to be extremely significant, often deadly, in the distribution of justice. As Winfree and Abadinsky (1996) point out, power often determines law, and laws seem to protect the vested interest of the powerful, or those who define and re-define the laws, often to the disadvantage of those who have little or no power. In the context of this assertion, it is worth noting Lord Action's famous observation that power corrupts, and absolute power corrupts absolutely. The truth is, however, that absolute power may corrupt absolutely, but individuals with absolute power are seldom officially defined as criminals, and thus rarely punished (Hobbes, 1950). In fact, law has created many crimes of the poor and powerless, and too few crimes of the rich and powerful (Lynch and Groves, 1986).

And, indeed, the significance of power is well illustrated by capitalist Cornelius Vanderbilt, who was noted as saying, "Law! What do I care about law! Hain't I got the power?" Who has power; who does not; who uses power, and who are its victims, then, becomes the focal point. As Karl Marx (1967:763) once said, "one capitalist always kills many." Thus, as the perspectives above indicate, in order to better understand the functions, distribution, and history of racial and ethnic punishment and death sentence outcomes in the United States, the emergence and changes in specific forms of punishment and sentencing must be examined in reference to the various historical factors.

According to criminal justice historian Samuel Walker (1994:36), "there is no one system" of justice, and Kappeler, Blumberg, and Potter (1996) characterize the criminal justice system as a "dual" system of justice. I would argue, though, that the United States criminal justice system is actually divided into four very distinct systems: one for the poor and defenseless, one for the rich and powerful, one for Euro-Americans, and one for African Americans and Latinos, particularly Mexicans.

With this in mind, we will now explore racial and ethnic influences on death sentence outcomes focusing on African Americans, Caucasians, Cubans, and Mexicans in the United States. This will provide a rich qualitative dimension and sound hypotheses.[76]

First of all, it is important to emphasize that while many poor and powerless Caucasians have received long and/or harsh sentences, including death, states like Florida and Texas have applied longer and/or harsher sentences, and perhaps more executions to African Americans and/or Latinos. Blalock (1967:167), for instance, observes that, "The South has an official defensive ideology that is turned on and off according to the degree and nature of the threat to white dominance." Thus, the low rate of executions in states like California may be influenced more by resource considerations than threats.

Sentencing disparities, even among the equally poor may be partly attributed to the fact that Euro-American criminals (or "created criminals") might be poor, but they are still "white," even though they are often referred to as "white trash." The historical record clearly indicates that the "white trash" status is not lower nor equivalent to the second-, third- or fourth-class status of Mexicans or African Americans. In fact, the "white trash" economic label is the primary, and often sole, characteristic that distinguishes "white trash" from wealthier Caucasians. In actuality, then, their status (e.g., poor, powerless, illiterate) has been a doubled-edge sword. On the one hand, their "white trash" status has prevented them from being treated as equals, and by extension, several would be expected to receive longer and/or harsher sentences over the years. On the other hand, this same "white trash" status in and of itself and the fact that they do not pose a major political, economic, or social threat, it might be expected that they have not received longer and/or harsher sentences. Thus, I would classify this segment of the population as "los desafortunados" (the unfortunate ones). Lastly, since this population poses no major threat in the near future, there is a high probability, as already observed, that punitiveness for this group of individuals will increase slightly in the near future, due to the current punitive trend.

The case of Cubans is also a unique one, but in a very different manner. Recall that the experiences of Cubans, especially the first wave of Cubans, have been very different from those of other Latinos (Mexicans and obviously Puerto Ricans) as well as African Americans. As mentioned earlier, the Cuban community is small, located mostly in Florida, especially concentrated in Miami, and is mostly conservative. On average, Cubans are economically better off than other Latino groups, and are higher on the racial, social, economic, and political status than the "white trash." Additionally, this community not only considers themselves above the other Latino groups and African Americans, but is also viewed as "superior" by Euro-Americans, indicated by the several issues/events (e.g., the symbiotic relationship between the two groups) discussed herein. Cubans are not encumbered with the stereotypes that characterized other Latinos. And, indeed, Cubans can actually be characterized as "los avanzados" (literally, the advanced ones).

Perhaps because they are viewed as a "superior" race by Euro-Americans, they have not, to this day, been viewed as a major economic, political, social, or ethnic threat. In fact, the opposite has been the case. The U.S. government has gone to great lengths to help Cubans. Thus, given the fact that they view themselves and are actually viewed by their Caucasian supporters "almost" as equals, as well as their economic and political status, it would be expected that few, if any, have received extremely long and/or harsh sentences, including executions, in the past in the United States, especially in Florida. If some Cubans have been executed, they were probably the "undesirable" Cubans (the dark-skinned Cubans who are not part of the first wave of immigrants). And, given their resources (including current economic and political status), there is a high probability that few Cubans will be sanctioned harshly (e.g., executed) in the near future. Again, the few who will end up under the control of the criminal justice system or executed will probably be the "undesirable" Cubans. Thus, Cubans have the advantage of being viewed as superior, not being viewed as a significant threat by Euro-Americans, and, therefore, able to make use of their "privileged" status.

Lastly, the case of African Americans and Mexicans is also different. Both groups have been and continue to be stereotyped in every possible way. These two communities, overall, continue to have limited resources. As indicated by the information discussed herein, they are plagued with poverty and are virtually politically powerless (Acuna, 1988; 1998; see also Healey, 1995; Moore and Pinderhughes, 1993).[77] Like war criminals, African Americans and Mexicans have been hunted all along. Thus, these two populations can be characterized as "los de abajo" (literally, the ones at the bottom).

Recall that during "hard times," many Mexicans have been thrown out of the United States, especially California and Texas where the Mexican population is highly concentrated. Actually, even during "good times," some Mexicans have not been allowed to stay. Often, after the crop has been picked, Mexican workers are shipped back to Mexico. Thus, while the state has helped Cubans all along, it has only pretended to help Mexicans. In the end, help to Mexicans has been mostly a "smoke screen." In fact, the Mexican community has been viewed at various points in time and place as a "surplus" population as well as a social, ethnic, political and/or economic threat. Evidently, as Blalock (1967) observes, at certain times and places it is feasible or necessary to treat certain individuals harshly, either because the supply is plentiful or because it is economically and politically rational to take such actions. Not surprisingly, then, Mexicans have not only run the risk of "morir ohogados" (being drowned), but also "ejecutados" (executed).

Several years ago, the Chicano movement became a "threat" to those who were interested in maintaining the status quo and in preserving their positions (see Marin, 1991). In recent years, some have expressed concern by the claims that the so-called Mexican "sleeping political giant" is threatening to wake up. Keep in mind that Latino youth outnumber African American youth.[78] Nonetheless, politicians at all levels have become aggressively hungry for the Mexican vote. In fact, it is not uncommon for politicians, including former President Clinton and President Bush, to make use of a phrase or two in Spanish. Often, depending upon the audience, their first phrase is in Spanish.

Underneath all of this, however, it appears that in recent years a higher number of Mexicans have received longer and harsher sentences, including executions (see Tables 1 and 2). One could logically speculate that, with few exceptions, the majority of the Latinos who are on death row or who have been executed in the past have been people of Mexican descent. And, given their historical status, and the fact that they are now not only viewed as an economic, social, and/or ethnic threat, but also a political threat, one could logically argue that the level of punitiveness will increase in the near future for the Mexican community.

African Americans, as Mexicans, have been considered a "surplus," "problematic," and "threatening" population (Chiricos and Delone, 1992; Cooper, 1988; Crawford et al., 1998; Williams, 1997). At all times, they have been under the watchful eye of the criminal justice system. At first, there was the brutal violence of the slave patrol (Walker, 1980; see also Anderson, 1995b). Then, there has been a combination of the "curbside" justice of the billy-club, violence, lynchings, jails, prisons, and long and/or severe sentences, including the death sentence (Aguirre and Baker, 1990; 1999; Baldus, Woodworth, and Pulaski, 1980; Franklin and Moss, 1988; Griffin, 1961; Walker, 1980).

African Americans' struggle for equal justice, especially the Civil Rights Movement, attracted not only high publicity, but also retaliation–e.g., the assassination of Martin Luther King, police surveillance, and violence against the African American community (Anderson and Hevenor, 1987; Goldberg, 1996; see also Gates and West, 1997; Williams, 1997). African Americans have been viewed by some observers as an economic, political, social and racial threat (Crawford et al., 1998; see also Blalock, 1967; Liska 1992; Spitzer, 1975). Liska (1992), for instance, observes that the effect has been strongest in Southern states where African Americans historically have been associated with political, economic, and social threats.

African Americans have been receiving longer and/or harsher sentences in recent times (Irwin and Austin, 1997; Tonry, 1995). For example, the number of "legal" executions for African Americans has increased in recent years (see Marquart et al., 1994). It appears, then, that even after years of reform efforts, some states, especially states like California, Florida and Texas, are reacting with extremely punitive sanctions against African Americans, as a result of being considered a potential threat (e.g., economic, political) in combination with the historical factors that continue to haunt African Americans (Chiricos and Delone, 1992; Hochstetler and Shover, 1997; see also Kappeler et al., 1996; Mann, 1993; Mauer, 1990; Reiman, 1995). And, given the current political climate, it appears that while the rate of punitiveness for this population might not increase drastically in the near future, it will not decrease significantly either. The level of executions, commutation denials, and sentence and/or conviction appeals rejected are responses to political, economic, social, and racial threats in combination with various historical factors. As a form of social control, it is evident that as threats increase, executions, commutations, and sentence and/or conviction overturns are critical decisions in the minds of decision-makers such as governors, judges, and parole boards. Let us turn to the development of specific hypotheses for each ethnic and racial group within each state following the four-threat theory and taking the numerous historical factors into consideration.

A New Dimension: The Four-Threat Theory of Death Sentence Outcomes and its Applicability to Three Southern States: California, Florida and Texas

First, as mentioned in Chapter II, each threat in and of itself has its own merits, but the final outcome is the product of various historical and intertwining factors operating in a complex fashion, depending on time and space. As the historical record clearly indicates, threatening conditions need to be explored from various angles. Thus, by broadening the scope of the analysis, we have a more holistic perspective while yielding similar, but stronger hypotheses. After taking the various historical factors, the complex multitude of threatening conditions, and the specific histories of relations between Caucasians, Cubans, Mexicans, and African Americans into consideration, the four-threat theory of death sentence outcomes suggests two perspectives, that in California, Florida, and Texas (in ascending order):

1. African Americans are slightly more likely to be executed than Mexicans, definitely more likely than Cubans, and, certainly more likely than their Caucasian counterparts.
2. African Americans are slightly less likely to be granted a commutation than Mexicans, definitely less likely than Cubans, and certainly less likely than their Caucasian counterparts.

As in the previous sets of hypotheses, before stating three additional hypotheses, it is important to emphasize that the four-threat theory of death sentence outcomes leads to competing hypotheses. One could reasonably predict that in California, Florida, and Texas (in ascending order):

1. African Americans are slightly less likely to have their sentence declared unconstitutional by State or U.S. Supreme Court than Mexicans, definitely less likely than Cubans, and certainly less likely than their Caucasian counterparts.
2. African Americans are slightly less likely to have their sentence overturned by an appellate court than Mexicans, definitely less likely than Cubans, and certainly less likely than their Caucasian counterparts.
3. African Americans are slightly less likely to have their conviction and sentence overturned by an appellate court than Mexicans, definitely less likely than Cubans, and certainly less likely than their Caucasian counterparts.

However, given the nature of the decision-making process, the opposite may also be possible. As mentioned above, African Americans, Cubans, and Mexicans may be more likely to receive these death sentence outcomes than their Caucasian counterparts due to the high possibility of "errors" during the conviction/sentencing stages and/or lack of resources (e.g., financial, political), which set grounds for overturning the sentence and/or conviction by the courts, in capital trials involving minority defendants. Given this, it is reasonable to make the following three predictions, that in California, Florida, and Texas (in ascending order):

1. African Americans are slightly more likely to have their sentence declared unconstitutional by State or U.S. Supreme Court than Mexicans, definitely more likely than Cubans, and certainly more likely than their Caucasian counterparts.
2. African Americans are slightly more likely to have their sentence overturned by an appellate court than Mexicans, definitely more likely than Cubans, and certainly more likely than their Caucasian counterparts.
3. African Americans are slightly more likely to have their conviction and sentence overturned by an appellate court than Mexicans, definitely more likely than Cubans, and certainly more likely than their Caucasian counterparts.

The type of relationships described above are more likely if the offender is an unmarried male and has prior felony convictions. In addition, the type of relationships described above will increase as the offender's education (years of schools completed) decreases, the number of years under the death sentence increases, and the age of the offender when the offense was committed increases.

Notice that the type of relationships described above are most likely in Texas, an extremely punitive state with a high concentration of Mexicans and a fair number of African Americans but where few Cubans live; less likely in Florida (but only slightly), a punitive state where the majority of Cubans are concentrated and with a high concentration of African Americans but where few Mexicans live; and least likely in California, a less punitive state (in terms of executions) with a high concentration of Mexicans and a fair number of African Americans but where few Cubans live.

Also, notice that the theory suggests that on the punitive sanction scale, African Americans are followed by Mexicans, Cubans, and Caucasians in descending order in each relationship. Thus, African Americans stand on the far end of the "harsh side" of the scale, and Caucasians stand on the far end of the "lenient" side of the scale. Also, African Americans and Mexicans are close by and stand on the harsh side of the punitive sanction scale, Cubans and Caucasians are close by and stand on the lenient side of the scale. Since Cubans, especially light-skinned elites, do not pose a substantial "threat" to the Anglo majority, I expect their death sentence outcomes to be very close to their Caucasian counterparts.

In sum, in the constant struggle to determine which race and ethnic groups are to survive and prosper, Mexicans and African Americans have been labeled by a multitude of sources (e.g., the media, politicians, academicians, authorities) as pathological, uncontrollable brutes, incapable and/or unwilling to comprehend social limits. Additionally, since African Americans and Mexicans are often viewed as pariahs and treated as scapegoats for society's ills and failures, one could reasonably predict that Mexicans and African Americans, often viewed as criminals by nature, will be controlled at whatever cost. Thus, one could logically predict that African Americans and Mexicans, the two largest minority groups in the United States (comprising approximately 1/4 or 25% of the total U.S. population in 2000), are the two groups most likely to be executed, least likely to be granted a commutation, least likely to have their sentence declared unconstitutional, and least likely to have their sentence and/or conviction overturned by the courts.

Additionally, since African Americans seem to be emerging as a kind of a great global surplus, and viewed as a threat, one could logically predict a disproportionate number of African American males receiving extremely harsh sanctions. And, since Mexicans have not been considered fully human or fully civilized, rather perceived as a threat, allowing U.S. political leaders and control agents to use punitive sanctions as a "safety valve" when times are tough, one could reasonably predict that the Mexican community has suffered and will continue to suffer the most punitive sanctions within the Latino community, placing them next to the African American community.

    Lastly, one needs to emphasize that by applying such methods of formal social control to threatening individuals not only segregates them from society but identifies and reinforces the parameters of actions that social control agents find socially acceptable. The legal system provides the structural opportunity for control agents (e.g., legislators, governors, judges, parole boards) to operate interdependently to control individuals defined as threatening by the dominant Caucasian majority, including social control agents and some segments of society at large.

VIENDOLO BIEN

The inevitable conclusion is that while the four-threat theory of death sentence outcomes contains competing hypotheses, as for "general predictions" (see Chapter II), the rate of long and/or harsh sentences in the United States has increased drastically in recent years. As indicated by disproportionate confinement data, most of those receiving such sanctions have been African American and Mexican males, most of whom are disadvantaged (e.g., poor, illiterate, powerless). In short, based on the proposed "death sentence outcomes typology," death sentence outcomes in the United States will largely depend on the defendant's resources (e.g., economic, political), status, threatening conditions of the day, a multitude of historical factors, the economic and political current of the day, the social control ideology of the day, and the winds of luck. A few years ago, in *The Punishment Response* Graeme Newman (1985:6) summed up the situation clearly when he said, "society is not divided into groups of 'equals.'"

    Finally, death sentence outcomes research must be based on an appreciation of history, an understanding of the implementation of punishment, and the realization that the distribution of (in)justice is quite a dynamic phenomenon. In the next chapter the methods for the current study will be discussed.

CHAPTER 5

The Present Study

This study will utilize a data set that was obtained from the Inter-university Consortium for Political and Social Research (ICPSR #6956). The principal investigator for the data set, *Capital Punishment in the United States, 1973-1995*, is the U.S. Department of Justice, Bureau of Justice Statistics (1997).

Capital Punishment in the United States, 1973-1995 provides annual data on inmates under the sentence of death, as well as those who had their sentence commuted or vacated and prisoners who were executed. The data set includes several basic sociodemographic variables (e.g., age, sex, race, ethnicity, martial status at the time of imprisonment, level of education, state and region of incarceration). Criminal history data includes prior felony convictions and prior convictions for criminal homicide and the legal status at the time of the capital offense. Additional information is provided on those prisoners removed from death row by year end 1995.

The data set contains a total of 6,228 cases, and provides information on prisoners whose death sentences were removed, in addition to information on those inmates who were executed. The data set also provides information about inmates who received a second death sentence by year end 1995 as well as prisoners who were already on death row.

As mentioned earlier (see Tables 1 and 2), it is difficult to locate studies that include Latino/a, along with African American and/or Caucasian, subjects in their analysis. On the few occasions that Latinos (e.g., Mexicans, Cubans) have been included, researchers have treated this diverse population as a whole, usually under the broad label of "Hispanic," or "Latino."

Thus, one of the primary goals of this research project will be to disaggregate the Hispanic/Latino categories. It is important to underscore the fact that the ultimate objective would be to disaggregate the data for each category, recode the data, and compute the analyses. However, due to limited time and resources, such a task is beyond the scope of this study. Given the fact that most published material usually includes only the race of the offender and not the ethnicity, one would need to search not only each individual case but also various non-conventional sources of information that require a number of resources. Thus, in the current study, the focus will be on disaggregating the Latino category for those who were executed between 1975 and 1995. One objective will be to find out the exact ethnicity of all the Latinos who were executed in the United States between 1975 and 1995.

It should be pointed out, though, that in keeping with federal regulations, the data (disaggregated Latino category) will not be recoded with the exact ethnicity of the individual. The results will be utilized for descriptive purposes. Additionally, based on the obtained results, however, we should be able to make a few tentative conclusions as to the nature of death sentence outcomes: executions, commutations (usually granted by the state governor), and overturned sentences and/or convictions by the U.S. Supreme Court or state appellate court.

In the search to determine the exact ethnicity of executed Latinos between 1975 and 1995, several sources of information were contacted and/or analyzed. These include newspapers (including foreign newspapers), magazines, journal articles, textbooks, radio and TV stations, journalists, attorneys and judges, consulates, state attorneys general, and departments of corrections. By contacting these various sources, I was able to find out not only the exact ethnicity of those executed, but also to develop a reliable data base.

The objective will be to assess whether race and ethnic differences in death sentences and death sentence outcomes are amplified in "threatening" contexts discussed herein. Recall that based on the literature (theoretical and empirical) discussed in Chapters II, III, and IV, there are three general hypotheses that can be made. First, the odds of being executed are highest for African Americans, followed by Latinos (both "black" and "white" Latinos) and Caucasians. Second, the odds of receiving a commutation are highest for Caucasians, followed by Latinos and African Americans. Third, the odds of having a death sentence and/or conviction overturned by the U.S. Supreme Court or state appellate court is highest for Caucasians, followed by Latinos and African Americans. And lastly, among the Latino population, Mexicans have received the least justice in each category.

Thus, we will extend the analysis of executions, commutations, and overturned death sentences and/or convictions by the U.S. Supreme Court or state appellate court by exploring the role of race and ethnicity in distinctive contexts specified by sociodemographic variables and criminal history records. Specifically, of the 37 variables in the data set, eight independent variables, the most relevant in the data set for this particular study, were selected to operationalize our hypotheses. And, indeed, based on prior research, these are legitimate case characteristics that need to be controlled for. To simplify and facilitate the analysis, some of these variables were re-coded, and a few moderate modifications were made.

STATES UNDER STUDY: CALIFORNIA, FLORIDA, AND TEXAS

For variable 7 (Q1: State), only the three selected states (California, Florida, and Texas) were analyzed. The variable was named STATE, and dummy variables were created for California (0/1) and Florida (0/1). Texas was selected as the reference category since Texas, after Delaware, has the most state executions per capita.

These three states were selected for three reasons: (1) each has the death penalty, a large population under the sentence of death, and often implements the death penalty; (2) California, Florida, and Texas are important because these states set a national trend; and (3) since the exact ethnicity of inmates is not known, these states will be used as a proxy for studying two of the three largest Latino/a groups in the country–i.e., Mexicans and Cubans. According to 2000 census figures, Cubans constitute the largest Latino minority group in Florida, and Mexicans constitute the largest Latino minority group in California and in Texas.[79]

In addition, the high courts in California, Florida, and Texas spend a substantial amount of time on capital appeals, and have a highly developed capital jurisprudence. Lastly, because state correctional policies and agencies, such as paroling authorities, determine length of stay in correctional facilities, states are the appropriate unit for examining death sentence outcome disparities as operationalized herein.

Before spelling out the operationalization of other variables in the study, especially the dependent variables, it would be wise to provide a discussion of two historical landmark decisions and the various possible death sentence outcomes in the United States. It should be emphasized that such an examination is not only critical in the operationalization of the dependent variables, but also in selecting the time frame for the present study.

GETTING OUT FROM UNDER THE SENTENCE OF DEATH IN THE UNITED STATES

Before analyzing the possible death sentence outcomes, one needs to make note of a few extremely important U.S. historical events which are relevant to the current study.

Two Landmark Decisions: *Furman* and *Gregg*

On June 29, 1972, the U.S. Supreme Court set aside death sentences for the first time in its history. In its decision in *Furman v. Georgia, Jackson v. Georgia*, and *Branch v. Texas* (hereafter referred to as the *Furman* decision), the Court held that the capital punishment statutes in those three cases were unconstitutional because they gave the jury complete discretion to decide whether to impose the death penalty or a lesser punishment in capital cases. It is important to underscore the fact that the U.S. Supreme Court did not rule that the death penalty itself was unconstitutional, only the way in which it was being administered. To be more specific, *Furman* declared the Georgia statute unconstitutional because of its lack of precision and not because of the method of execution. All other existing state statutes were very similar. Thus, one by one those state supreme courts declared their own statutes unconstitutional under the *Furman* reasoning. This process took a year or two (Streib, 1999). Given these factors, some critical questions follow:

First, as a result of the *Furman* decision in 1972, a challenge was launched by a 26-year-old African American male with a sixth-grade education, who was diagnosed as having some degree of mental defeat. Hence, what exactly happened to all of the inmates who were on death row at that particular time? The judicial response to the Furman decision was that the sentences of 631 defendants awaiting execution under pre-Furman discretionary statutes were vacated (Wolfgang, 1978). In another words, the practical effect of the *Furman* decision was that the Supreme Court voided nearly all death penalty laws then in effect (in some 35 states), and all death row inmates (over 600 men and women) had their death sentences overturned to life imprisonment with opportunity of parole. Some of those inmates were eventually paroled, but many of them were not (Bohm, 1999; Bohm and Haley, 1997).

It is important to emphasize that the U.S. Supreme Court did not directly order that all death sentences be vacated. Rather, challenges were filed in the different states under the authority of *Furman,* and state courts and the lower federal courts granted relief to the prisoners. Thus, this action occurred through measures taken by the various state courts for the most part (Acker, 1999). *Furman* did not set a "fixed" date for the states to carry out the order. It simply said that these defendants could not be executed (Streib, 1999). Thus, different states used different approaches. Some just converted the death sentence(s) to life imprisonment, while others set new sentencing hearings for each offender. But, again, the bottom line is that they all received either life without parole or some form of life with a parole option (Streib, 1999).

Second, was anyone allowed to be placed on death row between the *Furman* (1972) and *Gregg* (1976) decisions? Yes. The legislative response was reinstatement of the death penalty along the lines suggested by Chief Justice Burger. In fact, by the fall of 1974, 30 states had enacted new death penalty statutes that were designed to meet the Court's objections. Following the enactment of the new death penalty statutes, the number of individuals sentenced to death soared. Death sentences began to be imposed under these new laws as early as 1973.

According to Bohm (1999), by early 1973, just a couple of months after *Furman*, the Florida legislature met in special session to enact a new death penalty statute. Florida was the first state to do so. According to Professor James Acker (1999), it was not only Florida that reinstated the death penalty through new legislation (as early as late 1972), but many more did so during 1973. Hence, as Acker (1999) points out, the year-end total of death row inmates for 1972 would reflect the prisoners sentenced to death before *Furman*, and the year-end total for 1973 could reflect those sentenced to death under the post-*Furman* legislation. So there probably was very little time during which no one was sentenced to death. In fact, in 1975 alone, 285 defendants were condemned to death, more than double the number sentenced (mostly for murder, but some were sentenced for rape and kidnapping) in any previously reported year (Bohm and Haley, 1997). According to Wolfgang (1978), by Spring 1976, 34 states had passed new death penalty statutes and, as of January 2, 1976, there were 407 individuals sentenced to death under the new statutes. Although the number under the sentence of death declined (42 in 1973) as a result of *Furman*, the national death row census never dropped to zero. This is because each state implemented and responded to *Furman* at a different pace between 1972 and 1973. By December 31, 1972, most states had no one under a "valid" sentence of death (Streib, 1999).[80] However, many states, Florida included, immediately passed a new death penalty statute and began sentencing offenders under it as soon as they could.

The constitutionality of those death sentences and of the new death penalty statutes was quickly challenged, and on July 2, 1976, the U.S. Supreme Court announced its rulings in five cases. In *Woodson v. North Carolina* and *Roberts v. Louisiana*, the Court rejected "mandatory" statutes that automatically imposed death sentences for defined capital offenses. But, in *Gregg v. Georgia, Jurek v. Texas*, and *Proffitt v. Florida* (hereinafter referred to as the *Gregg* decision), the Court approved several different forms of "guided-discretion" statutes.

Those statutes, the Court noted, struck a reasonable balance between giving the trial jury some guidance and allowing it to consider the background and character of the defendant and the circumstances of the crime. In short, state legislatures then began passing new death penalty statutes between 1972 and 1974. And, trial courts began sentencing offenders to death under these new statutes. A few of these 1972 to 1973 sentences finally worked their way up to the U.S. Supreme Court in 1976 in *Gregg*. The most dramatic effect of the *Gregg* decision was the resumption of executions under the "new guideline" on January 17, 1977, when Utah executed Gary Gilmore by firing squad.

Third, no one was executed during the four-year period between the *Furman* decision in 1972 and *Gregg* in 1976. In fact, Gary Gilmore's January 17, 1977 execution was the first in the United States since 1967 (Acker, 1999). And while people were being placed on death row as a result of new state statutes, no one was executed due to their laws' unconstitutionality. One important caveat to all of this is the fact that some offenders were sentenced to death under federal law, and thus were not eligible for a commutation by the state Pardon Board or the governor (Vandiver, 1993). Between 1973 and 1975 nine individuals were sentenced to death under federal law, but none were executed during this time frame. Also, military authorities carried out additional executions during the period under study: 160 between 1930 and 1995. Practically, then, (and contrary to popular belief), not all death sentences were commuted to life imprisonment, nor were all executions ended as a result of *Furman*. Note: If you are wondering: where did the actual defendants in the three cases decided togther under the heading of *Furman* (1972) and the five decided together under the heading of *Gregg* (1976) end?, see Urbina (2002a).

Based on what happened in the aftermath of *Furman*, the present analysis should be limited to 1975 through 1995. Specifically, given all the variability in what occurred (e.g., the timing when states enacted new statutes and when death sentencing resumed in death penalty states), and the fact that only 11 individuals were sentenced to death in 1973 (including cases for California, Florida, and Texas only) and 48 in 1974, it is best to exclude sentencing years 1973 and 1974. As a result of *Gregg*, however, there was no consistent pattern (death sentences or death sentence outcomes) across states. It is important to point out that all death sentences before 1972 were vacated as a result of *Furman*. In 1975, 83 individuals were sentenced to death in the three states under study. After 1975, every year has 80 or more individuals sentenced to death except 1977 (49) and 1979 (62). And after 1979, most years are 100 or more. Thus, to avoid the *"Furman* effect" on the dependent variables in the analysis, the current study will cover the years 1975 to 1995. Because the focal point of the proposed research is to analyze racial and ethnic differences in death sentence outcomes: executions, commutations, sentences declared unconstitutional, and sentences and/or convictions overturned in Texas, California, and Florida between 1975 and 1995, the sub-sample will only consist of death penalty cases (2001), the unit of analysis, covering these three states from 1975 to 1995.[81]

Getting off Death Row: Who Decides? Why?

There are several official "ways" (besides execution) that an inmate may be removed from under the sentence of death in the United States. The most common are clemency, commutation, and appellate actions. Only a selected few "actors" have the power/authority to make such decisions. This section explains these processes.

Clemency

Clemency is a discretionary executive power (Ammons, 1994). The clemency power is not inherent in any particular branch of government, although it is usually associated with the executive branch.[82] Radelet and Zsembik (1993) note that rationales underlying clemency include unrestricted mercy, a "free gift" of the executive, needing no defined justification or pretense of fairness; a quasi-judicial rationale indicating that governors and clemency officials may consider factors that were not presented or considered by trial judges, prosecutors, juries, or appellate courts; and a retributive notion of clemency, which is intended to ensure that only the most deserving among those sentenced to death are actually executed. [83]

The reasons for granting clemency include doubts of guilt, changes in the political climate, and laws that reflect societal enlightenment concerning the nature and scope of certain behavior. In other words, clemency is an instrument of equity in the criminal law, designed to promote the general welfare by preventing injustice. Clemency is considered an appropriate means of reducing wrongful convictions or sentences that are too severe for a given offense. Radelet and Pierce (1991) note that historically, the most frequent reasons for extending clemency in capital cases were issues such as the fairness of the trail, the disparities in sentencing, and the geographic equalization of sentences, all of which may relate to racial (and ethnic) disparities. In short, reasons for clemency vary widely, but often fall into the following three categories: (1) to promote justice where the reliability of the conviction is in question; (2) to promote justice where the reliability of the sentence is in question; and (3) to promote justice where neither the reliability of the conviction nor the sentence is implicated (Palacios, 1996).

Clemency decisions are made personally by elected officials, the President or a state governor. The most common, though, is a state governor granting clemency in the form of a sentence reduction, usually to life imprisonment, or pardon (invalidating both guilt and sentence). In fact, in most states today the governor has primary authority to grant clemency. The clemency power gives a governor the final word as to whether a convicted individual will remain in prison, for how long, or whether the death sentence will be carried out. In other words, governors have the choice of either reducing the sentence, delaying an execution, or totally forgiving the convicted individual.

In most states, the governor may either make clemency decisions directly or exercise this power in conjunction with an advisory board. A few states have parole or pardon boards that make clemency decisions, and in several states this power is shared between the governor and a parole or pardon board. The mayor of the District of Columbia also has clemency powers. Clemency, however, does not indicate that an inmate will automatically be released from prison. And, indeed, while some have received clemency in the past, few have actually received a pardon (Ammons, 1994).

Commutation

Executive clemency is extended to inmates serving death sentences usually in the form of a commutation, often because of errors that occur during the bifurcated trial. In Texas, for instance, a death sentence can be imposed only by unanimous vote of the trial jury; that is, every jury member has to agree. If an error occurs at the sentencing phase of a trial, the case cannot be remanded for a new sentencing proceeding. And Texas Court of Criminal Appeals has indicated that it may not reduce the punishment assessed by the trial jury. Instead, if the jury fails to agree, a mistrial shall be declared. If the sanction was erroneously imposed, the case stands in the same position as if the jury had failed to reach a verdict and the entire case must be retried from the beginning.

According to Palacios (1996), errors occur at every point in the conviction and sentencing process. A commutation could be a result of plea bargaining, to avoid the time and expense of a retrial. A commutation, usually by a governor, reduces the original sentence, if considered to be inappropriate, to a lesser degree of punishment, usually life imprisonment. At any stage in the appeals process, the governor could step in and issue a commutation. In Florida, for instance, the governor, who is not required to specify precise reasons for clemency, must have the approval of three cabinet members to commute a sentence. The governor could overturn the death sentence to one of life imprisonment either with an extended mandatory term or without possibility of parole. Most governors, though, have not welcomed commutation petitions (see Ledewitz and Staples, 1993). According to Radelet, Lofquist, and Bedau

(1996), the rate of commutations in American capital cases has fallen to a fraction of the rate seen in earlier years in the United States, mostly due to the conservative political climate and fear of voter reprisal.

Former Texas Governor, George W. Bush, says that he limits his decisions on whether to intervene to two matters: (1) if there is any doubt about an individual's guilt or innocence, and (2) whether the courts had ample opportunity to review all legal issues in the case. Technically, Mr. Bush could only grant a death row inmate a 30-day reprieve from execution. However, as governor, Bush appointed the Texas Board of Pardons and Parole, giving its members the authority to grant clemency requests (e.g., commutations). But, the Board never varied from Bush's position on the 113 executions and one act of clemency granted during his five-year tenure as governor. In fact, Bush approved more executions than any other governor in any state since the death penalty was reinstated in 1976.

Bush had the authority, though he never used it, to overrule an act of clemency by the Board. In Florida, former Republication Governor Robert Martinez was the first governor in the history of Florida who, given the opportunity, failed to use his clemency powers in any of the 90 capital cases he reviewed (Radelet and Pierce, 1991). Moreover, the Florida Pardons and Parole Board holds no public hearings, votes by phone or fax, and does not explain its reasoning.

Notice that a commutation, while a more limited form of clemency, shares many attributes of its parent power; yet clemency and an acquittal is not the same thing. For instance, clemency in states like Ohio cannot be granted until after an individual has been convicted. Guilt must first be established.

Thus, the question is whether an individual will be granted total forgiveness or a qualified degree of mercy by reducing the death sentence to a lesser charge. Being acquitted means that the suspect did not commit a crime. A grant of commutation is not a declaration that no crime took place, but only that the capital sentence will be reduced. In the case of a pardon, the results of conviction will no longer be in effect. (A guarantee of acquittal is not a prerequisite for granting clemency.)

Finally, in addition to the above death sentence outcomes, there are three additional death sentence outcomes that should not be overlooked. For this reason, in addition to executions, commutations (the most common form of executive clemency), these last three possible death sentence outcomes, which are extremely important, will be included in the analyses of the current study.

Capital Sentence Declared Unconstitutional by State or U.S. Supreme Court

The central question, then, would be: why would a capital sentence be declared unconstitutional by a State or U.S. Supreme Court and what would it mean for the inmate? A detailed response to this question (and to the next two questions) is beyond the scope of this study. There are too many procedural issues to begin to catalogue, and a few substantive ones, such as no death penalty for rape of an adult, no death penalty for offenders under 16 years of age. Suffice it to say that a death sentence could be declared unconstitutional for several reasons, but mostly for some type of error during the guilt/innocence and/or sentencing stages of the trial process. Acker (1999), for example, notes that a death sentence could be declared unconstitutional for issues dealing with evidentiary irregularities, inadequate jury instructions, prosecutorial misconduct, defense attorney errors, improper exclusion of jurors and many more.

Another condition under which this could take place is when the sentence and/or conviction (usually just the sentence) is overturned as a result of death penalty statutes being void. The practice of removing individuals from a sentence of death because of statutes being struck down on appeal occurred mostly between *Furman* and *Gregg*. This, however, does not mean that the guilt/innocence of the individual will be affected, but it could be. Thus, when this occurs their death sentences will be vacated to life imprisonment with opportunity of parole.

Conviction Affirmed, Sentence Overturned by Appellate Court

The central questions in this case would be: why would a conviction be affirmed, but the sentence overturned by appellate court? And, what is the end result for the inmate? According to attorney Alan Clarke (1999), who has handled death penalty cases from beginning to end, this is partly due to the nature of capital sentencing: bifurcated trials, which allow room for error. It is important to underscore the fact that trials in capital cases are split in two. There is a guilt phase and a penalty phase. The jury first determines the guilt or innocence of the accused; followed by another proceeding in which the same jury decides the sentence. Here, it is important to note that when federal judges, who are appointed, reverse death sentences (usually to life imprisonment) affirmed by a State Supreme Court Justice, it's usually because of ineffective assistance of counsel, a common practice in California (Elias and Fried, 1999). Thus, appeals courts could vacate death sentences while upholding the convictions of the lower courts.

Conviction and Sentence Overturned by Appellate Court

Why would a conviction and sentence be overturned by appellate court and what would that mean for the inmate? Along with error, this is partly due to the two-stage process of capital cases. For instance, insufficient evidence in the first stage (conviction) could create problems in the second stage (sentencing) and thus could lead to a new trial and/or re-sentencing (Clarke, 1999). Additionally, if either the conviction or the sentence is vacated (e.g., during review) by the State's highest appellate court, the case could be remanded to the trial court for additional proceedings or for retrial. However, as a result of retrial or re-sentencing, the death sentence could be reimposed. Thus, given the nature of death penalty cases, appeals courts could vacate sentences while overturning the convictions.

In short, these decisions take place for various reasons, but mostly for some type of error during the bifurcated trial. Errors could lead to a retrial and/or new sentencing, even an acquittal. Errors do not only happen in capital cases (e.g., murder cases), they also happen in other felony cases, such as robbery. And while there are various possible outcomes for these decisions, the most common one is a death sentence overturned to life imprisonment, at times with the possibility for parole. All this being said, let us now turn to the operationalization of the variables in the present study.

RESEARCH VARIABLES FOR CURRENT STUDY

Dependent Variables

Variable 31 (Q14C1: Reason for inmate's removal from under sentence of death), the dependent variable, was originally divided into 9 categories: (1) executed, (2) deceased by other causes, (3) capital sentence declared unconstitutional by State or U.S. Supreme Court, (4) sentence commuted, (5) conviction affirmed, sentence overturned by appellate court, (6) conviction and sentence overturned by appellate court (7) other [removals], (8) information not available at this office, and (9) unknown/NA. While the last category is coded as missing, the cases actually constitute individuals who are still under the sentence of death. Thus, the last category is actually a possible death sentence outcome. Since no action has taken place, this is an indication, by default, of life imprisonment for those who still remain under the sentence of death.

Based on the previous section and an examination of the data for Texas, Florida, and California, the following five dichotomous dependent variables representing death sentence outcomes are the most appropriate for the analysis in the present study:

1. Those executed versus those still sentenced to death in 1995.
2. Sentence commuted versus those executed, plus those still sentenced to death in 1995.

3. Capital sentence declared unconstitutional by State or U.S. Supreme Court versus those executed, plus those still sentenced to death in 1995.

4. Conviction affirmed, sentence overturned by appellate court versus those executed, plus those still sentenced to death in 1995.

5. Conviction overturned (and therefore also the sentence overturned) by appellate court versus those executed, plus those still sentenced to death in 1995.

For the first dichotomous dependent variable, the variable was renamed as CAPPUN. The first category was left in its original form, and coded as 1 under the label of executed, and the 9th category was recoded as 0 under the label of not executed. Since the circumstances in which the decisions for categories 3 through 8 take place is different from category 9, they were excluded from the model. Excluding such categories will allow for a valid sentencing outcome comparison between those executed and those still under the sentence of death in 1995. (Since no cases fall under the 8th category, it is irrelevant.) Also, since the second category contains individuals (52) who died of other causes [natural cause (22), suicide (19), murdered by another inmate (3), other (3), unknown/NA (5)], it was deleted from the analysis. This category, for instance, reveals nothing in terms of death sentence outcomes and the decision-making process.

The second dichotomous dependent variable was renamed COMMUT. The 4th category was recoded as 1 under the label of commuted, and the 1st and 9th categories were combined and recoded as 0 under the label of not commuted. The 3rd and 5th through 8th categories were excluded from the model. The third dichotomous dependent variable was named UNCONSTI. The 3rd category was recoded as 1 under the label of unconstitutional, and the 1st and 9th were combined and recoded as 0 under the label of not unconstitutional. The 4th through 8th categories were excluded from the model.

The fourth dichotomous dependent variable was named SENOVERT. The 5th category was recoded as 1 under the label of sentence overturned, and the 1st and 9th categories were combined and recoded as 0 under the label of sentence not overturned. The 3rd, 4th, and the 6th through 8th

categories were excluded from the analysis. Lastly, the 5th dichotomous dependent variable was renamed CONSENOT. The 6th category was recoded as 1 under the label of conviction sentence overturned, and the 1st and 9th categories were combined and recoded as 0 under the label of conviction sentence not overturned. The 3rd, 4th, 5th, 7th, and 8th categories were excluded from the model.

The dependent variables in these analyses, then, are death sentence outcomes: (1) execution (CAPPUN), (2) commutation (COMMUT), (3) sentence declared unconstitutional (UNCONSTI), (4) sentence overturned (SENOVERT), and (5) conviction and sentence overturned (CONSENOT). The coding will be 0/1. For instance, whether a defendant gets executed (yes=1) or not, and, whether a defendant receives a commutation (yes=1) or not. The two types of independent variables (sociodemographic variables and criminal history variables) that will be included in logistic regression models will be discussed next.

Criminal History Data (Independent Variables)

Based on the theoretical discussion (i.e., normative theory) in Chapter II, it is important to control for criminal history of the offender because conservatives often argue that race and ethnicity differences in outcomes are due to differences in the criminal history. In addition, theoretically, a prior history record influences the perception of job opportunities and thus the risk of recidivism, regardless of the individuals' job history. Thus, sentencing decisions may be guided by the belief that a prior criminal history is a clear indication of recidivism, as indicated by Bedau (1964; 1965), and Vandiver (1993; see also Farrell and Swigert, 1978; Swigert and Farrell, 1977).

Given the fact that several prior studies have included the offender's criminal history information in their analyses (see Tables 1 and 2), and have found such variables to be statistically significant in this type of analysis, and the claim that the inmate's official prior criminal record is often a mandatory consideration in deciding whether the inmate should be granted a commutation (Ammons, 1994), a criminal history variable will be included in the current analyses.

Variable 19 (Q10A: Prior felony convictions) was originally divided into four categories: (1) yes, (2) no, (3) unknown, and (4) unknown/NA. The variable was renamed as PRFELCON. It should be underscored that since this variable contains missing data, which could create problems (e.g., unreliable estimates) in the regression models if the proper precautions are not taken, a few modifications need to be made. One common and efficient option is to replace missing values with the mean value of the variable, and to use a dummy variable for each variable that has missing values, which describes the data as either missing or present. Dummy variables will allow us to test whether the cases with missing values on the presence of prior felonies differ significantly from the cases without missing data. If systematic differences do exist, dummy variables should control for them and the model can be interpreted appropriately. In short, a dummy variable will be created for "prior felony" missing data, coded 0 when the data are not missing and 1 when they are. In addition, missing data for "prior felony" will be coded with the mean value of the variable. Thus, the third category (156 cases) and the last category (65 cases), were recoded and given the mean value of the variable. Also, by recoding these two categories with the mean value of the variable, no cases will be lost; and therefore will not have an effect on the dependent variable(s). The first two categories were left in their original form, but recoded as 0/1.

Sociodemographic (Independent) Variables

Offender's race and ethnicity, which have been used as a proxy for racial and ethnic threat and have been linked to punitive measures by the U.S. criminal justice system, will be the variables of principal interest in this research. A number of studies (see Tables 1 and 2) have shown that race and ethnicity play a significant and substantial role in death sentences and death sentence outcomes. Thus, the following two variables, which are of critical importance in our analyses of death sentencing, are being used to create a new variable: RACE/ETHNIC.

To be more specific, variable 9 (Q4A: Race) was originally divided into five categories: (1) white, (2) black, (3) American Indian or Alaskan Native, (4) Asian or Pacific Islander, and (5) other. The third and fourth categories were recoded as missing because of the small number of cases (5 and 16 respectively) and the fact that the focus of the study is on African Americans, Caucasians, and Latinos.[84]

Variable 10 (Q4B: Hispanic origin) was originally divided into four categories: (1) Hispanic, (2) non-Hispanic, (3) not known, and (4) unknown/NA. Given the fact that the third and fourth categories contain missing cases (127 and 55 cases, respectively), it will not be possible to include all of the cases.

The RACE/ETHNIC variable included Latinos [both black (1) and white (241)], African Americans (636), and Caucasians (873), the "reference" group/category, for a total of 1,751 cases. While the data indicate that the skin color of an individual is an influential factor in how one is treated, the data also indicate that country of origin, culture, and race are also influential factors in how one is treated. Thus, given this and the fact that there are only seven black Latinos, it was decided to combined both white and black Latinos (242).

Since threat theory suggests that criminal male offenders are more likely to receive the worst sanctions, another variable to include would be sex, especially since there is widespread disagreement as to whether there is a clear pattern of sex discrimination in death sentence and death sentence outcomes. However, due to the small number of female defendants, sex was not included in the analysis. Nonetheless, recall that in Bedau's (1964) study of New Jersey, only one female received a death sentence in the 53 years covered by his study, and her sentence was commuted. Similarly, in the 51 years covered by Bedau (1965) in Oregon, only three females were sentenced to die, and all three sentences were commuted. Also, in the 68 years cover by Marquart et al. (1994) in Texas, the three women with death sentences were commuted. And, in Maryland, only one female in 25 years was sentenced to death and her sentence was commuted (McCafferty, 1992). Lastly, Pridemore's (2000) study showed similar findings.

Another critical variable to the current analysis is level of education. Given the limitations of the original data, this variable will serve as an indicator for "class," income, and employment, which have also been linked to punitive measures by political and economic elites. According to some estimates, approximately 90% of those charged with capital murder are indigent when arrested, and virtually all are indigent by the time their cases reach the appellate courts (Vick, 1995). Adequate resources are among the most significant factors influencing the outcome of death penalty cases, and education is one of them. As with prior felony convictions, education influences the perception of job opportunities and thus the risk of recidivism (self reported or offical).

Variable 17 (Q8: Education at first conviction of capital offense) was originally divided into 13 categories: (1) 7th grade or less, (2) 8th grade, (3) 9th grade, (4) 10th grade, (5) 11th grade, (6) 12th grade/GED, (7) 1st year of college, (8) 2nd year of college, (9) 3rd year of college (10) 4th year of college (11) more than 4 years of college, (12) not known, and (99) unknown/NA. The variable was renamed as EdLEVEL and recoded to reflect the number of years of completed school. The 1st category was recoded as 7, the 2nd as 8, the 3rd as 9, the 4th as 10, the 5th as 11, the 6th as 12, the 7th as 13, the 8th as 14, the 9th as 15, the 10th as 16, and the 11th as 17. The 12th category (295 cases) was combined with the last category (76 cases) and then coded with the mean value of the variable, representing missing data. Additionally, as with "prior felony," a dummy variable has been created for missing data.

Since prior research has indicated that marital status may play a role in the final disposition of a death sentence, a marital status variable is included in the current analysis. Theoretically, marital status is an indication of stability, and thus, viewed as a measure of future recidivism. Pridemore (2000), for instance, found that capital offenders who are married are less likely to be executed than those who are not.

Variable 16 (Q7: Marital status) was originally divided into six categories: (1) married, (2) divorced, (3) widowed, (4) never married, (5) not known, and (6) unknown/NA. The variable was renamed as MARRIED and recoded to separate the married from the unmarried. The first category was left in its original form, coded as 1. The second, third, and fourth categories were combined and recoded as 0. The last category was coded with the mean value of the variable, representing missing data, and, as with prior felony and education, a dummy variable was created for missing data.

Also, in view of the increase in the rate of executions as inmates' legal appeals are exhausted, a decrease in availability of federal appellate review due to recent habeas corpus modifications, and the concomitant decline in executives exercising their power to commute, the time under a death sentence is critical. The number of years under a death sentence were also included in the analysis as a control variable, since the longer the inmates are on death row, the more likely their execution, given that they were sentenced in different years. The "reason for inmate's removal from under sentence of death" (variable 31) and "year of inmate's removal from under of sentence of death" (variable 33) were utilized to calculate this new variable: IMPRISON. For those whose death sentence was removed (for whatever reason), years under a death sentence is equal to the year the sentence was removed minus the year they were sentenced to die. For those still under a death sentence in 1995, years under a death sentence is equal to 1995 minus the year sentenced to die.

Thus, no modifications have been made to variable 33 (Q14C3: Year of inmate's removal from under sentence of death), which ranges from 1975 to 1995 (1975-1995 cases only for California, Florida, and Texas). Additionally, since this variable is only going to be used to create an additional variable, and it will not be included in the regression, the missing values (1,184 cases in the last category, 99: unknown/NA) will not affect the regression estimates. Notice that in this case, the "missing values" are individuals who are still under the sentence of death.

Lastly, historically age when the offender committed the crime has been an influential factor in death sentence and death sentence outcome decisions. Recall that empirical studies have shown that age plays a role in the execution and commutation decision-making process (Bedau, 1964; 1965; Pridemore, 2000; Wolfgang et al., 1962). This variable, then, serves as an indicator for youth, which, as the other variables herein, has been perceived as a threat not only to political and economic elites but to 'mainstream America' and has been linked to punitive measures. Thus, the next three variables were used to calculate the approximate age of the offender when s/he committed the capital offense, which is not in the data set.

As for the previous variable, no modifications were made to variable 12 (Q5B: Date of birth–year), which ranges from 1917 to 1976 (1975-1995 cases only for California, Florida, and Texas), variable 22 (Q11B: Date of arrest for capital offense–year), which ranges from 1974 to 1995, and variable 24 (Q12B: Date of conviction for capital offense–year), which ranges from 1973 to 1995, since these variables were only used to create a new variable.

For cases with non-missing data on year of arrest, the age at time of offense was estimated by year of arrest minus the year of birth. And, when year of arrest was missing (n=566), age at time of offense was estimated by year of conviction minus year of birth. There are several missing cases for year of arrest, which would be closer to the time when the offense was committed than the year of conviction, but since the calculated correlation between age arrested and age convicted is .978, this is a legitimate proxy for age at time of arrest.

ANALYTICAL PROCEDURES

Once the proper modifications were made, both tabular analysis and logistic regression analysis (the next subject matter), the principal analytic technique used, was performed on the three selected states separately (different models for each state) if it was determined that the interaction effect of state and race/ethnicity was statistically significant.

Logistic regression is the method of choice when analyzing models with dichotomous dependent variables since performing multiple regression with a dichotomous dependent variable violates several OLS assumptions, which in turn leads to illogical predicted values and invalid hypothesis tests. Specifically, utilizing OLS regression with dichotomous dependent variables has four undesirable consequences: (1) illogical predicted probabilities, (2) heteroskedasticity, (3) non-normality, and (4) nonlinearity (Menard,1995).

For instance, coding the dependent variable, Y, 0 when the event/outcome is absent and 1 when the event is present results in the mean of the variable being equal to the proportion of cases having a value of 1, and the predicted value Y (i.e., the conditional mean of Y given the value of the independent variables, X's, assuming linearity) can be interpreted as the predicted probability of a case falling into the event/outcome present category, given its value on the X's.

Additionally, in the case of illogical predicted probabilities, predicted values of Y may be greater than 1 or less than 0, values that fall beyond acceptable values for predicted probabilities because such probabilities cannot be greater than 1 or less than 0 in the "real world." With heteroskedasticity, the size of the residuals will depend on the value of the X's. This results in unbiased estimates, but standard errors will not be efficient, thus affecting significance tests. And, there will be a systematic pattern in the residuals. In the case of nonnormality, the residuals will not be normally distributed, thus sampling variances/standard errors will not be correctly estimated, resulting in invalid significance tests and confidence interval estimates. Lastly, with nonlinearity, there is inherent nonlinearity in the relationships involving a dichotomous dependent variable. Thus, violation of OLS assumptions leads to invalid hypothesis tests and unreliable results.

Logistic regression that models the log of the odds ratio (i.e., logit) is the appropriate method to use with a dichotomous dependent variable. A logistic regression model has a binary response variable as the dependent variable (i.e., a variables having only two outcomes, 0 and 1). It is common to use the generic terms failure and success for these two outcomes. The sum of the scores in the sample is then the number of successes. The mean of the 0 and 1 scores, which is the sum divided by the total sample size, equals the proportion of successes (Agresti and Finlay, 1997; Blalock, 1979). In other words, coding the dependent variable, Y, 0 when the event/outcome is absent and 1 when it is present results in the mean of the variable being equal to the proportion of cases having a value of 1, and the predicted value Y (i.e., the conditional mean of Y given the value of the independent variables, X's, assuming linearity) can be interpreted as the predicted probability of a case falling into the event/outcome present category, given its value on the X's.

The Statistical Package for the Social Sciences (SPSS) allows flexible and exhaustive ways to perform logistic regression. For example, it allows us to include both continuous and categorical variables, and it allows for automatic dummy and effect coding of categorical variables. It also computes several of the diagnostic statistics that are familiar from OLS linear regression.

The odds ratios, which are the building blocks of the logistic regression model equals the probability of an event divided by the probability of no event equals the probability of an event divided by one minus the probability of an event:

odds ratio=probability of event/probability of no event
=probability of event/(1-probability of event).

Since probabilities (and odds ratios based on them) take an s-shaped nonlinear distribution, we take the natural log of the odds ratio to make the regression model linear in its parameters: log (probability of event/probability of nonevent)=log(odds ratio)=logit.

Additionally, since the logit (log-odds ratio) is the dependent variable in logistic regression, the following logistic regression equation is used to predict the log odds of an event happening and the odds ratio may be obtained by taking the antilog of the logit: $\log(\text{odds ratio})=B_0+B_1X_1+B_2X_2+ ... +B_kX_k$.

The interpretation of parameter estimates (B's), which are derived using maximum likelihood estimation are as follows: (1) B_0 is the intercept and shows the value of log odds when all X's are equal to zero, (2) the B's show how much the log odds increase or decrease with a unit change in X, and (3) the antilog of the B's, Exp(B), shows how much the odds are multiplied for a unit change in X. For example, an Exp(B) equal to 1 shows equal odds (odds are 50/50), thus indicating no effect of X on the odds. And, values of Exp(B) over 1 show that the odds are increased for a unit change in X; values less than 1 show that the odds decrease. It should be noted that the probability, the odds, and the logit are three different ways of expressing exactly the same thing.

As far as measures of goodness of fit, significance test statistics, etc., logistic regression provides measures that are analogues to OLS regression. For instance, D_m = -2 Log Likelihood for the model $\approx$ Sum of Squares Error, and it shows how poorly the model fits the data; G_m = $D_o - D_m \approx$ F-test (note: H_o: β s=0); Cox and Snell $R^2 \approx$ Adjusted R^2; Nagelkerke $R^2 \approx R^2$; and Wald statistic $\approx$ t-test statistic for H_o: β =0.[85]

The log-likelihood is the criterion of selecting parameters in the logistic regression model. To be more specific, maximum likelihood techniques are used to maximize the value of the function, the log-likelihood function, which indicates how likely it is to obtain the observed values of Y, given the values of the independent variables and parameters, $\alpha, \beta_1, ..., \beta_\kappa$.

Thus, logistic regression is especially appropriate for the analysis of dichotomous and unordered nominal polytomous dependent variables. In logistic regression, the emphasis is on whether the classification of cases into one or the other of the categories of the dependent variable can be predicted by the independent variables. Instead of trying to predict the arbitrary value associated with a category, it may be helpful to reconceptualize the problem as trying to predict the probability that a case will be classified into one as opposed to the other of the two categories of the dependent variable. In logistic regression analysis, one may not only be interested in the frequency of correct as opposed to incorrect predictions of the exact value of the dependent variable, but one may also be interested in how well the model minimizes errors of predictions. With a finite number (usually only two) of the possible values of the dependent variable, one may sometimes be more concerned with whether the predictions are correct or incorrect than with how close the predicted values (predicted conditional means, which are equal to the predicted conditional probabilities) are to the observed (0 or 1) values of the dependent variable.

It should be noted that in logistic regression, if our principal concern is with how well the model fits the data, we use G_M and R^2_L, based on -2LL, to test for statistical and substantive significance. If our concern is less with the overall fit of the model and more with the accuracy with which the model predicts actual category membership on the dependent variable, the binomial d and one of the three indices of predictive efficiency (λ_p, τ_p, or ϕ_p) are used to assess the statistical and substantive significance of the model. Above all, we need to emphasize that when the assumptions of logistic regression analysis are violated, calculations of a regression model may result in biased coefficients, inefficient estimates, or invalid statistical inference (Menard, 1995).

In short, the dichotomous dependent variable (e.g., executed or not) makes logistic regression a more appropriate method than other estimating procedures available. This technique allows the conversation of logit coefficients into "odds ratios," the antilogs of logit coefficients, indicating how much more likely an outcome is for a specific predictor category. For dichotomous predictors, odds ratios indicate how much more likely an outcome is for one category as opposed to another. For continuous predictors, the odds ratio indicates how much more likely an outcome is when the predictor increases by one unit (Aldrich and Nelson, 1986). Thus, logistic regression analysis is well suited for the analyses of the five selected dichotomous dependent variables. Finally, while the principal focus of these analyses is the odds ratio for African American and Latino defendants, controlling for other relevant variables, the odds ratios for all independent variables will be discussed.

LIMITATIONS

As Curran and Renzetti (1994) point out, no study is characterized by complete objectivity; that is, free of bias. For this particular study, there are three limitations to address. The first will be disaggregating the Latino category. From government documents to newspapers and even academic literature, Latinos are seldom identified by their exact ethnicity.[86] However, by making use of the latest sophisticated technology and the various sources of information available we should be able to identify the specific ethnicity of the Latinos who were executed between 1975 and 1995, which will be used for descriptive purposes. And, based on INS records and the latest Bureau of Census statistics (2000), states may be used as proxies for ethnicity. The latest figures show that the Latino/a population in Florida is predominately Cuban. In California and Texas, the Latino/a population is predominately Mexican.

The second limitation will be missing data. However, given the fact that a number of "remedies" have been applied, it is expected that the estimates, if altered, will not be affected substantially nor significantly. As Pridemore (2000) points out, the dummy variables included in the model for prior felony convictions, education, and marital status enable one to determine whether the data are missing at random or whether the cases with missing data somehow are systematically different from those for which data are provided. And, if there is a significant difference between sets of cases with data missing and those with available data, the inclusion in the model of each of these dummy variables control for this systemic component.

The third limitation, and perhaps the most critical, is the fact that multiple regression models may give conflicting results, depending on what variables are included in the analysis, how they are measured, and what period of observation is employed.[87] In this particular case, since the data have already been collected and coded, we are forced to work with the selected variables, the selected time frame, and the given population.

As Pridemore (2000) points out, the aggravating and mitigating factors of the act may help to determine the seriousness of the offense in the mind of decision-makers, and thus may be an influential factor in the final disposition. And, although data on type of counsel, the relationship between victim and offender, and the victim characteristics are widely available for executed inmates, such information is not collected in a central database for capital offenders whose death sentences have been commuted. Thus, since such data are not readily available, one would need to examine the individual files of all individuals with commuted death sentences, a task that is beyond the scope of this study. Similarly, the lack of data on the victim's race in the current study adds an additional shortcoming, since, as mentioned earlier, strong evidence of racial and ethnic disparities in both the charging and sentencing stage have been shown in past studies that address these issues.

Recall that past research has identified type of legal counsel (see Bedau, 1965; Bridge and Mosure, 1961; Wolfgang et al., 1962), relationship to victim (see McCafferty, 1962; Marquart et al., 1994; Vandiver, 1993), victim's race (see Allredge, 1942; Bridge and Mosure, 1961; McCafferty, 1962; Vandiver, 1993; Wolfgang et al., 1962), and whether the murder occurred together with a felony (see Vandiver, 1993; Wolfgang et al., 1962) as important predictors of the decision to execute or commute the sentence. A failure to test for or control for a legitimate case characteristic could introduce a risk of errors in the analysis if, for instance, the omitted variable is correlated with the outcome of interest. One should be especially aware of the possibility that omitted variables may interact with variables in the system, producing nonadditive relationships. However, while additional variables could be utilized, a more representative sample of the selected categories and perhaps a longer time frame could enhance the analysis, the existing data will suffice to conduct the study and provide tentative conclusions.

Lastly, while not directly related to this particular study, it is important to acknowledge that state-by-state comparisons are not likely to reveal much about the effect of capital punishment, because states differ in many ways, including their willingness to execute. Still, careful analysis will be performed in the hope of improving the study's validity and reliability. And, indeed, since the analysis will be highly historical, qualitative and quantitative, the data help to indicate the types of findings that support or refute the hypotheses.

Having addressed these concerns and issues, the present study seeks to determine: (1) which ethnic Latino members are on death row; (2) which ethnic Latino members have been executed; and (3) how severe the death sentence outcome (execution, commutation, sentence and/or conviction being overturned by the courts as well as remaining under the sentence of death) disparities are among various ethnic groups. In short, from this analysis, we are able to obtain a more realistic picture of the distribution of death sentence outcomes in California, Florida, and Texas for the years 1975 to 1995.

CHAPTER 6

Latinos Executed in the United States Between 1975 and 1995

The history of executions in the United States is a story shaped by race and ethnicity of the offender (and victim), as well as various other factors at different points in time and space. Additionally, to debunk historical myths about racial and ethnic differences in death sentence outcomes in the United States, one needs to treat each group accordingly.

In a non-death penalty study, Zatz (1984) found that prior record, type of offense, especially homicide and rape, and mode of disposition (but not race and ethnicity of defendant) are of special importance in distinguishing between sentence lengths for Chicanos and members of other race and ethnic groups.

Zatz (1984:165) also found that prior record was "used primarily against Chicanos, perhaps because they are seen as specializing in drug trafficking from Mexico." Furthermore, based on her determinate sentencing study, where the "dangerousness" of an offender was most ambiguous, Chicanos received longer prison sentences than Caucasians or African Americans. Kelly (1976), though, found that Chicanos (and Native Americans) convicted of homicide received lighter sentences than Caucasians and African Americans. This trend, however, may have changed historically, given the various recent threatening issues/events (e.g., immigration, job security).

Additionally, as Zatz (1984) points out, Latinos, like African Americans, have fewer financial resources with which to hire a private attorney than do Caucasians. In a related issue, LaFree (1985) found that while indigent Latino drug offenders in Tucson, Arizona had access to competent public defenders, Latino, mostly Mexican, defendants in El Paso, Texas did not have access to a system of competent public defenders.

Hebert's (1997:146) drug offense study found evidence suggesting that "acceptance of responsibility" or remorse varies by race and ethnicity. African American and Latino offenders, for a variety of reasons including cultural standards of appropriate behavior, quality of legal representation, and intercultural miscommunication, are thought to be less likely to express remorse than Caucasian offenders.

Thus, in interpreting the race and ethnic differences in executions, one needs to look beyond the traditional African American/Caucasian approach, which minimizes not only the Latino population, which is usually treated as a monolithic group, but also the various ethnic groups (e.g., Cubans, Mexicans) that constitute the Latino population. As a result of such an approach, little is known about executed Latinos. For instance, of what ethnic group were those Latinos who were executed between 1975 and 1995? What were the experiences and/or characteristics of the individuals who lost their lives at the hands of the state? Based on the above studies and the history of the relations between Caucasians, Cubans, and Mexicans in Chapter IV, I would expect that most, if not all, of the Latinos who were executed between 1975 and 1995 were of Mexican heritage. Additionally, I would predict that most, if not all, of the executions took place in Texas. Therefore, the main objective of this chapter is to go beyond the African American/Caucasian traditional approach by disaggregating the group of Latinos who were executed between 1975 and 1995 in the United States, focusing primarily (but not exclusively) on California, Florida, and Texas.

This chapter will begin by discussing the process and the various sources that were utilized to determine the ethnicity of the Latinos who were executed in the United States between 1975 and 1995. After describing the techniques used to collect evidence of ethnic identity, an examination of the evidence on ethnic identity will follow. This examination will provide insight into the existence of ethnic differences in executions. Additionally, if differential treatment exists, as predicted, the evidence will enhance our understanding of when, why, and how

Mexicans are more likely to be executed. After an examination of the "execution" evidence, a commutation analysis will follow. Such examination will provide insight into the struggle that some individuals have gone through in the hope of being granted a commutation. The chapter will then conclude by making predictions as to whether similar ethnic differences would apply to other death sentence outcomes: sentences and/or convictions being overturned.

IN SEARCH OF THE EVIDENCE

First, it should be noted that not all states keep information on race/ethnicity of inmates under a sentence of death other than "whites" and "blacks," and the majority of states do not differentiate between the different Latino groups. Additionally, record keeping methods vary widely across states. As a result, information on Latinos, especially for specific Latino groups, is scant and/or unreliable (see Aguirre and Baker, 1988; Baldus et al., 1998; Nixon, 1996). Given this set of circumstances, triangulated methods (multiple procedures) were used to gather evidence of ethnicity in order to reduce possible sources of error.

Specifically, in the hope of obtaining valid and reliable information, multiple published sources of information were utilized in determining the ethnicity of Latinos who were executed during the time under study.[88] In addition to multiple published sources, I sent out over 100 e-mail messages, made numerous phone calls, and sent several letters via U.S. mail to various government agencies (e.g., state offices of the attorney general, departments of correction, departments of criminal justice, police departments), political and professional organizations (e.g., League of Latin American Citizens or LULAC, National Association for the Advancement of Color People or NAACP, Amnesty International, Hispanic National Bar Association, American Civil Liberties Union, Mexican American Legal Defense and Educational Fund), individuals (e.g., attorneys, judges, authors), newspapers (both national and international), magazines (both Spanish and English), radio stations (Spanish), televison stations (Spanish), among others, in the hope of not only obtaining the needed information, but also reliable information. In some cases, I was able to obtain relevant information, but in most cases the information was not available. Several of these sources, though, served to confirm the identity of the executed Latinos.

Overall, though, the use of triangulated methods proved to be an efficient method. The findings of one method reinforced and validated the findings of another. Thus, it is particularly important to utilize multiple procedures in gathering evidence of ethnicity to reduce possible sources of error.

EXAMINATION OF THE EVIDENCE

An Historical Reminder

Don Reid (1973:109), a reporter who witnessed some 190 executions in Texas between 1923 and 1972 and who spent time talking with death row inmates, stated

> it took no study for me to accept that simple, ignorant men committed more crimes of violence than did sophisticated men of means. And, it took but little time to realize that when sophisticated men of means did commit crimes of violence, they seldom were executed for them. Those who were electrocuted were the blacks, Mexican-Americans, the poor whites and whites out of favor in their communities for one reason or another, having nothing to do with the criminal allegations for which they died.

This observation is consistent with Giardini and Farrow (1952), who found that Mexicans constituted the third largest group of individuals under the sentence of death in Texas between 1924 and 1952. Also, of the 506 men who were placed on death row between 1924 and 1964 in Texas, 361 eventually died in the electric chair: 229 African Americans, 108 Caucasians, and 23 Mexicans (*San Antonio Express News*, 1999; see also Aguirre and Baker, 1989; 1997). (Please see Tables 1 and 2 for additional ethnic studies.)

Los Ejecutados

First, it should be underscored that of the 313 executions between 1973 and 1995 in the United States, 17 were Latino inmates (NAACP Legal Defense Fund and Death Penalty Information Center, 1999). Other sources, however, claim that there were 19 Latino executions (Snell, 1996).

Second, the data show that 17 Latino executions took place in Texas (NAACP Legal Defense Fund and Death Penalty Information Center, 1999). The origin of the remaining two Latino executions (cited by Snell, 1996) is unclear, but based on the numerous sources mentioned above (including the fashion in which cases were treated in the media), it appears that one of these executions took place in Florida and the other in Utah.

Third, recall that while the focus of this chapter is on executed Latinos between 1975 and 1995 in the United States (particularly California, Florida, and Texas), no one was executed in the United States between 1973 and 1976. In fact, as noted in Chapter V, for the time frame under analysis (all states included), the first execution took place on January 17, 1977 and the last on December 12, 1995.

Fourth, of the 135 individuals who were executed during this 20-year period in the three states under analysis, two were executed in California, 29 in Florida, and 104 in Texas. Of these 135, 18 were Latinos, all identified as "white" Latino men. One Latino was executed in Florida and 17 in Texas.[89] Thus, of the 19 executed Latinos in the United States between 1975 and 1995, 18 were executed in the states under analysis. Of the 19 Latinos executed between 1975 and 1995, one was Dominican and 16 were of Mexican extraction.[90] The 16 Mexican defendants and one Dominican defendant were all executed in Texas.

One of the 16 Mexican defendants, executed on December 11, 1995, was once identified by a Yaqui-Mexican (who was once the defendant's neighbor) as part Yaqui Indian and part Mexican (Hayes, 1999b).[91] Additionally, some of the Mexican defendants could have been U.S. citizens but classified themselves as "Mexican" (Crocker, 1999; *New York Times*, 1985; Office of the Attorney General of Texas, 1999; Texas Department of Criminal Justice, 1999). Also, some of the executed

Mexicans were Mexican nationals (Amnesty International, 1999; Bentele, 1993; *Courier-Journal*, 1993; Halperin, 1997; *Houston Chronicle*, 1993c; *Los Angeles Times*, 1994; *New York Times*, 1993a; 1993b; *Sacramento Bee*, 1994; *San Francisco Chronicle*, 1993b).[92]

Lastly, the other two Latino executions are unique. As it was mentioned above, the evidence indicates that one execution (apparently under the identity of a "white" Latino) took place in Florida in 1989 and the other (apparently under the identity of a "black" Latino) in Utah in 1987. I, however, was unable to find evidence tying these individuals to a specific ethnic group or to Latino heritage (Kinder, 1982; *St. Petersburg Times*, 1989a; 1989b). These two cases, though, are worth noting for several reasons, especially the fashion in which they were treated by the media and the criminal justice system.

According to Hayes (1999a), who lived approximately 30 miles from where the Florida murder was committed and who attended the trial for several days, the defendant was born in New Mexico but moved to Florida as a small child. Hayes (1999a) found that the Florida School and State Employment records had "white-Hispanic" and "white-non-Hispanic" on the forms then, but everything in his records indicated strictly "white." Also, Hayes (1999a), who followed the case in various newspapers (e.g., *Ocala Star* and *Orlando Sentinel*), found no evidence of Latino heritage for the Florida execution.

The 1987 Utah execution is also worth noting. Based on the inmate's data file (including appeals), the defendant was born in Trinidad, and there is some indication that "he MAY have been 'Indian [and] Black' but nothing to indicate that he was in any way Hispanic" (Hayes, 1999a). Kinder (1982:81) notes that the defendant was once identified by an air force official as a "young black airman, a twenty-year old Trinidadian named . . . ." Also, Kinder (1982) found that the defendant was born in the isle of Tobago, which lies in the azure waters of the Caribbean east of Venezuela, and lived there until three. Twenty miles to the southwest of Tobago is Trinidad, where the defendant, who often received a "good licking" grew up (Kinder, 1982:238).[93] There are, however, three important caveats. First, he spoke some Spanish and while in San Antonio, Texas he "managed to fall in love with a Mexican . . ." (Kinder, 1982:250). This could have led to the "Latino" identification. Second, the charge to the county by his attorneys was "perhaps the lowest fee in the state's history for a case of this magnitude" (Kinder, 1982:290). Third, while a note was passed to a juror that read "hang the niggers," the judge denied a mistrial and he was convicted by an all-Caucasian jury (*Chicago Daily Law Bulletin*, 1992:1).

Thus, since I was unable to trace these last two executions to a specific ethnic group or to Latino heritage, I classified these two executions as not of known Latino origin. This conclusion is supported by Culver (1992:59) who claims that "Texas is the only state to have executed Hispanics" between 1977 and 1990. The bottom line, though, is that regardless of their ethnicity, in the eyes of the criminal justice system, they were identified as Latino and treated as such. In short, of the 19 executed Latinos: 16 were Mexicans (all in Texas), one Dominican (in Texas), and two unknowns (one in Florida and one in Utah).

Other Characteristics of Executed Latinos

The characteristics of the executed Latinos between 1975 and 1995 are consistent with observations made by Aguirre and Baker, Giardini and Farrow, and Reid, among others. First, the evidence shows that about half of the victims were Latino and the rest were non-Latino, mostly Caucasian. Second, most of them had prior criminal records. Third, while some defendants remained under the sentence of death for only a few months before the execution was carried out, most stayed on death row for several years before they were executed.

Fourth, all of the Mexican defendants had non-professional jobs, if employed prior to their arrest, were young at the time of the capital offense, were uneducated, and, at times, their income was "just barely enough to get by" (*Atlanta Journal and Constitution*, 1991; *Courier-Journal*, 1993; Halperin, 1997; *Houston Chronicle*, 1992a; 1992b; 1993a; 1993b; *Los Angeles Times*, 1985b; 1994; *New York Times*, 1985; 1987; 1993b; 1995b; *Phoenix Gazette*, 1995; Office of the Attorney General of Texas, 1999; *Sacramento Bee*, 1994; *San Diego Union-Tribune*, 1985a; 1985b; 1986; Texas Department of Criminal Justice, 1999; *Washington Post*, 1994). Not surprisingly, an attorney who witnessed one of the executions made the following observation: "I think it [death sentence] is at best extremely arbitrary, at worst extremely discriminatory against the poor" (*New York Times*, 1995a:24).

Fifth, based on the social history evaluations, where information was available, some of the Mexican defendants were "mildly mentally retarded" and suffered from "severe brain impairment" (*Baltimore Sun*, 1995; *Houston Chronicle*, 1992a; 1995; *Independent*, 1995; *New York Times*, 1995b; *Phoenix Gazette*, 1995; Office of the Attorney General of Texas, 1999). In one case, tests showed that the defendant had an IQ below 70, which is considered mentally retarded (*Baltimore Sun*, 1995; *Independent*, 1995; *Houston Chronicle*, 1995; *Phoenix Gazette*, 1995). Keyes, Edwards, and Perske (1999:3) found that this defendant "had an IQ estimated at 65, with adaptive skills of a 7 year old."

Sixth, some of the Mexican defendants had "a lengthy history of chronic inhalant abuse and extensive drug use" (*Houston Chronicle*, 1992b; 1993a; 1993b; *New York Times*, 1985; 1987; Office of the Attorney General of Texas, 1999; *San Diego Union-Tribune*, 1985a; 1985b; 1986; 1987).

Seventh, in some cases there was "no sign of remorse," which in part contributed to the execution (*New York Times*, 1986). Additionally, lack of remorse was perhaps due in part to other things, as in the following case of one of the executed Mexicans: ". . . I shot a man who shot me first" (*San Diego Union-Tribune*, 1985a:4). In another case, the final statement of an executed Mexican was: "I am innocent, innocent . . . make no mistake about this. I owe society nothing" (*Houston Chronicle*, 1993b:1). With few exceptions, most Mexican nationals currently on death row in Texas claim innocence (Halperin, 1997). It should not come as a surprise, then, that Mexico (as well as some other countries) have not extradited fugitives on a number of occasions unless the death sentence was waived in the United States (*Phoenix Gazette*, 1993), as illustrated by the recent Florida case involving Jose Luis del Toro.[94]

Lastly, in some cases, the Mexican defendants were not only represented by inadequate counsel, but at times no Mexican American or other minority jurors served on petitioner's trial jury (*Houston Chronicle*, 1992a; *New York Times*, 1986; Office of the Attorney General of Texas, 1999; *Sacramento Bee*, 1994; *Washington Post*, 1994). Their frustration was summed up by one of the Mexican defendants: "They call it equal justice, but is your justice . . . a Mexican life is worth nothing" (*New York Times*, 1985:11). Similarly, Pat Clark, executive director of Death Penalty Focus, made the following observation: "it's interesting that many folks consider the U.S. a more civilized country than Mexico and yet Mexico doesn't have such a barbaric penalty" (*San Francisco Chronicle*, 1993b:15).[95]

THE SIGNIFICANCE OF COMMUTATIONS IN THE STRUGGLE FOR LIFE

In a battle against time and the state to avoid execution, commutations have been viewed as "hope," as a "possibility" of not losing an additional life. However, while in some cases involving Mexican defendants, especially Mexican nationals, there was widespread pressure for commutation, based largely on claims of discrimination, violation of civil rights, innocence, violation of international treaties, lack of adequate legal and financial representation, mental illness, youth at the time of the offense, irreversibility of mistakes, and a history of chronic drug abuse and neglect of the defendant, the death sentences were carried out.[96]

The majority of foreign nationals sentenced to death in the United States have been convicted in violation of their rights under the Vienna Convention of 1963 (Amnesty International, 1999; Halperin, 1997; *National Law Journal*, 1998; Vandiver, 1999; Warren, 1999). Article 36, which requires authorities in the country where the person was arrested to notify his/her country (e.g., consulate, State Department) within 12 hours of the arrest, of the Vienna Convention on Consular Relations is an international treaty that became U.S. law in 1969.

Robert Brooks, a Virginia attorney who represented a Mexican national who was executed recently, points out that "the State Department maintains a double standard when applying Article 36" (Halperin, 1997:6). According to Brooks, while the "State Department insists on being notified whenever Americans are jailed abroad and that while failure to comply with Article 36 within 12 hours of an arrest is grounds for diplomatic protest, it allows the law to go unheeded when foreign nationals are arrested in the United States" (Halperin, 1997:6). In fact, "People are going to death in violation of every article . . . in every case,

Mexican consulates were not notified until after their citizens had been convicted and given the death sentence" (Halperin, 1997:6; see also Vandiver, 1999). Contrast this with the 1994 caning of Michael Fay, an 18-year old male from Ohio who was lashed four times on his bare buttocks with a rattan cane in Singapore for vandalizing cars. Before the sentence was carried out, there was an enormous outcry from Americans expressed in the U.S. media.

When Mexican nationals in Texas approached their execution dates, the Mexican government (including the President and state governors), protestors on both sides of the border (including organizations like the League of Latin American Citizens), and international groups called on the Governor (e.g., Ann Richards) to commute the sentences (*Los Angeles Times*, 1994; *Sacramento Bee*, 1994; *Phoenix Gazette*, 1993). On behalf of one Mexican national, the Mexican National Human Rights Commission, the Vatican, as well as the National Network of Civil Rights Organizations made up of more than 30 Mexican groups, called for a reprieve, not challenging his guilt, but only objecting to the death sentence, which was viewed as racist, repugnant, and barbarous (Bentele, 1993; *Courier-Journal*, 1993; *Houston Chronicle*, 1993c; *Sacramento Bee*, 1994; *San Diego Union-Tribune*, 1994; Tierney, 1992).

In the case of the second Mexican national, there were worldwide protestations, as indicated by various news stories. For instance, a director of Comite Nacional de La Raza explained:

> This is the global aspect–not only are we trying to save the life of an innocent man and how he was used as a scapegoat–but it's also a protest of the justice system that is discriminatorily used against people of color (Dieter, 1997; Edwards, 1993; *Los Angeles Times*, 1994; *New York Times*, 1993a; *Sacramento Bee*, 1994; Zuniga, 1993).

The case of a third Mexican (a U.S. citizen) who was executed in 1993 also brought national and international protestations on the grounds of innocence (Dieter, 1997; Edwards, 1993; *Houston Chronicle*, 1993b; *New York Times*, 1993b).

Yet, over the protestations of the Mexican government and various national and international organizations, Mexican defendants have been executed (Dieter, 1997; Edwards, 1993; Halperin, 1997; *Houston Chronicle*, 1993a; 1993b; 1993c; *Los Angeles Times*, 1985a; 1985b; 1994; *New York Times*, 1993b; *Phoenix Gazette*, 1993; *Sacramento Bee*, 1994; *San Diego Union-Tribune*, 1985a; 1993; 1994; *San Francisco Chronicle*, 1993b; *Washington Post*, 1993; 1994). In one case, outside the Texas' Walls Unit Prison where the execution took place, protestors held candles and chanted in Spanish, "Justice! and "Life, not death!" The demonstration was the largest in several years for a Texas execution (*Houston Chronicle*, 1993c). At other times, though, "there were no conferences . . . no Hollywood stars speaking out for [them] . . . no international attention riveted on [their] case . . . no speeches . . . no rallies" (*Washington Post*, 1993:9).

The bold headline across the front page of the daily newspaper *La Jornada* summarized the end result after the death sentence of a Mexican national was carried out in one word: "EXECUTED." Other Mexico City newspapers (e.g., *El Nacional*) made similar statements and criticized the execution on various grounds. In the United States, one defendant's lawyer made the following observation: "they have done everything you could ask a Government to do . . . unfortunately, to use the vernacular of Texas, Mr. [defendant's name] is a wetback who killed a white cop" (*Los Angeles Times*, 1994; *New York Times*, 1993b:19).

Symbolic Justice

As an additional symbol of insult, not only toward the executed Mexicans, but to all Mejicanos of the world, four Mexicans were executed close to major Mexican holidays, and one was actually executed (or perhaps I should say, sacrificed) on Diez y Seis de Septiembre (Mexico's independence day, September 16). Thus, the execution of a Mexican is not only an act against the individual, as Currie has pointed out, but the execution is carried out against Mexico, its people and governmental policy. Zavaleta points out that whichever way one puts it, the end result is clear: when such executions take place, the state is "shedding Mexican blood on American soil . . . [it is] like slitting the throat of a sacrificial lamb" (Halperin, 1997:4-5).

CONCLUSION

The evidence shows that all but one of the identified Latinos executed between 1975 and 1995 were of Mexican extraction, and all were executed in Texas. While Mexicans have been classified as "white," through the give and take of treaty making in *In re Rodriguez* (1897), the end results are quite different at the practical level. The Mexican government's call for "fair trials,"and statement that it "would like the sentences of . . . Mexicans condemned to death in the United States to be commuted to life imprisonment" on numerous occasions, achieved little (*Los Angeles Times*, 1994; *Phoenix Gazette*, 1993; *Sacramento Bee*, 1994; *San Diego Union-Tribune*, 1994; *San Francisco Chronicle*, 1993a:4). This may be because "it is easier to rationalize the harsh treatment of persons who are essentially 'outsiders'" (Blalock, 1967:206).

Protestations on behalf of Mexicans (documented and undocumented) were (and continue to be) not entirely the byproduct of the release of one Mexican who was under the sentence of death and the execution of another. Tony Garza, Texas Secretary of State, explains ". . . from the sense of the left and right, Mexico was being scapegoated" (Halperin, 1997:3). As Zavaleta points out, the war between the two countries may have ended 150 years ago, "but very hard feelings and serious grudges remain" (Halperin, 1997:4).

The data show that Latino and African American death sentence outcomes differ, not only from those of Caucasians, but also from each other. Variables that best explain variation in death sentence outcomes are different for African Americans, Caucasians, Chicanos, and Cubans. Unfortunately, as Gordon observes, "we haven't taken the time to understand Mexican culture the way we have taken (time) to understand the European culture" (Halperin, 1997:4).[97] Nonetheless, Zatz (1984:147) points out, "Chicanos constitute a separate group, distinct from both Blacks and whites [and Cubans, Puerto Ricans, and so forth], and must be treated accordingly in criminological research." Not only must one triangulate methodology, one must also triangulate perspectives.

In the next chapter, a quantitative analysis of death sentence outcomes will be provided. Specifically, the analysis includes African Americans, Caucasians, and Latinos, and goes beyond executions and commutations to include sentences and/or convictions overturned by the courts in California, Florida, and Texas between 1975 and 1995. Based on this chapter's evidence on executions (as well as the commutation struggle), I expect to find similar trends in all death sentence outcomes included in the quantitative analysis.

CHAPTER 7

Findings

This chapter presents the results of the tabular and logistic regression analyses that provide tests of the hypotheses derived from the four-threat theory discussed in chapters two and four.[98] The tabular results (Tables 3 to 7) are presented first followed by the logistic regression findings (Tables 8 to 16).

TABULAR ANALYSES

In Table 3 and the following tables, the chi-square (X^2) test statistic and its associated significance level (p) reveal whether derived cell frequencies differ significantly from the frequencies expected given the marginal distributions of the independent and dependent variables. Goodman and Kruskal tau (τ) and lambda (λ) are proportional reduction in error measures of association that give the strength of the relationship between the independent and dependent variables. The p-value reveals the level of statistical significance.

Table 3 presents the results of the cross-tabulation of death sentence disposition by state. Of all inmates removed from the sentence of death in California, 2.4% were executed, 10.6% had their sentences commuted, 62.4% had their sentences declared unconstitutional or overturned, and 24.7% had their convictions overturned. In Florida, 8.5% were executed, 1.5% had their sentences commuted, 64.4% had their sentences declared unconstitutional or overturned, and 25.7% had their convictions overturned. In Texas, 39.5% were executed, 14.8% had their sentences commuted, 6.3% had their sentences declared unconstitutional or overturned, and 39.5% had their convictions overturned.

Table 3

Cross-tabulation of Death Sentence
Outcomes by State

Disposition	California	Florida	Texas	Total Percent
Executed	2.4	8.5	39.5	19.3
Commuted	10.6	1.5	14.8	7.6
Sentence unconstitutional or overturned	62.4	64.4	6.3	42.4
Conviction overturned	24.7	25.7	39.5	30.7
Total Percent	100.0	100.0	100.0	100.0
N	85	343	256	684

X^2 = 259.504 λ = .216 τ = .163
P = .000   P = .000   P = .000

Table 3 shows marked differences in death sentence dispositions across states. Of all inmates removed from the sentence of death, 2.4% of those in California were executed compared with 8.5% of those in Florida, and 39.5% of those in Texas. Commutations also differed across states with 1.5% of cases in Florida receiving commutations, 10.6% in California compared with 14.8% in Texas. In Florida and California, the majority of cases (64.4% and 62.4%, respectively) had their death sentences overturned or declared unconstitutional by the courts while only 6.3% of the cases in Texas had a similar outcome. On the other hand, a higher percentage of cases in Texas (39.5%) had their convictions overturned, while 24.7% of the cases in California and 25.7% of the cases in Florida had their convictions overturned. The X^2 test indicates that the relationship between state and death sentence disposition is statistically significant. The τ and λ statistics show that the strength of the association between state and disposition is weak to moderate and statistically significant.

These results show that California carried out the lowest percentage of executions and granted a low percentage of commutations while it overturned a high percentage of death sentences as well as convictions. Florida granted the lowest percentage of commutations, but had the highest percentage of sentences being declared unconstitutional or overturned by the courts. Texas carried out the highest percentage of executions–20 times greater than California and five times greater than Florida–it also granted the highest percentage of commutations as well as convictions overturned, but a very low percentage of sentences declared unconstitutional or overturned. California and Florida had a similar pattern of dispositions.

Overall, these results provide partial support for predictions in Chapters II and IV. Predictions were made that Texas, followed by Florida, and California, would be: (1) more likely to execute; (2) less likely to commute; (3) less likely to declare a death sentence unconstitutional; (4) less likely to overturn a death sentence; and (5) less likely overturn a conviction. (Keep in mind that hypotheses 3 and 4 were combined.) The results provide support for hypotheses 1, 3 and 4. Also, in Chapters II and IV alternative hypotheses suggested that Texas, followed by Florida, and California, would be: (1) more likely to declare a death sentence unconstitutional; (2) more likely to overturn a death sentence; and (3) more likely overturn a conviction. (Again, keep in mind that hypotheses 3 and 4 (or 6 and 7) were combined.) Thus, the results provide support for the third alternative hypothesis.

Table 4 presents the cross-tabulation of death sentence disposition by race/ethnicity for all three states in the study combined. Of all Latinos removed from the sentence of death, 23.1% were executed, 11.5% had their sentences commuted, 28.2% had their sentences declared unconstitutional or overturned, and 37.2% had their convictions overturned. Of all African Americans removed from the sentence of death, 18.8% were executed, 6.1% had their sentences commuted, 44.1% had their sentences declared unconstitutional or overturned, and 31.0% had their convictions overturned. Of all Caucasian inmates removed from the sentence of death, 18.8% were executed, 7.8% had their sentences commuted, 44.3% had their sentences declared unconstitutional or overturned, and 29.1% had their convictions overturned.

Table 4

Cross-tabulation of Death Sentence Outcomes
by Race/Ethnicity

Disposition	Latino	African American	Caucasian	Total Percent
Executed	23.1	18.8	18.8	19.3
Commuted	11.5	6.1	7.8	7.6
Sentence unconstitutional or overturned	28.2	44.1	44.3	42.4
Conviction overturned	37.2	31.0	29.1	30.7
Total Percent	100.0	100.0	100.0	100.0
N	78	245	361	684

$$X^2 = 8.524 \qquad \lambda = .018 \qquad \tau = .005$$
$$P = .202 \qquad P = .327 \qquad P = .090$$

Table 4 shows some differences in death sentence dispositions by race/ethnicity. Of all inmates whose death sentences were removed, 23.1% of Latinos were executed compared with 18.8% of African Americans and 18.8% of Caucasians. Similarly, 11.5% of Latinos were granted commutations compared with 6.1% of African Americans and 7.8% of Caucasians. Turning to the death sentence being overturned or declared unconstitutional, 28.2% of Latinos received this disposition compared with 44.1% of African Americans and 44.3% of Caucasians. Finally, for convictions overturned, 37.2% of Latinos fell in this category compared with 31% of African Americans and 29.1% of Caucasians. Neither the X^2 test statistic nor the two measures of association were statistically significant; thus, there is no relationship between race/ethnicity and death sentence disposition.

Notice, however, that the distribution of dispositions for Caucasians and African Americans is nearly identical. Latinos, though, were most likely to be executed, have their sentences commuted, and have their convictions overturned, while they were much less likely to have their sentences overturned or declared unconstitutional by the courts. Thus, these results provide mixed support for the four-threat theory. Recall that in Chapter IV, the four-threat theory of death sentence outcomes suggested the following five points, that in California, Florida, and Texas (in ascending order): (1) African Americans would be more likely to be executed than Mexicans, definitely more likely than Cubans, and, certainly more likely than Caucasians; (2) African Americans would be less likely to receive a commutation than Mexicans, definitely less likely than Cubans, and certainly less likely than Caucasians; (3) African Americans would be less likely to have their sentence declared unconstitutional than Mexicans, definitely less likely than Cubans, and certainly less likely than Caucasians; (4) African Americans would be less likely to have their sentence overturned than Mexicans, definitely less likely than Cubans, and certainly less likely than Caucasians; and (5) African Americans would be less likely to have their conviction overturned than Mexicans, definitely less likely than Cubans, and certainly less likely than Caucasians.

It was also argued that the four-threat theory of death sentence outcomes leads to competing hypotheses. Given the nature of the decision-making process (e.g., trial errors, resources), the opposite could also be possible for the last three hypotheses. Thus, it was predicted that in California, Florida, and Texas (in ascending order): (1) African Americans would be more likely to have their sentence declared unconstitutional than Mexicans, definitely more likely than Cubans, and certainly more likely than Caucasians; (2) African Americans would be more likely to have their sentence overturned than Mexicans, definitely more likely than Cubans, and certainly more likely than Caucasians; and (3) African Americans would be more likely to have their conviction and sentence overturned than Mexicans, definitely more likely than Cubans, and certainly more likely than Caucasians. Thus, while the findings for African Americans and Caucasians, which are similar, are contrary to predictions in Chapters II and IV, the findings for Latinos provide partial support for the four-threat theory. The findings for Latinos do not support hypotheses 2 but partially support hypotheses 1, 3, and 4. Additionally, the findings for Latinos provide partial support for the third alternative hypothesis.

Table 5 presents the cross-tabulation of death sentence dispositions by race/ethnicity in California. Of all Latino inmates removed from the sentence of death, 7.1% had their sentences commuted, 64.3% had their sentences declared unconstitutional or overturned, and 28.6% had their convictions overturned. Of all African American inmates removed from the sentence of death, 7.1% had their sentences commuted, 64.3% had their sentences declared unconstitutional or overturned, and 28.6% had their convictions overturned. Of all Caucasian inmates removed from the sentence of death, 4.7% were executed, 14.0% had their sentences commuted, 60.5% had their sentences declared unconstitutional or overturned, and 20.9% had their convictions overturned.

Table 5

Cross-tabulation of Death Sentence Outcomes
by Race/Ethnicity in California

Disposition	Latino	African American	Caucasian	Total Percent
Executed	---	---	4.7	2.4
Commuted	7.1	7.1	14.0	10.6
Sentence unconstitutional or overturned	64.3	64.3	60.5	62.4
Conviction overturned	28.6	28.6	20.9	24.7
Total Percent N	100.0 14	100.0 28	100.0 43	100.0 85

X^2 = 3.436 λ = .000 τ = .007
P = .752   P = —a   P = .949

a. Cannot be computed because of the asymptotic standard error = 0.

Again, as in the previous table, Table 5 shows some differences in death sentence dispositions by race/ethnicity. Of all inmates whose death sentence was removed, 4.7% of Caucasians were executed, but no African American or Latino inmates were executed. For commutations, 7.1% of Latinos were granted commutations compared with 14.0% of African Americans and 14.0% of Caucasians. Also, for death sentences that were declared unconstitutional or overturned, 64.3% of Latinos and 64.3% of African Americans received this disposition compared with 60.5% of Caucasians. Finally, for convictions overturned, 28.6% of Latinos and 28.6% of African Americans fell in this category compared with 20.9% of Caucasians. Neither the X^2 test statistic nor the measures of association were statistically significant; thus, there is no relationship between race/ethnicity and death sentence disposition in California.

Overall, results provide mixed support for predictions in Chapters II and IV. Notice that the distribution of dispositions for African Americans and Latinos is identical. Caucasians were most likely to be executed, and have their sentences commuted, while they were slightly less likely to have their sentences overturned or declared unconstitutional as well as their convictions overturned by the courts. Thus, the distribution of commutations provide partial support for the four-threat theory of death sentence outcomes. Findings do not support hypotheses 1 and 3, but partially support hypotheses 2 and 4. Additionally, the findings provide partial support for all three alternative hypotheses.

Table 6 presents the cross-tabulation of death sentence dispositions by race and ethnicity in Florida. Of all Latino inmates removed from the sentence of death, 5.3% were executed, 68.4% had their sentences declared unconstitutional or overturned, and 26.3% had their convictions overturned. Of all African American inmates removed from the sentence of death, 6.8% were executed, 2.3% had their sentences commuted, 63.2% had their sentences declared unconstitutional or overturned, and 27.8% had their convictions overturned. Of all Caucasian inmates removed from the sentence of death, 9.9% were executed, 1.0% had their sentences commuted, 64.9% had their sentences declared unconstitutional or overturned, and 24.1% had their convictions overturned.

Table 6

Cross-tabulation of Death Sentence Outcomes
by Race/Ethnicity in Florida

Disposition	Latino	African American	Caucasian	Total Percent
Executed	5.3	6.8	9.9	8.5
Commuted	---	2.3	1.0	1.5
Sentence unconstitutional or overturned	68.4	63.2	64.9	64.4
Conviction overturned	26.3	27.8	24.1	25.7
Total Percent N	100.0 19	100.0 133	100.0 191	100.0 343

X^2 =   2.777 λ =   .000 τ =   .002
P   =   .836   P   =   —a   P   =   .949
a. Cannot be computed because of the asymptotic standard error = 0.

Table 6, like the previous tables, shows small differences in death
sentence dispositions by race/ethnicity. Of all inmates whose death
sentences were removed, 5.3% of Latinos were executed compared with
6.8% of African American and 9.9% of Caucasians. For commutations,
2.3% of African Americans were granted commutations compared with
1.0% of Caucasians. No commutations were granted to Latinos. Also, for
death sentences that were declared unconstitutional or overturned, 68.4%
of Latinos received this disposition compared with 63.2% of African
Americans and 64.9% of Caucasians. Lastly, for convictions overturned,
26.3% of Latinos fell in this category compared with 27.8% of African
Americans and 24.1% of Caucasians. As in the previous table, neither the
X^2 test statistic nor one of the measures of association were statistically
significant; thus, there is no relationship between race/ethnicity and death
sentence disposition in the state of Florida during the time under analysis.

Again, overall, these findings provide mixed support for our predictions in Chapters II and IV. Notice that the distribution of dispositions for African Americans and Caucasians is very similar. Caucasians were most likely to be executed, while they were less likely to have their convictions overturned by the courts. African Americans were most likely to have their sentences commuted and have their convictions overturned, while they were less likely to have their sentences overturned or declared unconstitutional. Latinos were most likely to have their sentences overturned or declared unconstitutional, while they were less likely to be executed, and have their sentences commuted. The distribution of dispositions, especially for sentences overturned or declared unconstitutional and overturned convictions, in California and Florida is very similar, and provide partial support for the four-threat theory. Specifically, the findings do not support hypotheses 1, 3, 4, and 5 but partially support hypothesis 2, and provide partial support for all three alternative hypotheses.

Table 7 presents the cross-tabulation of death sentence dispositions by race/ethnicity in Texas. Of all Latino inmates removed from the sentence of death, 37.8% were executed, 17.8% had their sentences commuted, and 44.4% had their convictions overturned. Of all African American inmates removed from the sentence of death, 44.0% were executed, 11.9% had their sentences commuted, 7.1% had their sentences declared unconstitutional or overturned, and 36.9% had their convictions overturned. Of all Caucasian inmates removed from the sentence of death, 37.0% were executed, 15.7% had their sentences commuted, 7.9% had their sentences declared unconstitutional or overturned, and 39.4% had their convictions overturned.

Table 7

Cross-tabulation of Death Sentence Outcomes
by Race/Ethnicity in Texas

Disposition	Latino	African American	Caucasian	Total Percent
Executed	37.8	44.0	37.0	39.5
Commuted	17.8	11.9	15.7	14.8
Sentence unconstitutional or overturned	---	7.1	7.9	6.3
Conviction overturned	44.4	36.9	39.4	39.5
Total Percent N	100.0 45	100.0 84	100.0 127	100.0 256

X^2 = 5.372 λ = .039 τ = .005

P = .497   P = .604   P = .748

Table 7, like the previous tables, shows some differences in death sentence dispositions by race/ethnicity. Specifically, of all inmates whose death sentences were removed, 37.8% of Latinos were executed compared with 44.0% of African Americans and 37.0% of Caucasians. For commutations, 17.8% of Latinos were granted commutations compared with 11.9% of African Americans and 15.7% of Caucasians. Also, for death sentences that were declared unconstitutional or overturned, 7.1% of African Americans received this disposition compared with 7.9% of Caucasians. Latinos had no death sentences declared unconstitutional or overturned. Lastly, for convictions overturned, 44.4% of Latinos fell in this category compared with 36.9% of African American and 39.4% of Caucasians. Neither the X^2 test statistic nor the two measures of association were statistically significant; thus, there is no relationship between race/ethnicity and death sentence disposition in the state of Texas.

Overall, these results provide partial support for our predictions in Chapters II and IV. As the table indicates, the distribution, especially for sentences overturned or declared unconstitutional, for African Americans and Caucasians is very similar. Caucasians were most likely to have their sentences overturned or declared unconstitutional, while they were less likely to be executed. African Americans were most likely to be executed, while they were less likely to have their sentences commuted and have their convictions overturned. Latinos were most likely to have their sentences commuted and have their convictions overturned, while less likely to have their sentences overturned or declared unconstitutional.

Finally, note that the distribution of dispositions for California and Florida–which is similar, especially for sentences overturned or declared, sentence unconstitutional and overturned convictions–differs in each category from Texas' disposition distribution. California is less likely to execute, and Florida is less likely to commute. Texas, though, is most likely to execute, grant commutations, and overturn a conviction, but less likely to overturn a sentence or declare a sentence unconstitutional. Also, these findings show that the experiences of Latinos differ from those of African Americans and Caucasians, whose experiences are similar.

These findings provide partial support for the four-threat theory of death sentence outcomes. Thus, while the findings are not statistically significant, the distribution of dispositions in California, Florida and Texas between 1975 and 1995 for African Americans, Caucasians, and Latinos suggests that the possibility of discrimination in death sentence outcomes remains. In the next section, the results of a more advanced analytical technique, logistic regression, are presented.

LOGISTIC REGRESSION ANALYSIS

The multivariate analysis in this chapter is used to investigate the apparent race/ethnicity and state effects suggested in the cross-tabulations. In contrast to these bivariate tabulations, multivariate analysis allows for the study of simultaneous effects for many different factors, and the unique, independent contribution of each factor also can be determined. This allows us to unravel the effects of the variables concerned, such as demographic characteristics and criminal history.

As indicated in Chapter V, the main explanatory variables used in the analysis are state of disposition and offender's race/ethnicity. Additional control variables include offender's age, education, prior felonies, marital status, and years on death row.

Three of the variables, education, prior felonies, and marital status, contain missing data for a large number of cases. To prevent loss of these cases from the analysis, missing values were replaced with the mean of their corresponding variables. In addition, a dummy variable was included for each of those three variables, which indicates if each value is missing (dummy=1) or present (dummy=0). This method allows us to control for any significant differences between cases that did not have missing data and those where the mean value was used.

Four logistic models were run. All the models used the same set of nine explanatory variables described in Chapter V, plus the three dummy variables for missing data.[99] The four models were run twice, first using Caucasians and then African Americans as the reference category, respectively.[100]

In addition, to check for possible multicollinearity, correlation matrices, tolerances and variance inflation factors were computed. The results obtained do not indicate problematic relationships among the variables included in the models. For instance, tolerance statistics range from low (.729) to high (.960) and variance inflation factors range from low (1.041) to high (1.371), indicating low levels of multicollinearity among the independent variables. Given these results, we proceeded to test for interaction effects.

Logistic Regression Results

Table 8 presents the results of tests for interaction between state and race-ethnicity. In this table, X_1^2 is the X^2 obtained for the model containing the main effects of all independent variables mentioned above; X_2^2 is the X^2 obtained when the interaction effects between state and race/ethnicity are added to the model; diff is the difference between X_2^2 and X_1^2; and significance is the p-value associated with the differences between X_2^2 and X_1^2. A statistically significant difference between X_2^2 and X_1^2 indicates that the effect of race/ethnicity on the disposition of interest differs across states, necessitating estimation of separate models for each state.

Table 8

Tests for Interaction Effects: Race-Ethnicity × State

Disposition	X_1^2	X_2^2	Diff	Significance
Execution	185.5	189.5	4.0	0.403
Commutation	96.1	99.9	3.8	0.430
Sentence overturned	300.5	307.4	6.9	0.139
Conviction overturned	176.8	180.4	3.6	0.462

Contrary to our expectations, Table 8 reveals that none of the tests for interaction between state and race/ethnicity were statistically significant. These tests indicate that the effects of race-ethnicity on death sentence dispositions did not differ across states. Thus, logistic regression models can be estimated pooled across states.

Logistic Regression Using Caucasians and Texas as the Reference Groups

Table 9 presents the results of the logistic regression that estimates the probability of a person under a death sentence being executed versus remaining under a death sentence. The first column in Table 9 gives the logit coefficients that show how much the log of the odds of execution increase for a unit increase in the independent variable; the second column shows the odds ratios, antilogs of the logit coefficients, that express how many times the odds or probability of execution is multiplied for a unit change in the independent variable; the third column displays the standard error estimates associated with the logit coefficients; the fourth column gives the Wald test statistics, the statistical significance of which are indicated by the asterisks in column six; column five contains the R coefficients which, like standardized coefficients in OLS regression, allow comparison of the relative importance of the independent variables in predicting the probability of execution; and the final column contains the probability difference coefficients which express the change in the probability of execution for each unit change in the independent variable as a percentage. Since the logit, odds ratio, and probability difference coefficients merely are different ways of expressing the same effect, the discussion of the logistic regression results will focus on the probability difference coefficients, which are the most interpretable, and the R coefficients that assess the relative strength of the predictors.

Table 9

Multivariate Logistic Regression Model: Executed/Under Death Sentence

Variable	Logit (B)	Odds Ratio (Exp(B))	S.E.	Wald	R	Prob[a] Diff
Race-ethnicity:						
African Americans	-0.17	0.85	0.23	0.54	0.00	-4.17
Latinos	-0.13	0.88	0.31	0.17	0.00	-3.25
Time under death sentence	0.11	1.12	0.02	23.77	0.16	2.74**
Prior felony convictions	0.80	2.23	0.28	7.95	0.08	19.01**
Age at time of offense	0.02	1.02	0.01	2.79	0.03	0.56*
Marital status	-0.01	0.99	0.22	0.00	0.00	-0.36
Education	-0.02	0.98	0.05	0.18	0.00	-0.56
State:						
California	-4.08	0.02	0.72	32.25	-0.19	-48.35**
Florida	-1.40	0.25	0.24	34.36	-0.20	-30.16**
Dummies for missing data:						
Education	-0.16	0.85	0.38	0.17	0.00	-3.91
Marital status	-1.75	0.17	1.08	2.66	-0.03	-35.22
Prior felony conviction	0.50	1.65	0.43	1.37	0.00	12.31
Constant	-2.94	-	0.77	14.69	-	-**

N = 1,199   **p < .05
X^2 = 185.52**   *p < .01
a. Probability difference=((odds ratio/(1+odds ratio)) -.5)*100

Contrary to expectations, African Americans and Latinos were not significantly more likely to be executed than Caucasians. Holding all other independent variables constant, African Americans were 4.17% less likely to be executed than Caucasians, while Latinos were 3.25% less likely to be executed than Caucasians, but these differences were not statistically significant at the P<.05 level. Instead, the R coefficients and Wald tests indicate that state was the most important statistically significant predictor of the probability of execution. The probability difference coefficients reveal that California was 48.35% less likely than Texas to execute inmates under a sentence of death, while Florida was 30.15% less likely to carry out the death penalty. The remaining statistically significant predictors of the probability of execution include time under the death sentence, prior felony convictions, and approximate age at the time of the capital offense. Consistent with normative theories, having a prior felony conviction increased the odds of execution by almost 20 percent (19.01%), while the probability increased nearly 3 percent (2.74%) for every year spent on death row. Finally, for every year increase in the age of the offender at the time of the capital offense, the odds of being executed increased by approximately one half of one percent (.54%).

The results in Table 9 are consistent with our earlier cross-tabular results. For example, in Table 3 there were marked differences in the propensity of states to actually carry out the death sentence by executing the offender, with Texas executing nearly 40 percent of inmates removed from under the sentence of death during the 1975-1995 period. On the other hand, Table 4 showed no difference in the percentage of African Americans and Caucasians executed (18.8% in each category), while 23.1% of Latinos were executed.

In addition, the findings in Table 9 provide support for theories that suggest legal and criminal justice process variables are the primary determinants of execution, while extra-legal variables are irrelevant. Here, race/ethnicity variables failed to be significant, while years under the sentence of death, prior felony convictions, and age at time of the capital offense proved to be significant predictors of the probability of execution.

Finally, the significant X^2 statistic in Table 9 indicates that the model provides a good fit to the data. However, an examination of the classification table shows that the model correctly classifies non-executions more than executions. Only 2 of the 132 executed in the three states (i.e., 1.52%) were correctly classified as having been executed. Taken together, these findings indicate that, while the model fits the data reasonably well, there are other factors not in the model that influence the probability of being executed.

Table 10 presents the results of the logistic regression that estimates the probability of an individual under a death sentence receiving a commutation versus executed plus remaining under a death sentence. As in the previous table, contrary to expectations, African Americans and Latinos were not significantly more likely to receive a commutation than Caucasians. Holding all other independent variables constant, African Americans were 9.25% less likely to receive a commutation than Caucasians, while Latinos were 16.39% less likely to be commuted than Caucasians, but these differences were not statistically significant at the P<.05 level. Instead, the R coefficients and Wald tests indicate that the dummy variable for prior felony convictions was the most important statistically significant predictor of the probability of commutation. The remaining statistically significant predictors of the probability of commutation include time under the death sentence, education, dummy variable for missing education, and state. The probability difference coefficients reveal that California was 23.57% less likely than Texas to grant a commutation to inmates under a sentence of death, while Florida was 38.71% less likely to commute a death sentence. Also, for every year of additional education, the odds of commutation decreased by 6.23%. However, the dummy variable for education shows that the odds of commutations increased by 25.55% for inmates with missing data on education. For every year spent on death row, the odds of receiving a commutation decreased by 3.95%.

Table 10

Multivariate Logistic Regression Model: Commuted/ Executed and Under Death Sentence

Variable	Logit (B)	Odds Ratio (Exp(B))	S.E.	Wald	R	Prob Diff
Race-ethnicity:						
African Americans	-0.37	0.69	0.37	1.05	0.00	-9.25
Latinos	-0.68	0.51	0.46	2.24	-0.02	-16.39
Time under death sentence	-0.16	0.85	0.04	13.13	-0.16	-3.95**
Prior felony convictions	0.05	1.05	0.40	0.01	0.00	1.22
Age at time of offense	-0.03	0.97	0.02	1.28	0.00	-0.65
Marital status	0.15	1.16	0.36	0.17	0.00	3.68
Education	-0.25	0.78	0.10	6.11	-0.10	-6.23**
State:						
California	-1.02	0.36	0.41	6.20	-0.10	-23.57**
Florida	-2.06	0.13	0.52	15.92	-0.18	-38.71**
Dummies for missing data:						
Education	1.13	3.09	0.42	7.31	0.11	25.55**
Marital status	-1.14	0.32	0.71	2.61	-0.04	-25.80
Prior felony conviction	2.02	7.57	0.37	30.54	0.26	38.33**
Constant	1.40	-	1.25	1.24	-	-

N = 1,199   **p < .05

X^2 = 96.11**   *p < .01

The results in Table 10 are consistent with earlier cross-tabular results. For example, Table 3 showed marked differences in the propensity of states to grant commutations, with Texas commuting nearly 15 percent of inmate's death sentences during the 1975-1995 period, while California and Florida commuted a much lower percentage of death sentences, especially Florida, (10.6% and 1.5%, respectively). Table 4, however, showed no substantial difference, especially between African Americans and Caucasians having their sentences commuted.

The findings in Table 10 provide support for theories that suggest legal and criminal justice process variables are the primary determinants of commutations, while, as in the previous table, extra-legal variables are irrelevant. In this particular model, race/ethnicity variables failed to be significant, while years under the sentence of death, and education proved to be significant predictors of the probability of commutation.

The significant X^2 statistic in Table 10 indicates that the model provides a good fit to the data. An examination of the classification table, however, shows that the model correctly classifies non-commutations more than commutations. Only 3 of the 52 commutation received in the three states (i.e., 5.77%) were correctly classified as having been commuted. Taken together, these findings indicate that, while the model fits the data reasonably well, there are other factors not in the model that influence the probability of receiving a commutation.

Table 11 presents the results of the logistic regression that estimates the probability of individuals having their death sentences overturned or declared unconstitutional by the courts versus those executed plus those remaining under a death sentence. Contrary to expectations, African Americans were not significantly more likely to have their sentences overturned or declared unconstitutional than Caucasians. However, Latino inmates were significantly less likely to have their sentences overturned. Holding all other independent variables constant, Latinos were 17.36% less likely to have their death sentences overturned than Caucasians, a statistically significant difference at the .05 level. African Americans were 2.03% less likely to have their death sentences overturned than Caucasians, but as mentioned above, this difference was not statistically significant at the P<.05 level. The R coefficients and Wald tests indicate that state was the most important statistically significant predictor of the probability of having a death sentence overturned or declared unconstitutional. The probability difference coefficients reveal that California was 27.87% more likely than Texas to overturn a sentence of death, while Florida was 43.79% more likely to overturn a death sentence. The remaining statistically significant predictors of the probability of having a death sentence declared unconstitutional or overturned include time under the death sentence, prior felony convictions, marital status, education, and the dummy variable for education. Consistent with normative theories, having a prior felony conviction decreased the odds of having a death sentence declared unconstitutional or overturned by almost 13 percent (-12.43%), while the probability decreased over 2 percent (-2.26%) for every year spent on death row. Being married increased the odds of having a death sentence declared unconstitutional or overtured by nearly 15 percent (14.63%), while the probability decreased over 3 percent (-3.25%) for every additional year of education. The dummy variable for education missing, however, indicates that missing data on education increased the odds of having a death sentence declared unconstitutional or overturned by the courts by over 18 percent (18.44%).

The results in Table 11 are consistent with earlier cross-tabular results. Table 3 showed marked differences in the propensity of states to overturn a death sentence, with California and Florida overturning over 60 percent (62.4% and 64.4%, respectively) of the death sentences removed during the 1975-1995 period, while Texas overturned 6.3% of the death sentences removed. Table 4 showed only a slight difference in the percentage of African Americans and Caucasians having their sentences overturned or declared unconstitutional (44.1% and 44.3%, respectively), while 28.2% of Latinos had their death sentences declared unconstitutional or overturned by the courts.

Table 11

Multivariate Logistic Regression Model: Sentence Overturned/ Executed and Under Death Sentence

Variable	Logit (B)	Odds Ratio (Exp(B))	S.E.	Wald	R	Prob Diff
Race-ethnicity:						
African Americans	-0.08	0.92	0.16	0.26	0.00	-2.03
Latinos	-0.72	0.48	0.27	7.23	-0.06	-17.36**
Time under death sentence	-0.09	0.91	0.02	27.65	-0.13	-2.26**
Prior felony convictions	-0.51	0.60	0.16	9.55	-0.07	-12.43**
Age at time of offense	-0.01	0.99	0.01	2.22	-0.01	-0.36
Marital status	0.60	1.83	0.17	12.26	0.08	14.63**
Education	-0.13	0.88	0.04	9.28	-0.07	-3.25**
State:						
California	1.26	3.52	0.30	17.40	0.10	27.87**
Florida	2.71	15.10	0.28	97.29	0.25	43.79**
Dummies for missing data:						
Education	0.77	2.17	0.19	16.64	0.10	18.44**
Marital status	-0.17	0.84	0.34	0.25	0.00	-4.25
Prior felony conviction	-0.02	0.98	0.32	0.00	0.00	-0.38
Constant	-0.79	-	0.59	1.82	-	-

N = 1,199   **p < .05

X^2 = 300.46**   *p < .01

The findings in Table 11 provide support for theories that suggest legal and criminal justice process factors are the primary determinants of having a death sentence declared unconstitutional or overturned, while extra-legal variables are important, but not the most important. In this case, the race/ethnicity variable for African American failed to be significant, while Latino, years under the sentence of death, prior felony convictions, marital status, and education proved to be significant predictors of the probability of having a death sentence declared unconstitutional or overturned by the courts.

The significant X^2 statistic in Table 11 indicates that the model provides a good fit to the data. An examination of the classification table, though, shows that the model correctly classifies sentences not overturned more than those overturned. Only 57 of the 290 death sentences declared unconstitutional or overturned in the three states (i.e., 19.66%) were correctly classified as having been overturned. Taken together, these findings indicate that, while the model fits the data reasonably well, there are other factors not in the model that influence the probability of having a death sentence declared unconstitutional or overturned by the courts.

Table 12 presents the results of the logistic regression that estimates the probability of a conviction being overturned in death penalty cases by U.S. courts versus executed plus remaining under a death sentence. As in Tables 9 and 10, contrary to our expectations, African Americans and Latinos were not significantly more likely to have their convictions overturned than Caucasians. Holding all other independent variables constant, African Americans were 3.22% more likely to have their convictions overturned than Caucasians, while Latinos were 8.29% less likely to have their convictions overturned than Caucasians, but these differences were not statistically significant at the P<.05 level. Instead, the R coefficients and Wald tests indicate that the number of years under the sentence of death and dummy variable for prior felony convictions were the most important statistically significant predictors of the probability of the conviction being overturned. The remaining statistically significant predictors of the probability of the conviction being overturned include marital status, education, dummy variable for education missing, and the state of California. The probability difference coefficients reveal that California was 29.16% less likely than Texas to overturn a conviction of those under a sentence of death, while Florida was 1.06% more likely to overturn a conviction. Also, being married, increased the odds of having a conviction overturned by over 16 percent (16.13%). For every year of additional education, the odds of having a conviction overturned decreased by 1.93%. However, for the dummy variable for education missing, the odds increased by 10.46% for those with missing data on education. Similarly, the dummy variable for prior felony conviction showed that having missing data on a prior felony conviction increased the odds of having a conviction overturned by 31.18%. For every year spent on death row, the odds of an overturned conviction decreased by 3.48%.

The results in Table 12 are also consistent with earlier cross-tabular results. For example, Table 3 showed marked differences in the propensity of states to overturn a conviction, with Texas overturning the convictions nearly 40 percent of the death sentences removed during the 1975-1995 period, while California and Florida overturned a much lower percentage (24.7% and 25.7%, respectively) of convictions. Table 4, however, showed no substantial difference, especially between African Americans and Caucasians having their convictions overturned in death penalty cases by the courts.

As in the previous three tables, the findings in Table 12 provide support for theories that suggest legal and criminal justice process factors are the primary determinants of having a conviction overturned in death penalty cases, while, as in Tables 9 and 10, extra-legal variables are irrelevant. As noted above, in this particular model, race/ethnicity variables failed to be significant, while years under the sentence of death, marital status, and education proved to be significant predictors of the probability of having a conviction overturned in death penalty cases.

Table 12

Multivariate Logistic Regression Model: Conviction Overturned/ Executed and Under Death Sentence

Variable	Logit (B)	Odds Ratio (Exp(B))	S.E.	Wald	R	Prob Diff
Race-ethnicity:						
African Americans	0.13	1.14	0.18	0.51	0.00	3.22
Latinos	-0.33	0.72	0.25	1.76	0.00	-8.29
Time under death sentence	-0.14	0.87	0.02	40.54	-0.18	-3.48**
Prior felony convictions	-0.23	0.79	0.20	1.38	0.00	-5.74
Age at time of offense	0.01	1.01	0.01	1.29	0.00	0.28
Marital status	0.67	1.95	0.18	13.68	0.10	16.13**
Education	-0.08	0.93	0.04	3.00	-0.03	-1.93*
State:						
California	-1.33	0.26	0.26	25.54	-0.14	-29.16**
Florida	0.04	1.04	0.18	0.05	0.00	1.06
Dummies for missing data:						
Education	0.42	1.53	0.23	3.43	0.03	10.46*
Marital status	-0.34	0.71	0.38	0.80	0.00	-8.48
Prior felony conviction	1.46	4.31	0.23	40.45	0.18	31.18**
Constant	-0.52	-	0.59	0.78	-	-

N   =   1,199   **p < .05
X^2 =   176.76**   *p < .01

The significant X^2 statistic in Table 12 indicates that the model provides a good fit to the data. An examination of the classification table, though, shows that the model correctly classifies convictions not overturned more than those that were overturned. Only 38 of the 210 overturned convictions in the three states (i.e., 18.10%) were correctly classified as having been overturned. Taken together, these findings indicate that, while the model fits the data reasonably well, there are other factors not in the model that influence the probability of having a conviction overturned in death penalty cases.

Logistic Regression using African Americans and Texas as the Reference Groups

Tables 13-16 present the second set of results, which utilized African Americans and Texas as reference groups. Since the only major alterations as a result of switching the reference group are the coefficients for the race-ethnicity variables (and the constant), only the findings for African American, Latino, and Caucasian variables are discussed. As in Table 9, Table 13 presents the results of the logistic regression that estimates the probability of a person under a death sentence being executed versus remaining under a death sentence.

As in Table 9, the race-ethnicity variables are not statistically significant. Caucasians and Latinos were not significantly more likely to be executed than African Americans. Holding all other independent variables constant, Caucasians were 4.17%, as in Table 9, more likely to be executed than African Americas, while Latinos were 0.93% more likely to be executed than African Americans, but these differences were not statistically significant at the P<.05 level.

Table 13

Multivariate Logistic Regression Model:
Executed/Under Death Sentence

Variable	Logit (B)	Odds Ratio (Exp(B))	S.E.	Wald	R	Prob Diff
Race-ethnicity:						
Caucasians	0.17	1.18	0.23	0.54	0.00	4.17
Latinos	0.04	1.04	0.33	0.01	0.00	0.93
Time under death sentence	0.11	1.12	0.02	23.77	0.16	2.74**
Prior felony convictions	0.80	2.23	0.28	7.95	0.08	19.01**
Age at time of offense	0.02	1.02	0.01	2.79	0.03	0.56*
Marital status	-0.01	0.99	0.22	0.00	0.00	-0.36
Education	-0.02	0.98	0.05	0.18	0.00	-0.56
State:						
California	-4.08	0.02	0.72	32.25	-0.19	-48.35**
Florida	-1.40	0.25	0.24	34.36	-0.20	-30.16**
Dummies for missing data:						
Education	-0.16	0.85	0.38	0.17	0.00	-3.91
Marital status	-1.75	0.17	1.08	2.66	-0.03	-35.22
Prior felony conviction	0.50	1.65	0.43	1.37	0.00	12.31
Constant	-3.11	-	0.76	16.87	-	-**

N = 1,199   **$p < .05$

X^2 = 185.52**   *$p < .01$

Table 14 presents the results of the logistic regression that estimates the probability of an individual under a death sentence receiving a commutation versus being executed plus remaining under a death sentence. As in Table 10, the race-ethnicity variables are not statistically significant. Caucasians and Latinos were not significantly more likely to have their death sentence commuted than African Americans. Holding all other independent variables constant, Caucasians were 9.25%, as in Table 10, more likely to have a death sentence commuted than African Americas, while Latinos were 7.61% less likely to be granted a commutation than African Americans, but these differences were not statistically significant at the P<.05 level. Thus, the results indicate that as far as commutations, African Americans, Caucasians, and Latinos were treated similarly in California, Florida, and Texas.

Table 14

Multivariate Logistic Regression Model: Commuted/ Executed and Under Death Sentence

Variable	Logit (B)	Odds Ratio (Exp(B))	S.E.	Wald	R	Prob Diff
Race-ethnicity:						
Caucasians	0.37	1.45	0.37	1.05	0.00	9.25
Latinos	-0.31	0.74	0.49	0.40	0.00	-7.61
Time under death sentence	-0.16	0.85	0.04	13.13	-0.16	-3.95**
Prior felony convictions	0.05	1.05	0.40	0.01	0.00	1.22
Age at time of offense	-0.03	0.97	0.02	1.28	0.00	-0.65
Marital status	0.15	1.16	0.36	0.17	0.00	3.68
Education	-0.25	0.78	0.10	6.11	-0.10	-6.23**
State:						
California	-1.02	0.36	0.41	6.20	-0.10	-23.57**
Florida	-2.06	0.13	0.52	15.92	-0.18	-38.71**
Dummies for missing data:						
Education	1.13	3.09	0.42	7.31	0.11	25.55**
Marital status	-1.14	0.32	0.71	2.61	-0.04	-25.80
Prior felony conviction	2.02	7.57	0.37	30.54	0.26	38.33**
Constant	1.02	-	1.23	0.70	-	-

N = 1,199   **$p < .05$

X^2 = 96.11**   *$p < .01$

Table 15 presents the results of the logistic regression that estimates the probability of individuals having their death sentence overturned or declared unconstitutional by the courts versus those executed plus those remaining under a death sentence. As in Table 11, the race-ethnicity variable for Latinos is statistically significant, while the race variable for Caucasians is not statistically significant. Caucasians were not significantly more likely to have their death sentences declared unconstitutional or overturned than African Americans, while Latinos were significantly less likely to have their death sentences declared unconstitutional or overturned by the courts than African Americans. Holding all other independent variables constant, Caucasians were 2.03%, as in Table 9, more likely to have their death sentences declared unconstitutional or overturned by the U.S. courts than African Americas, but again, this difference was not statistically significant at the P<.05 level. Latino inmates were 15.55% less likely to have their death sentences declared unconstitutional or overturned than African Americans, a statistically significant difference at the P<.01 level. It should be underscored that the difference is more substantial between Latinos and Caucasians (-17.36%) than Latinos and African Africans (-15.55%).

Table 15

Multivariate Logistic Regression Model: Sentence Overturned/
Executed and Under Death Sentence

Variable	Logit (B)	Odds Ratio (Exp(B))	S.E.	Wald	R	Prob Diff
Race-ethnicity:						
Caucasians	0.08	1.08	0.16	0.26	0.00	2.03
Latinos	-0.64	0.53	0.28	5.36	-0.05	-15.55*
Time under death sentence	-0.09	0.91	0.02	27.65	-0.13	-2.26**
Prior felony convictions	-0.51	0.60	0.16	9.55	-0.07	-12.43**
Age at time of offense	-0.01	0.99	0.01	2.22	-0.01	-0.36
Marital status	0.60	1.83	0.17	12.26	0.08	14.63**
Education	-0.13	0.88	0.04	9.28	-0.07	-3.25**
State:						
California	1.26	3.52	0.30	17.40	0.10	27.87**
Florida	2.71	15.10	0.28	97.29	0.25	43.79**
Dummies for missing data:						
Education	0.77	2.17	0.19	16.64	0.10	18.44**
Marital status	-0.17	0.84	0.34	0.25	0.00	-4.25
Prior felony conviction	-0.02	0.98	0.32	0.00	0.00	-0.38
Constant	-0.87	-	0.57	2.31	-	-

N   =   1,199   **p < .05
X^2 =   300.46**   *p < .01

224

Table 16 presents the results of the logistic regression that estimates the probability of a conviction being overturned in death penalty cases by the courts versus executed plus remaining under a death sentence. The race-ethnicity variable for Latinos, which was not statistically significant in Table 12, is statistically significant, while the race variable for Caucasians is not statistically significant. Caucasians were not significantly more likely to have their convictions overturned than African Americans, while Latinos were significantly less likely to have their convictions overturned by the courts than African Americans. Holding all other independent variables constant, Caucasians were 3.22%, as in Table 12, less likely to have their convictions overturned than African Americas, but again, this difference was not statistically significant at the P<.05 level. Latinos were 11.39% less likely to have convictions overturned than African Americans, a statistically significant difference at the P<.01 level.

Table 16

Multivariate Logistic Regression Model: Conviction Overturned/ Executed and Under Death Sentence

Variable	Logit (B)	Odds Ratio (Exp(B))	S.E.	Wald	R	Prob Diff R
ace-ethnicity:						
Caucasians	-0.13	0.88	0.18	0.51	0.00	-3.22
Latinos	-0.46	0.63	0.26	3.17	-0.03	-11.39*
Time under death sentence	-0.14	0.87	0.02	40.54	-0.18	-3.48**
Prior felony convictions	-0.23	0.79	0.20	1.38	0.00	-5.74
Age at time of offense	0.01	1.01	0.01	1.29	0.00	0.28
Marital status	0.67	1.95	0.18	13.68	0.10	16.13**
Education	-0.08	0.93	0.04	3.00	-0.03	-1.93*
State:						
California	-1.33	0.26	0.26	25.54	-0.14	-29.16**
Florida	0.04	1.04	0.18	0.05	0.00	1.06
Dummies for missing data:						
Education	0.42	1.53	0.23	3.43	0.03	10.46*
Marital status	-0.34	0.71	0.38	0.80	0.00	-8.48
Prior felony conviction	1.46	4.31	0.23	40.45	0.18	31.18**
Constant	-0.39	-	0.57	0.47	-	-

N   =   1,199   **p < .05
X^2 =   176.76***   *p < .01

SUMMARY OF FINDINGS

While the death sentences disposition results for race (i.e., African Americans, Caucasians) are not statistically significant, some results for the ethnicity (i.e., Latino) variable are statistically significant. After controlling for time under the death sentence prior felony convictions, age at time of the offense, marital status, education, and state (and the inclusion of three dummy variables for missing data), the results for the Latino variable are statistically significant for two dispositions: (1) death sentence declared unconstitutional or overturned by the courts; and (2) death sentence conviction overturned by the courts.

In Tables 11 and 15, the results show that Latinos who were under the sentence of death in California, Florida, and Texas between 1975 and 1995 were less likely to have their death sentences declared unconstitutional by state or U.S. Supreme Court or overturned by an appellate court than both African Americans and Caucasians. Table 16 shows that Latino inmates were less likely to have their convictions overturned by an appellate court during this 20-year period in the three states than African Americans and Caucasians. While the death sentence disposition results for African Americans are contrary to the first five hypotheses discussed in Chapter IV, which suggested that African Americans would be the group most disadvantaged, the findings for Latino inmates do not provide support for hypotheses 1 and 2 (on executions and commutations), but provide partial support for hypotheses 3, 4, and 5, which suggested that Latinos would be less likely to have a death sentence declared unconstitutional or overturned, and less likely to have a conviction overturned than Caucasians. Overall, the findings provide partial support for the four-threat theory of death sentence outcomes.

The logistic regression results presented in this chapter provide support for the orthodox theories discussed in Chapter II. Several legal factors (e.g., prior felony conviction, time under the sentence of death, and age at the time of offense) were statistically significant in several models. These findings indicate that while all the models fit the data reasonably well, there are other factors not in the models that influence the probability of execution, commutation of the death sentence, having a death sentence declared unconstitutional or overturned, and having a conviction overturned. In short, the findings indicate that differential treatment in death sentence dispositions is not completely a phenomenon of the past. And, while the death sentence disposition results for African Americans are contrary to our hypotheses, the results for Latino inmates provide partial support for the four-threat theory of death sentence outcomes.

CHAPTER 8

CONCLUSION

CONTINUING DEBATE ON JUSTICE

Scholars in a variety of disciplines continue to debate the following questions with great passion: (1) is justice and punishment being equally distributed in the United States?; and (2) if justice and punishment are not being equally distributed, what are the origins of disparities? Given the global nature of these questions, though, the goal of this study was to seek an answer to two more specific questions that are at the center of the debate: (1) were there race and ethnic differences in death sentence dispositions in California, Florida, and Texas between 1975 and 1995?; and (2) if yes, what were the most influential factors affecting these outcomes?

One argument could be made that given modern judicial reform, discrimination has disappeared. Another argument, though, could be made that given the historical relationships between groups, discrimination continues to be present in the American criminal justice system. The goal of this project was not to propose an "answer" to the evils of prejudice and discrimination; rather, the objective was to seek preliminary explanations to both questions by utilizing alternative methodologies and perspectives. Ideally, this project would serve as a guide for those who are interested in developing and implementing remedies and solutions to existing social ills.

FINDINGS IN THEORETICAL PERSPECTIVE

The findings indicate that no statistical variation was found by race-ethnicity across states could be attributed to a number of factors. One possible explanation for not finding race and ethnic differences in death sentence dispositions across states could be that states do not differ significantly in terms of the number of violent crimes. Alternatively, the proxies used to represent Cubans (i.e., Latinos in Florida) and Mexicans (i.e., Latinos in California and Texas) are not sensitive enough to pick up differences in the treatment of Cubans and Mexicans. There is a possibility that Florida has a larger Mexican population than expected, and many of the Latinos sentenced to death there were Mexican rather than Cuban.

The results also show that there is no difference in death sentence dispositions between African Americans and Caucasians could also be attributed to a several factors. One explanation could be that, as discussed in Chapter IV, Caucasians on death row are those identified as "white trash." They are "lower class whites" who do not have the resources to avoid death row. These "whites," like African Americans, were socially and politically disadvantaged, with fewer resources with which to hire private attorneys and pay bail or fines than richer defendants. Perhaps they are viewed as a segment of society who are not worth the expense of an execution, but who society does not want out in the streets. Their experiences in terms of resources and how they are viewed are perhaps similar to those of African Americans. This may be a homogenous population that is viewed by the courts in a very similar fashion regardless of their race-ethnicity. In short, class differences between African American and Caucasian inmates on death row could be very similar; and thus, there is no statistical difference in death sentence dispositions between these groups in California, Florida, and Texas.

The finding that Latinos are the most disadvantaged group and not African Americans, as predicted, could be attributed to several historical and legal factors including that where there is a high concentration of people of Spanish origin, Latinos replace African Americans as the most oppressed group in the community.

Another question raised by the findings here is why did a group that has been identified as "white" suffer the worst injustice in sentences and convictions being overturned, but not in executions and commutations? One explanation could be that legal discretion, which seems to be most critical in the sentencing stage, occurs in later stages for Latino inmates. Most of the defendants were of Mexican heritage, and may be perceived as specializing in narcotics trafficking from Mexico and thus too dangerous to be out in the streets even in the future (see Zatz, 1984). For instance, if paroled, there is the possibility that Latino, especially Mexican, offenders will leave the country given the close proximity to Mexico. Also, international treaties make it difficult to bring offenders back to the United States, and countries such as Mexico do not have the death penalty. Furthermore, given the close proximity to Mexico, differences in treatment could be partly attributed to southern culture and beliefs discussed in Chapters IV and VI (see Marquart et al., 1994). The fact that some acts took place in border states (e.g., California, Texas) where the heritage of Mexican land grants and immigration pattens from Mexico (and South and Central America, among other countries) are the strongest, could have an impact on the decision to overturn a sentence and/or conviction. Lastly, and perhaps most important, the fact that these two dispositions do not receive the kind of local, state, national, and international attention, especially from the offenders' country of origin, nor the resources (e.g., economic, political) that executions and commutations attract, as discussed in Chapter VI, could have a detrimental impact in whether a death sentence is declared unconstitutional or overturned and whether a conviction is overturned by the courts, but not in execution and commutation cases.

As Rodriguez (1999) points out, another possible influential factor in the decision making-process is the law itself. For instance, in "INS law means lengthy sentences for convicted immigrants" Rodriguez claims that INS law for convicted immigrants, especially those who are illegally in the country, is a nightmare for those who have no place to go (i.e., when their country of origin refuses to take them back). Or, if defendants are illegally in the country, they either accept deportation or remain in prison for however long it takes to appeal their case. Rodriguez (1999:2) adds that according to Arthur Helton, a law professor at New York University,

INS law ". . . subjects individuals to arbitrary detention . . . ." However, as immigration attorney Jose Macedo argues, ". . . Congress has no sympathy for immigrants" (Rodriguez, 1999:3). This claim is supported by the harsh treatment of Los Marielitos by the U.S. government (including the INS), discussed in Chapter IV.

Thus, while INS law might not have a direct impact (in terms of deportation) on some convicted offenders, the law has a detrimental influence on others. As mentioned in Chapter VI, there were a number of foreign nationals (e.g., Mexicans) under the sentence of death in the United States. There is a possibility that the legal decision-making process was partially influenced by immigration law. There is also the possibility that the decision to overturn a death sentence and/or conviction of a Latino inmate was influenced by the immigration law itself and the fear of possible ramifications (e.g., recidivism).

Latinos may have more difficulty filing appeals than African Americans and Caucasians due to limitations such as fluency in English, a situation that in some cases contributed to their death sentence (Texnews, 1999). In some cases Mexican defendants signed homicide confessions written in English that they could not read (Texnews, 1999).

Race-ethnicity differential treatment in death sentence dispositions could also be attributed to the fact that, with the exception of Cubans, Latinos, as noted in Chapter IV, have historically been a scapegoat. In the case of Mexicans, differential treatment could be partly attributed to historical factors, as discussed in Chapter VI. As Zavaleta (Texnews, 1999:1) points out, the Mexicans under the sentence of death, particularly in border states (e.g., Texas) is a "continuous symbol of the differences that exist and the grudges that exist between the two nations."

LIMITATIONS AND PROPOSITIONS

As mentioned in Chapter V, there are some limitations that should not be overlooked. First, in this study, executed Latinos between 1973 and 1995 in the United States were identified. For the remaining four death sentence dispositions, proxies were used to represent Cubans in Florida, and Mexicans in California and Texas. However, as mentioned above, there is a possibility that the proposed proxies were invalid indicators of

Latino heritage. Thus, to control for this possible discrepancy, one would need to disaggregate the entire population under the sentence of death to identify their exact ethnicity.

Second, while the results indicate that all the models fit the data reasonably well, there are other factors not in the models that influence the final disposition. Of the more relevant factors, I would think, to include in the logistic regression analyses would be race-ethnicity of victim(s), number victims, number of prior felony convictions, socio-economic status of defendant and victim, country of origin of the defendant, occupation, employment status, relationship between victim and defendant, family background, whether drugs were involved, and type of counsel (i.e., private or court appointed).

Lastly, and perhaps most important, this study showed that Latinos (i.e., Cubans and Mexicans) constitute separate groups, distinct from both African Americans and Caucasians; and by extension, do not receive the same type of treatment by the criminal justice system. Latinos must be treated accordingly, not only in death sentence dispositions research, but also in all future sociological and criminological research, whenever possible.

THE GLOBAL NATURE OF CAPITAL PUNISHMENT

Discrepancy in death sentence dispositions could be largely due to the fact that when it comes to race and ethnic differences in punishment/sentencing, law is a double-edged sword: it creates one set of conflicts while it attempts to resolve others. Although some perceived *Furman* as the end of the death penalty in America, including sentencing disparities, the decision has questionable effects on death sentence dispositions, especially sentences and convictions being overturned for Latino inmates.

The historical overview of relationships between minority groups and Caucasians indicate that past reform often boils down to "symbolic justice." Elected and appointed officials support capital punishment as a symbol for their toughness on crime. Support for the death penalty has become a litmus test, especially for politicians, to determine how tough one is willing to be on crime. Opposition to this appealing and deadly sanction invariably is interpreted as symbolic of softness on violent crime.

The wide discretion that led to the *Furman* (1972) decision, which supposedly was reduced by *Gregg* (1976), has not been eliminated. These decisions attempted to remedy the capricious element in processing capital cases at the sentencing stage, but not for later stages: death sentence dispositions (i.e., sentences being overturned and convictions being overturned).

In the application of capital punishment, there is empirical evidence of disparities in death sentencing as well as in final dispositions. Unfortunately, in the 1987 *McCleskey* case, the U.S. Supreme Court refused to accept statistical evidence to support a claim that the death penalty had been applied in a racially discriminatory fashion (see Baldus et al., 1980; Gross, 1985; Hubbard, 1985; Wolfgang, 1978). Evidently, "impartial application of the laws is . . . a myth in the case of homicide" (Kappeler, Blumberg, and Potter, 1996:159:237). According to Kramer (1994:32), "despite the many supposed safeguards, what matters most is who you are, who you kill, and who your lawyer is."

Unquestionably, as Reiman (1995) points out, from whatever angle the situation is analyzed, the criminal justice system reserves its harshest sanctions for the lower classes. Based on his analysis, prisons and jails were built to punish poor criminals and not each and every criminal, as some observers like to believe. Kappeler, Blumberg, and Potter (1996:326) add that "it [capital punishment] is disproportionately applied to the poor, illiterate, African-Americans and Hispanics." William Rentschler (1994:19) states that:

> The death penalty is so widely accepted largely because it provides a measure of seeming certainty to a society greatly frustrated by its inability to solve its most vexatious problems. But it is a simplistic answer, akin to the primitive law of the jungle. It is evidence of a society unwilling and incapable of coming to grips rationally with hard challenges. Capital punishment makes a mockery of such noble legal canons as equal justice under law. . . . The death penalty is reserved exclusively for society's little people, its powerless, its rabble, its

dregs. This alone makes capital punishment wrong in a just society.

Rentschler (1994) points to the O.J. Simpson and the Menendez brothers cases as illustrations of the fact that fame, wealth, and community standing support the Russian proverb: "No one is hanged who has money in his pocket." Or, "If you've got the capital, you don't get the punishment" (Page, 1995:15). Bohm (1989:192) adds that "capital punishment offers a simplistic and believable solution to a complex phenomenon of which the public is frightened and of which it is generally uninformed." And, of course, as the saying goes: "reform consists in taking the bone away from a dog" (Newman, 1985:149).

According to Black (1989), all efforts to change discriminatory patterns have failed. He suggests that perhaps an appropriate solution would be to eliminate the death penalty as an option for punishment. This proposition, however, is very unlikely, given the current political climate. For instance, in 1986, in his last remaining days, New Mexico Governor Toney Anaya stirred major controversy by granting executive clemency to all five prisoners on New Mexico's death row (Anaya, 1993). More recently, Republican Governor George Ryan received harsh criticisms for commuting the death sentences of 167 inmates (including three Mexicans) to life in prison after concluding that the capital punishment system in Illinois was "haunted by the demon of error" (Pierre and Lydersen, 2003:1A). Like Anaya, Ryan took action (January 11, 2003) just a few days before leaving office. To the disappointment of many, Ryan announced in a televised speech: "Because our three-year study has found only more questions about the fairness of sentencing, because of the spectacular failure to reform the system, because we have seen justice delayed for countless death row inmates with potentially meritorious claims, because the Illinois death penalty system is arbitrary and capricious–and therefore immoral–I no longer shall tinker with the machinery of death."[101] Hugo Bedau, a professor at Tufts University who has studied the matter extensively for over 40 years, called Governor Ryan's decision "the most remarkable political act against the death penalty by any governor in our history" (Pierre and Lydersen, 2003:14A). As expected, the resulting debate was partly fueled by the perception that a governor who commutes a death sentence verges on committing political suicide (Vick, 1995; see also Urbina, 2002a; 2002b).

In sum, the following statement by Casey Groves (1991:111) demonstrates the continuous pattern of injustices within the U.S. criminal justice system:

> People are inclined to personalize evil, to employ it, to stuff it into another human being. That way we can find the culprit, detect the enemy. This is psychologically tempting. It allows us to 'locate' evil, to see it, spit at it, hate it, blame it, perhaps even to kill it. This is one 'logic' behind the death penalty.

REFLECTIONS ON THE GLOBAL NATURE OF LEGAL SANCTIONS AND JUSTICE

According to Currie (1985:169), "Around the world, at every level of economic development, increasing equality goes hand in hand with lower risks of homicide." Kovandzic, Vieraitis, and Yeisley (1998:569) add that "the results suggest that both inequality and poverty have significant and independent positive effects on rates of homicide in U.S. cities following the largest increase in the economic gap between rich and poor in our nation's history." Yet, policymakers continue to call for more jails and prisons, longer and harsher sentences, and the death penalty for more offenses.

The historical record indicates that the notion of equality is more of a dream than a reality. As Thrasymachus once stated, "In every case the laws are made by the ruling party in its own interest. . . . By making these laws they define as 'just' for their subjects whatever is for their own interest, and they call anyone who breaks them a 'wrongdoer' and punish him according." Consequently, injustices continue to fall on the most disadvantaged individuals. "From the beginning," Clarence Darrow has informed us, "a procession of the poor, the weak, and the unfit, have gone through our jails and prisons to their deaths. They have been the victims."[102]

Given the various issues raised in this work, how will mainstream America respond to these "unmelted minorities"? Latinos/as, the largest minority group in the U.S., have a high poverty rate and a high unemployment rate (Acuna, 1998; Colon, 1999). Latino/a youth now outnumber African American youth, and the Mexican population is fairly young (LatinoLink, 1999). According to the Bureau of Census, the median age for the total U.S. population was 35.3 years in 2000. Among the Latinos/as, median ages ranged from 24.3 years for Mexicans to 40.1 years for Cubans. What will be the fate of *los de abajo*? As we have seen, the notion of *sal si puedes* has been more of a dream than a reality. What will be the fate those Mexican workers who live *sin techo* (literally, without a roof over their heads)? Will the historical paradigm of prejudice, hate, hypocrisy, vindictiveness, discrimination, and ignorance disappear someday?

First, we need to come to the realization that the system cannot be improved by simply passing more laws. We need to be cautious of policies that promise an easy fix to difficult situations. While some policies (e.g., "English only") might be politically appealing, they often led to ramifications. As the saying goes: "every time we gain a language, we gain a world." In retrospect, every time we lose a language, we lose a word. Additionally, we need to be careful about accepting the "culture explanation" as a last resort approach to complex social problems. Second, we need to seek and approach possible remedies with honesty and positive attitudes. Third, instead of neglecting people and making it (more) difficult for them to express their views, concerns, and experiences, we should listen to their stories. For instance, individuals under the control of the criminal justice system have their own story to share. Un/documented people who work the fields have their own unique story to share. People in elite positions/institutions have their own story to share. To the person in prison, one concern could be getting legal presentation; to the person in the fields, one concern could be getting medical attention; and to the person in the elite world of, say, academia, one concern could be being respected. According to Reyes and Halcon (1988:307), "what appears to be at the heart of the objection to brown-on-brown-research is not the credibility of our research, but an unspoken objection to a potential undermining of White expertise on minority issues." Fourth, we need to make an honest effort to see the "others'" world through their own eyes–however sweet, however sour. More fundamentally, we need to truly understand the "others'" world before making judgments or generalizations about their views, behaviors, and experiences. Too often, we are too quick to make final judgement. For instance, during the 2002 Fall semester, two graduate students argued in my *Punishment* course that some segments of society live under extreme social conditions by choice. Interestingly, the two students proceed to argue that not only do some segments of society live in extreme poverty by choice, but that they are actually happy. To these potential policymakers, there is no need to alter or improve the social existence of these individuals. Fifth, we need to be cautious of the fact that injustices are often difficult to detect–in that they are not labeled. Hence, we should never forget that cruelty has a human face. Sixth, we should be excited about living in a democratic country. However, we should never forget that when people regularly experience injustices, democracy is of little utility. Lastly, it is my hope that this project inspires understanding, coraje (righteous anger), hope, justice, and peace. As Jovita Idar beautifully wrote in 1911, "Hay que trabajar juntos en virtud de los lazos de sangre que nos unen."

Appendix
THEORETICAL PROPOSITIONS

The following are some of Blalock's (1967:204-220) theoretical propositions concerning various issues, some of which are central to the current study:

1.   Resources depend primarily on the motivation and goals of the persons over whom power is being exercised, whereas mobilization is a function of the goals and expectations of the persons exercising the power. This means that classifications of resources should be in terms of the "motive base" of those over whom power is being exercised.

2.   To the extent that one possesses those resources necessary for obtaining his most important goals he becomes less subject to control by others.

3.   If resources for a given goal are unavailable or insufficient, then one can gain greater independence from, as well as control over, others by renouncing the goal.

4.   Whenever A can limit B's access to a given goal, a certain restriction is placed on B's power over A with respect to other goals. Therefore, although power is always relative to particular goals, power in any one area depends on the availability of resources for achieving other goals. This means that ordinarily power is easily generalized, and that power in one area can be used to beget power in another.

5.   In general, the greater the resources, the larger is the number of alternative means or paths that are ordinarily open for the achievement of objectives.

6.   According to the flexibility principle, the possession of resources, by permitting greater flexibility of choice, therefore reduces the probability that the objective or goal in question will dominate choice behavior. This suggests that in many situations persons who are in the best position to discriminate (e.g., persons who have secure high statuses) may be less motivated to do so because of other available alternatives.

7.   Persons who lack the resources to achieve important objectives are more likely than those who do possess these resources to develop strong personality needs to dominate or control the behavior of other individuals.

8.   To the degree that the development of competitive resources requires special adaptive mechanisms and a distinctive minority subculture, minorities that possess effective competitive resources are likely to become "perpetual minorities" if the economy is such that the minority occupies a special "niche" in the economic structure (e.g., a merchant class), if the minority's subculture is highly ethnocentric, with strong beliefs in its own superiority (e.g., the chose people), and if the minority develops a strong internal organization, with a leadership dedicated to the perpetuation of endogamy and a distinctive subculture.

9.   The wider the range of a man's alternative means, the more difficult it is to control his behavior through the use of the punishment power alone.

10.   Minority (or dominant-group) mobilization is a multiplicative function of the strength of one's goals and the perceived probability of achieving those goals.

11.   If it can be assumed that resistance remains constant, and if the (mI) component also does not change, then the amount of power actually mobilized should be a nonlinear function of one's resources. The form of this function should be that of a positive relationship with an increasing slope. If, under the above assumptions, a minority's resources continually increase linearly, we would expect to find that power will be exerted by the minority at an accelerating rate.

12.   The motivational component (mI) is more likely to decrease with progress toward the achievement of objectives defined as continuous, as contrasted with objectives defined as discrete. In the former case, there is more likely to be a "saturation" effect or a point of diminishing returns.

13.   As resources increase, the amount of power exerted will also increase until a point of diminishing returns is reached (in the case of continuous objectives). At this point, the (mI) component will decrease toward zero, and power will no longer be exerted even though the necessary resources are available. This proposition does not imply that a minority will case to press for any changes, or that it will disappear as a distinct group. It may simply mean that energies will be directed elsewhere or that goals may be modified. For example, it is even conceivable that the minority might attempt to attain elite status.

14.   Economic and status factors are most likely to be major determinants of minority discrimination if both of the following hold: a) there is a relatively small number of means to status and economic goals that are perceived to be efficient; and b) discriminatory behavior is perceived to be instrumental, either for large numbers of persons or for influential elites, in achieving status objectives by these most efficient means.

15.   Given a situation in which there is displaced aggression, minorities are likely to be selected as targets for aggression to the degree that such aggression can serve as a means to other goals. In particular, minorities are especially likely to be selected as targets if: a) aggression serves the purpose of reducing competition with the minority or of handicapping potential competitors; b) aggression serves to facilitate the exploitation of the minority by making it more tractable; c) the minority is perceived as the actual source of the frustration, or as being in an alliance with the actual source.

16.   A minority that deviates from important group norms is especially likely to become a target for displaced aggression to the degree that: a) the deviance increases the visibility of the minority; b) the deviance is in itself a frustration to members of the dominant group; c) the deviance constitutes a threat to sacred traditions; d) the deviance makes it easier to rationalize aggression, thereby reducing the amount of guilt or self-punishment; and e) the deviance leaves the minority unprotected by the larger society and therefore vulnerable to aggression.

17.   If there are two parties, one dominant and the other subordinate, the fewer the resources of the subordinate party, and the fewer its realistic alternatives, the greater is the number of alternatives available to the dominant party in controlling the behavior of the subordinate party.

18.   Provided that the weaker group cannot profitably be exploited by the stronger group,

the greater the imbalance of power and the less likely it is that effective retaliation will take place, the greater is the probability of extreme measures on the part of the more powerful group.

19.   If exploitation is not possible, extreme violence and extermination are likely to the degree that; (a) the weaker group cannot easily be removed from the area (e.g., to "reserves") due to a scarcity of even marginal land; (b) the weaker group insists on retaliatory action which is not sufficiently serious to lead to a military "stalemate" but which serves as an additional source of frustration and anxiety to members of the more powerful group; and (c) the greater the physical and/or cultural differences between the two groups, making rationalizations for extreme aggression more plausible.

20.   A positive nonlinear relationship with a decreasing slope is most likely whenever there is a labor surplus and/or a period of prolonged economic depression.

21.   To the degree that a fear of the minority's power underlies prejudice, there should be a positive nonlinear relationship with an increasing slope between minority percentage and motivation to discriminate.

22.   If the minority is not defined as a distinct sociological group, and if identifying characteristics are defined along a continuum (e.g., skin color), then the power-threat factor is not likely to be important, and nonlinearity of the form predicted in 21 is not likely.

23.   Under the "continuum" conditions of 22, the power-threat factor is likely to be minimized by: (a) the absence of legal discrimination, and the difficulty of locating individuals or groups responsible for discrimination; (b) the possibility of upward social mobility, making it easier to "co-opt" potential minority leaders into the elite group; and (c) the lack of an explicit racist ideology.

24.   Nonlinear relationships with increasing slopes, as predicted by the power-threat argument, are especially likely in the case of the following kinds of discrimination: (a) restrictions on minority suffrage; (b) symbolic segregation; and (c) threat-oriented beliefs and control mechanisms.

25.   Nonlinear relationships as predicted in 24 are likely in the case of the following specific forms of threat-oriented beliefs and control mechanisms: (a) degree of endorsement of stereotypes stressing threatening minority characteristics; (b) degree of hostility toward outsiders who are defined as potential allies of the minority; (c) degree to which deviants are defined as traitors, and there is a closing of ranks on potentially divisive issues; (d) degree of hypersensitivity to outside criticism; and (e) degree of adherence to an "official" ideology justifying the system as inevitable or morally superior to other systems.

26.   Minority mobilization should be low if either of the following two conditions hold: (a) there is a low perceived probability of success in reducing discrimination through such mobilization; or (b) there is a high probability of extreme negative sanctions being applied by the dominant group.

27.   Minority mobilization is likely to be greatest whenever the minority is intermediate in size, being neither too small to exert any influence at all nor so large as to constitute a major power threat.

Endnotes

1. At the practical level, until recently, it was difficult to identify a population of criminal defendants that included sufficient numbers of Latinos/as. At the ideological level, Hawkins (1994:105) attributes the inattention to ethnic group differences in legal sanctions to "biases and themes inherent in extant theories of social control in the United States."

2. For a discussion of the origin as well as the social, economic, and political significance of language (terms) identification, see Acuna (1988), Oboler (1995), and Rodriguez and Cordero-Gusman (1992).

3. According to Blumstein (1982:1264), "the differential involvement of blacks as arrestees, particularly for the offenses of homicide and robbery . . . accounts for 80% of the disproportionality between black and white incarceration rates." This suggests that African Americans will be incarcerated at disproportionately higher rates than Caucasians in areas where African Americans have disproportionately higher rates of arrest for serious and violent acts than Euro-Americans.

4. Based on stratification theories, racial differences in imprisonment are usually created by the following three conditions of the legal process that afford Caucasian offenders less severe sanctions than African Americans, even among individuals committing similar types of acts: (1) racial discrimination may take place overtly in legal decisions, with judges and other officials often granting Euro-American defenders more lenient dispositions than African Americans (Davis, 1969; Quinney, 1970a); (2) class biases enter into the legal processing of cases in terms of the economic resources required to obtain an effective criminal defense; and (3) racial discrimination in legal processing is created by organizational or institutional aspects of the legal system that have the consequences of ensuring that minority defendants receive harsher dispositions than Euro-Americans (Lizotte, 1978; Swigert and Farrell, 1977).

5. The argument for proportionality involves three steps: "the State's sanctions against proscribed conduct should take a punitive form; that is, visit deprivations in a manner that expresses censure or blame . . . the severity of a sanction expresses the stringency of the blame . . . and hence, sanctions should be arrayed according to the degree of blameworthiness (i.e., seriousness) of the conduct" (von Hirsch, 1993:15).

6. Seriousness has two major elements: harm and culpability (von Hirsch, 1981). Harm can be measured by the typical impact of the conduct on an individual's living-standard, and culpability by the conduct's degree of purposefulness or carelessness (von Hirsch, 1993).

7. According to von Hirsch (1993:106), "it is not necessary to seek and try to reflect precisely a social consensus." A substantial degree of consensus has been found in the ranking of criminal behavior, and there was little variation in response among different racial, occupational, and educational subgroups (von Hirsch, 1981).

8. According to von Hirch (1981), the reason for treating the first offense less seriously is that recidivism alters the degree of culpability that may be ascribed to the defendant. In assessing a first offender's culpability, it ought to be borne in mind that the offender was, at the first, the individual who committed the act, only one of a large audience to whom the law impersonally addressed its prohibitions.

9. From a predictive perspective, the more often an offender has offended in the past, the

243

more likely s/he is to repeat the offense. From a deterrence viewpoint, having continued to commit criminal acts despite previous sanctions, recidivists as a class might require a greater sentence to induce them to conform.

10.   Gross (1981) proposes a dessert-based theory of sentencing that under certain circumstances allows sentences to be made more lenient than a principle of just desserts alone would indicate, but which precludes sentences harsher than what is deserved for the act.

11.   One might be led to insert a series of intervening variables between percent of Caucasian, and non-Caucasian, education, and income.

12.   Three general types of prejudice or discrimination in which the power-threat hypothesis should predominate are the restriction of the minority's political rights, symbolic forms of segregation, and a threat-oriented ideological system.

13.   According to Liska (1992), the premier indicator of "status" within southern communities during the late 19th and early 20th centuries was one's race.

14.   Liska (1992) notes that while the exact number and position of the inflection points may depend on the specific form of threat and social control mechanisms, the general functional form of the curve (e.g., third-degree polynomial) may operate across specific forms of threat and social control.

15.   Some have noted that what is responsible for mushrooming correctional populations is the punitive initiatives maneuvered by politicians at a time when economic inequality and job insecurity have jumped to the highest levels since the Great Depression of the late 1920s and early 1930s (Barlett and Steele, 1992; Lind, 1995; Thurow, 1995). In addition, Massey and Denton (1993) and Wilson (1987) point out that a vast urban "underclass" has become increasingly segregated from "mainstream" America.

16.   Although problem populations are defined (and redefined) in terms of the threat and costs that they pose to the social relations of the production, such populations are far from "isomorphic with a revolutionary class" (Spitzer, 1975:642).

17.   Spitzer (1975) states that there are two additional, distinct, and opposite groups: (1) the social junk who, from the dominant majority point of view, is a costly but relatively harmless burden to the country; and (2) the social dynamite who has the potential to call into question established relationships, especially those of production and domination.

18.   Our data make it impossible to control for class, income, or even employment status. However, at the sentencing stage of the judicial process, class is virtually constant. There are few defendants eligible for death sentencing who are not low income, "working class," or part of a labor surplus that is either unemployed or not in the labor force (Crawford et al., 1998).

19.   "Antagonism" encompasses all levels of intergroup conflict including ideologies and beliefs (e.g., prejudice and racism), behaviors (e.g., discrimination, lynchings, riots), and institutions such as laws perpetuating segregation (Bonacich, 1972).

20.   According to Barlett and Steel (1992) and the *New York Times* (1996), the rapid infusion of other minorities (Latinos/as, Asians) in the labor force and popularly documented trends of disinvestment, downsizing, and capital mobility have likely diffused the perceived sources of economic threat.

21.   The claim that individuals who have sufficient resources to become elites generally come from a fairly rich country and have resources of their own will be explored in Chapter IV.

22. Exclusion and caste are similar reactions to a split labor market, claims Bonacich (1972). One common exclusion movement is against undocumented Mexican workers.

23. Bonacich (1972) claims that Mexican nationals in the United States have received little protection from the Mexican government. For a more sophisticated analysis of Mexican workers in the U.S., see Gutierrez's *Between Two Worlds: Mexican Immigrants in the United States* (1997). Also, she states that African states were unable to intervene on behalf of slaves brought to the United States.

24. According to Bonacich (1972), color differences in the initial price of labor only seem to be a factor due to the fact that resources have historically been roughly correlated with color.

25. Melossi (1989:317) has argued that "dangerous classes" have come to be "defined by a mix of economic and racial, ethnic and national references" so that unemployed young African Americans males have become a "privileged target group for imprisonment" in the United States. According to Blalock (1967:147), one might "expect a nonlinear positive relationship, with a decreasing slope, between the minority percentage and economically motivated discrimination based on the threat of competition." However, the rapid infusion of other minority groups (e.g., Latinos/as, Asians) into the labor force and the now popularly documented trends of disinvestment, downsizing, and capital mobility have diffused the perceived sources of economic threat (Barlett and Steele, 1992). Quinney (1977:131) states that the "criminal justice system is the modern means of controlling surplus population." Increasing anxiety and resentment in the ranks of criminal justice may fuel harsher punishment during drastic economic declines and at times of rising unemployment (Hochstetler and Shover, 1997). Box and Hale (1982:26) propose that the relationship between unemployment and imprisonment will be strongest for young males. The relationship between labor surplus and punishment has underscored the human agency and ideology of criminal justice personnel, particularly judges and prosecutors. According to Melossi (1985:183),

> in periods of economic decline, a 'discursive chain' of punitiveness and severity spreads across society, linking the attitude of 'moral panic' expressed by business leaders and 'moral entrepreneurs' to the ways in which citizens, police, courts and correctional authorities perceive behavior as deviant and/or criminal.

Lewis Coser once characterized this phenomenon as a "safety value" (Levin and McDevitt, 1993). Specifically, when times are hard, hostilities that might otherwise be directed at the community leaders of a society are instead aimed squarely at its most marginalized individuals, those located at the bottom-most rungs of the socioeconomic hierarchy.

26. Even when no ethnic differences exist, split labor markets may create ethnic antagonism (Bonacich, 1972).

27. According to Gross (1981:278),

> the remedy is not a more ample and discriminating presentation of facts by competent lawyers. What is lacking that must be supplied is a uniform set of sentencing standards that conform to principles of criminal justice; that prevent any exercise of discretion not supportable under those principles; and that, like any proper body of legislative provisions, is law formulated with sufficient clarity to allow a higher legal authority to tell, on appeal, whether or not the law has been followed.

28.   Morris (1981:264) states that dessert is a limiting principle and not a defining one. The concept of a just dessert limits the maximum and the minimum of the sentence that may be applied for any illegal act and helps to define the legal sanction relationships between criminal acts, but "does not give us more fine tuning to the appropriate sentence than that."

29.   Perhaps economic inequality and the concentration of African Americans are associated with prior criminal involvement. African American defendants may be more likely than Euro-Americans to have severe histories of criminal behavior and thus, to be sanctioned more severely for criminal behavior. States that sanction career criminals or habitual offenders more severely than other offenders would, therefore, apply longer prison sentences for African American offenders. According to Bridges and Crutchfield (1988:719), "habitual offender laws advantage neither blacks or whites." To them, the relatively low levels of disparity in the South associated with disproportionately low rates of African American imprisonment implies that explanations centered mainly on class-based prejudice and racism against African Americans are inadequate.

30.   One caveat that is worth noting is Blalock's (1967) claim that as the percentage of minorities approximates 50%, minorities assume more positions of political power. And, as a result, minorities will no longer be viewed as a threat by local authorities. In my view, this is an indication that the Caucasian dominant majority has, to a certain degree, accepted the presence of minorities, but they are still the ones who set the agenda. My observations have been that if one looks closely at the power structure of communities that have a large number of minorities, the political agenda continues to be set by Anglo elites.

31.   In this section the focus will be exclusively on minorities vis-a-vis Caucasians. In Chapter IV, though, "other problem populations" will be included in the discussion.

32.   Baldus et al.'s (1998:1717-1718) analysis of outcomes of prosecutorial and jury decision making show that

> in both the analysis of all jury penalty trials and the analysis of the jury weighting decisions, the contrast in the treatment of these two groups [Caucasians and Latinos] versus the black defendants was more substantial for the Hispanic white defendants than it was the non-Hispanic white defendants.

Baldus at el. (1998: 1718), however, also found that

> the race-of victim effect estimated in an analysis of jury death sentencing for failure to find mitigation after finding statutory aggregation suggest comparable levels of treatment of defendants whose victims are non-Hispanic whites and defendants whose victims are Hispanic whites.

33.   In a related issue, Marquart et al. (1994) found a statistically significant occupational differences between death sentences and life sentences between 1941 and 1971 for convicted murderers. In addition, Marquart et al. (1994:172) claims that data from 1974 to 1988 show that "contrary to the idea that only the poor are sentenced to die, 'professionals' were more likely to received the death sentence, once convicted, than were offenders whose occupation was categorized as 'other'"–82% compared with 76% (likelihood ratio chi-square=.4655).

34.   Bentele (1985:591), who conducted a qualitative comparison of 85 homicide cases of defendants who were sentenced to life in prison and defendants who were sentenced to death by the Georgia Supreme Court in 1981, concluded that "Georgia's death row population is no more fairly selected now than the one 'freakishly' chosen in *Furman*."

That is,

> the new law has failed to bring about fair and evenhanded imposition of sentences. The safeguards that the *Gregg* plurality relied on to avoid discriminatory and freakish application of the penalty have not performed that function (Bentele, 1985:638).

35.   Johnson (1957) also found that among killers, the highest execution rate (72%) was exhibited when a crime for economic gain was involved. The most frequent themes found in commutation statements by governors for murderers and rapists included the failure of the case to meet legal requirements, mental abnormality, lack of premeditation, evidence was deemed doubtful or otherwise inappropriate, bad reputation of the victim, the victim's contribution to the crime, the defendant's socially underprivileged status, requests for commutations by court and other officials and/or by the jurors. Also, occupational data showed that capital offenders were more heavily representative of the labor class.

36.   McCafferty (1962) also found that of the 27 rape cases, six were Caucasian and 21 were African American. Of the 52 homicide cases, 11 were Caucasian and 41 were African American. Additionally, the extent to which commutation was used was proportionately lower for murderers, 31.1%, as contrasted to those convicted of rape, 36.6%. Individuals born in Maryland appeared to have a better chance to escape execution than those born in other states, whether the offense was murder or rape.

37.   Johnson (1970) further found that in addition to the number of African Americans put to death by the state of Louisiana, there were three others put to death in Louisiana by the U.S. government. This made a total of 40 African Americans executed for rape, compared to two Caucasian men. In short, of the Caucasians convicted of rape and sentenced to death, two were executed and two were commuted. Of the African Americans convicted of rape and sentenced to death, 37 were executed and 3 were commuted. Thus, the total number of African Americans executed in Louisiana between 1900 and 1950 for rape totaled 40.

38.   Bedau (1964) found that among Caucasian killers sentenced to death, felony murder was significantly correlated with execution; among non-felony killers, previous criminal record was significantly related with execution. No statistically significant relation was found between execution and foreign born, or occupation.

39.   Bedau (1965) also found that of the 65 death sentences that were issued to native-born, 39 were executed and 18 were commuted; of the nine foreign-born whites, eight were executed and one was commuted. And, by far the largest number–43% of all executions–were given to the group labeled "laborer." Of the 25 felony cases, 18 were executed and five were commuted; and of the 66 non-felony cases, 40 were executed and 17 were commuted. Of the 46 cases involving court-appointed counsel, 33 were executed and ten were commuted; and of the 22 private counsel cases, 11 were executed and six were commuted. In a related vein, of the 40 in which the jury had mandatory sentencing power, 24 were executed and 12 were commuted; and of the 52 involving discretionary power, 34 were executed and 11 were commuted.

40.   Wolfgang, Kelly, and Nolde (1962) further found that proportionately more felony murderers than non-felony murderers actually suffered the death penalty, and more non-felony cases had their sentences commuted.

41.   Johnson (1957) observed that his data do not support the common assumption that death row population is composed of the most hardened criminals (i.e., those with previous prison sentences).

42.   Bridge and Mosure (1961:54) further found that "the most important single determinant of which murderers shall be executed in Ohio is discretionary sentencing by juries or three-judge courts." Of those commuted, 30.6% had court-appointed counsel and 44.4% had private counsel. Of those executed, 57.2% had court-appointed counsel and 50% had private counsel.

43.   Johnson (1957) found that one of the most frequent themes found in commutation statements by governors for murderers and rapists was extreme youth or elderliness of the offender.

44.   McCafferty (1962) also found that among inmates executed, laborers accounted for about six out of ten, and for those commuted, the ratio of laborers was five out of ten. When an inmate was sentenced to death for killing during a robbery or burglary, there was a greater chance that the defendant would be executed than for murders committed for other reasons.

45.   Giardini and Farrow (1952) also found that of the 399 inmates under the sentence of death in Pennsylvania, 64.2% were Caucasian, 35.6% were African American, and one was Mongolian. Of the 350 inmates under the sentence of death in Texas, regardless of the offense, 30% were Caucasian, 58.9% African American, and 10.8% included 38 Mexicans and one Indian. When considering the 269 Texas cases convicted of homicide, 32.7% were Caucasian, 54.6% were African American, and 12.3% included 33 Mexicans and one Indian. When considering the 73 Texas cases convicted of rape, 16.4% were Caucasian, 76.7% were African American, and 6.9% were Mexican. When considering the eight Texas cases convicted of robbery, 62.5% were Caucasian and 36.5% were African American. It should be emphasized that when analyzing studies, especially early studies, the numbers for African Americans and Latinos could be skewed. Since only "legal death sentences" and "legal executions" are considered, the figures for African Americans and Latinos, especially Mexicans, are underestimated. Lynchings, for example, are seldom mentioned in research. Further, the disposition of the cases whose death sentence was commuted to life imprisonment varies by state. Of the two cases discharged in Texas, one was by order of court and the other by the governor. The 41 cases conditionally released in Pennsylvania included five that were released for deportation. Only one case was released for deportation in Texas. Of the 41 Pennsylvania cases that were conditionally released, 31 were Caucasian and ten were African American. Of the 22 Texas cases, eight were Caucasian, 11 African American, and three Mexican.

46.   Marquart et al. (1994) also note that in eight cases, the death sentence was reversed or dismissed, two died while under death sentence awaiting execution, and the death sentences of 47 inmates were vacated by the Supreme Court's *Furman* decision in 1972. (It is important to keep in mind that the Furman releases were card-blanche and the others had specific release or execution dates.)

47.   Marquart et al. (1994) also remind us that there is some indication that Latino offenders may have been less likely to be convicted of capital rape.

48.   It should be underscored that variation could be due in part to the fact that the age of legality varies from state to state (e.g., in some states the legal age at which an individual may be executed is 18, by statute).

49.   It should be emphasized that death penalty discrimination is not restricted to the South (Baldus et al., 1998). This indicates that race differences in death sentence outcomes will vary by state and region. Thus, African Americans may be more likely to be executed in the South, but only if they are the dominant majority. In California, Florida, and Texas, it will

be ethnic discrimination; that is, Latinos will be the group being discriminated against.

50.   For a detailed discussion on the rationales and ramifications of using a dichotomous approach of theorizing and conducting research, see Perea (1997).

51.   Trujillo (1974) found that only 18 studies focused on Mexicans between 1900 and 1940, and Savitz (1973) found over 500 studies that focused on African Americans and the criminal justice system during the same time period (see also Holmes and Daudistel, 1984; Romero and Stelzner, 1985).

52.   According to Rex (1983), the first blacks to be introduced into the United States in 1619 were not legally defined as slaves in the complete sense in which the status of slavery eventually came to be defined.

53.   It should be noted that this kind of belief and treatment is also true with respect to women. Not only do many individuals believe that God has blond hair and blue eyes, but God is also male.

54.   According to Acuna (1998), the ultraconservative, racist Pioneer Fund underwrote much of the research for the *Bell Curve* and *Race, Evolution, and Behavior.*

55.   These acts are an indication of vigilante law, a prominent part of U.S. "legal" history. These cruelties may be viewed as "death sentences" by popular demand. However, since these were not considered legal executions, they do not count as a form of death sentencing. Thus, the fact that numerous studies have found no statistically significant relationship between the number of African Americans and Caucasians executed is due, in part, to incomplete data.

56.   Although there is no official date as to when the "war on drugs" started, it appears that the Anti-Drug Abuse Act of 1986 set the tone for the prosecution of drug related offenses. Some scholars, however, claim that the law was not designed to be applied evenly (Irwin and Austin, 1997; see also Currie, 1993; Tonry, 1995; Walker, 1994). Currie (1993:31) claims that "the drug war has been overwhelmingly targeted at the communities of the poor and near-poor, especially the minority poor." Furthermore, classifying the war on drugs as the "American Nightmare," Currie (1993:10) argues that "twenty years after the drug war began in earnest, we are far worse off than when we started." On this end, contrary to the popular belief that mandatory minimum sentences for drug offenses ensure that drug "kingpins" get locked up for a substantial amount of time, one out of every three federal prisoners incarcerated under mandatory laws for drug offenses are low-level offenders (U.S. Department of Justice, 1994).

57.   Given the current American social arrangements, it is evident that the dominant Caucasian race is not sufficiently motivated to stop intra-racial homicides.

58.   In fact, as time progressed, Reagan seemed unable to distinguish fact from fiction. Once, after watching *Rambo*, Reagan declared that he knew what to do about the terrorists.

59.   Latino/a youth now outnumbers African American youth (LatinoLink, 1999), and based on 2000 census figures, Latinos/as recently bypassed African Americans and became the nation's largest minority group for the first time in history. Together African Americans (34.7 million or 12.3%) and Latinos/as (35.3 million or 12.5%) constitute approximately 70 million residents–approximately 1/4 (or 25%) of the total U.S. population (281,421,906). (This does not include the 3.8 million Latino/a residents of Puerto Rico.) Also, based on 2000 census figures, Mexicans constitute the largest (20,640,711 or 7.3%) Latino/a group in the United States, Puerto Ricans constitute the second largest (3,406,178 or 1.2%), and Cubans constitute the third largest (1,241,685 or 0.4%) Latino/a group in the United States.

Other Latinos/as (e.g., Central and South Americans) combined constitute 10,017,244 (3.6%) of the population. More specific, the figures for these Latinos/as in 2000 were: 1.7 million of Central American descent, 1.4 million of South American origin, 765,000 of Dominican heritage, 100,000 of Spanish background, and 6.1 million of other Latino/a origins. Hence, people of Mexican heritage constitute 58% of the total Latino/a population, and an increase of 7.1 million since 1990. Togther, Mexican Americans and Puerto Ricans, who are concentrated in New York and New Jersey, account for 68% of the nation's Latinos/as and an even a greater percentage of the nation's Latino/a citizens (see also Garcia, 1994). Furthermore, according to the March 2000 Current Population Survey, more than one-quarter of the foreign-born population was from Mexico, which had the largest share of any country. However, along with Mexico, Cuba, and Puerto Rico, the Dominican Republic and El Salvador also ranked among the ten leading countries of foreign birth in the United States. Also, base on the 2000 census, about three in four Latinos/as lived in seven states with one million or more each: California, Texas, New York, Florida, Illinois, Arizona, and New Jersey.

60.   Keep in mind that based on the latest census figures, in Texas and California (two of the three states included in the analysis), Mexicans constitute the largest Latino minority group, and in Florida (the third state included in the analysis) Cubans constitute the largest Latino minority group (see also *San Diego Union-Tribune*, 1993; Spohn and Holleran, 2000). It is important to emphasize that since Puerto Ricans are concentrated in states that have few individuals under the sentence of death (in comparison to California, Florida, and Texas, the three states with the most people under the sentence of death), this Latino group will not be included in the analysis. Additionally, Puerto Ricans are concentrated in states that are less likely to execute, in comparison to California, Florida, and Texas, especially the latter two.

61.   It has been argued that the first Latinos settled in the continental United States in 1598, when Juan de Onate established a small colony at Santa Fe in what is now the state capital of New Mexico. Interestingly, based on the 2000 census figures, 42% of New Mexico's population was Latino/a in 2000, highest of any state.

62.   While little is known about the various class and skin color divisions among the Mexican population, especially those of Euro-Spanish decent and Indian decent, there is an indication that the experiences of Euro-Spanish decedents and Indian decedents have been different in Mexico and in the United States, including name labels, stereotypes, and actual discrimination. Some scholars have stated that there has been an almost caste-like distinction between the two groups historically (Acuna, 1988; Meyer and Sherman, 1995).

63.   I have always been astonished by the responses I get when I have asked the questions: "What does a Mexican look like?" "Do I look Latino?" "Do I look Mexican?"

64.   Talking about figures that are seldom mentioned, consider the following statistics. According to the U.S. Census Bureau, Latinos owned 1.2 million businesses in the United States in 1997. These firms employed almost 1.4 million people and generated $186.3 billion in revenues. Latino-owned firms made up 6% of the nation's 20.8 million non-farm business. Among the minority-owned business in 1997, Latinos/as owned 39% of the firms, more than any other minority group. Among the Latino/a groups, Mexicans owned by far the highest number of Latino/a-owned firms. In 1997, 472,000 firms were owned by Mexicans. Among the Latino-owned firms in 1997, Latinas owned 28% of the business. Without going into great detail, I will caution that these figures could be very deceiving to some people. For instance, annual salary of $33,455 (discussed below) might sound high to

some observers. But, the Latino/a "household" is generally not composed of the traditional American family of two or three children.

65.　In a way, this is a form of "death sentence" and "executions." This contributes to an actual undercount of Mexicans sentenced to death (and executions) without due process (similar to police beatings in the Barrio and the ghetto).

66.　Based on 2000 census figures, 28 million of U.S. residents age five and over speak Spanish at home. Spanish-speakers constitute a ratio of more than 1-in-10 residents. Among all those who speak Spanish, slightly more than half also reported speaking fluent English.

67.　It is worth noting that, contrary to popular belief, the major beneficiaries of affirmative action were not African Americans and certainly not Latinos, but Caucasian women.

68.　During the 1980s and 1990s, the average Latino taxpayer in Los Angeles was earning approximately $10,000 a year, and African Americans were making about $12,000.

69.　Their experience is similar to Western Jews who migrated prior to World War II.

70.　On the surface, one could be led to believe that the negative relationship between Cubans (mostly professionals) and Mexicans (mostly migrant farm workers) in Florida, especially Miami, could be due in part to class, since there has been a positive and strong relationship between the ruling elite in Mexico and Cuba. A closer look at international politics and economics indicates that class might not be the primary factor. For instance, such a relationship has been, for the most part, "between ruling elites" and not between the general population. And, there is evidence that indicates that such a relationship has not been in the name of "good will," but in the name of "political and economic interests." The two countries have served as "safety nests" for runaway elites, especially politicians. Thus, such a relationship is not a reflection of the general public in Mexico and Cuba, and certainly not in the United States.

71.　It should be noted that despite popular misconceptions, not all Cubans are wealthy, even though they are more affluent as a group than other Latinos.

72.　It is important to recognize that harsh treatment against Latinos goes beyond that of Mexicans and Cuban Marielitos. The available data suggests that other Latinos are not immune to punitive legal sanctions by the criminal justice system. For instance, Puerto Ricans represent a unique case. First, in 1952 Puerto Rico (formally an organized territory) became a commonwealth (not a state) freely associated with the United States. Today, Puerto Ricans constitute the second largest–3,406,178 or 1.2%–Latino/a group in the United States. The 2000 census revealed that New York City's total population included 2.2 million Latinos/as. Those of Puerto Rican heritage comprised the biggest (37%) share of the city's Latino/a population (followed by Mexicans and Cubans, respectively); they were particularly concentrated in Bronx County and Kings County (Brooklyn), each of which contained more people of Puerto Rican origin than any other county in the nation. The data on Puerto Ricans is limited, but the existing data suggest that Puerto Ricans are being neglected and, at time, punished without due process.

　　　Also, as with African American women and Chicanas, other Latinas are being swept under the net (see Bourgois, 1995; Diaz-Cotto, 1996). In some cases, Latinas have received extremely harsh treatment. Consider, for instance, the case of Puerto Rican women radicals arrested between 1980 and 1983. Released after two decades in federal prisons, five Puerto Rican nationalists (Alejandrina Torres, Dylcia Pagan, Alicia Rodriguez, Carmen Valentin, and Ida Luz Rodriguez) were among the longest-serving political prisoners in this country. Some observers have documented that the jailing of the Puerto Rican nationalists is one of the most savage and remorseless acts of repression in recent history. No evidence was presented linking any of the accused to specific crimes. All young women were convicted on conspiracy and sedition charges on the grounds that they did not recognize the authority of the United States government. The sentences, ranging from 35 years to 98 years, were outrageous, even by the brutal standards of the American system, and were designed to intimate and silence militant political opposition. The sentences averaged 72.8 years, and were 19 times longer than the average sentence given out the same year (for crimes such as murder and rape). Furthermore, while in prison, they were subjected to sexual and physical abuse, constant surveillance, psychological torture, denial of medical services, and lengthy stays in solitary confinement. Yet, people who are prosecuted for bombing abortion clinics have been released on parole after serving only two years in prison. Perhaps because these prisoners were not guilty of any crimes, but were imprisoned simply because they fought for liberation, the Clinton Administration openly acknowledge that these women had received long sentences, with little justification. Still, the clemency (offered by former President Clinton) imposed significant restrictions on the political freedom of the prisoners (see Fernandez, 1994; Nebbia and McLaughlin, 1999). Of course, abuse and neglect against Puerto Ricans is not new. The history of ethnic differential treatment is reflected in *Gonzalez v. People of Virgin Islands* (1940). In *Gonzalez*, the court decided that since there was ample evidence that the defendant, a native of Puerto Rico, could speak English, the court did not abuse its discretion in refusing to appoint an interpreter.

73.   Rodolfo O. de la Garza, professor of political science at Columbia University and a leading expert on Latino/a political behavior, and his coauthors vividly and eloquently document the conservative agenda of Cuban Americans (see de la Garza and DeSipio, 1992; 1996; 1999; see also Lester, 2002). According to these observers, while Latinos, especially Mexicans, have a tradition of backing Democrats, Cubans have a tradition of backing Republicans at all levels. With few exceptions, Cubans have traditionally supported Republican candidates at local, state, and national elections for the last 20-plus years. In fact, some argue that Cubans have been among the most loyal voters for recent GOP Presidential candidates. Actually, the ties between the two groups can be characterized as a symbiotic relationship. For instance, Cubans have emerged as a group whose support is actively courted by a growing number of officeholders at all levels. And, the Cuban vote like in the 1992 elections have brought continued expansion for the Cuban conservative political base and enhanced the political incorporation of Cubans at the local, state, and federal levels. Case in point: When the 1992 elections were finally settled, there were no non-Cuban Republicans in the Dade delegation to either Tallahassee or Washington, reflecting the extent to which the GOP has been an effective vehicle for Cuban office seekers from south Florida. Thus, Cubans are making significant inroads in "elite politics" and are consistently building on their growing electoral clout to project themselves into the institutional processes that not only respond to narrow (and/or specific) group interests, but more broadly shape political and economic policy agendas at all levels of government. However, in modern times, Cuban voting patterns and Cuban loyalty to the Republican Party are not only contingent on an anti-Castro foreign policy or the enormous popularity of Ronald Reagan, but are also more (and more) dependent on the GOP's ability and willingness to address the social, political, and economic needs of the Cuban community. In short, the GOP has become increasingly identified with the issues of the Cuban community, and the GOP has benefitted from the creation of a Cuban enclave in south Florida, especially Miami, the relative prosperity of

Cubans in the U.S., and the political empowerment of the Cuban community in general–reinforcing the essential conservatism of the Cuban middle class and its political-economic unique culture. On this end, the GOP will probably be the main beneficiary of the growing strength of conservative Latinos/as, particularly Cubans. Of course, de la Garza and colleagues are not alone. Other observers have noted that the Cuban vote stands in stark contrast to that of other Latinos/as across the U.S. who have consistently backed the Democratic Party. Writing for *The Miami Heard*, Silva (2000) claims that current President, Republican George W. Bush, built his victory in Florida on the loyal conservative Cuban vote. Hence, like in previous elections, Cuban voters in Miami overwhelmingly supported Bush. The Republican candidate had support among Cubans that rivals former President Ronald Reagan's vote in the 1980s. In fact, some observers estimate that over 80% of Cubans in Miami voted for Bush, and others estimate that over 90% of Cubans in south Florida voted for Bush (see Faria, 2000). Writing for the *Sierra Times*, Miguel Faria Jr. (2000) sums the current political behavior of Cubans: "there was one ethnic group that voted for Bush even more heavily than any of the other conservative groups did–the Cuban-Americans of Miami and South Florida. This minority group, which is usually lost within the larger Democratic Hispanic constituency bloc, votes consistently and overwhelmingly for Republicans in national elections, depending on the ardor with which the candidates support conservative values and oppose Castro and international communism. This has been true since at least the time of President Richard Nixon and, more decidedly, since their participation in the Republication revolution of Ronald Reagan in 1980."

74.   Marilyn McShane observes that since the Cubans were "fleeing" Castro and communism, their mere presence here in the U.S. was a reinforcement of democracy and condemnation of Russian-backed cold war oppression. The Cubans, then, were paid well to be used and exploited to undermine Castro. McShane suggests that if a communist Russian-back Mexico had existed, a similar economic situation would of unfold.

75.   Here, a critical reader should contrast the image of the Cuban exile, bona fide political refugee, with the Mexican greaser or wetback. Additionally, contrast U.S. refugee policies toward Cubans with President Bill Clinton's policy of the forcible return of Haitian refugees, who have been regarded as economic refugees and repatriated. For an excellent illustration of a world of differential treatment in modern times, take a close look at the dynamics (e.g., legal, political, economic, ideological) surrounding the situation of the Cuban boy, Elian Gonzalez. For approximately five months, young Elian had people (including President Clinton, U.S. Attorney General Janet Reno, INS authorities, local, state, and federal officials, and religious leaders) across the country glued to television and newspaper coverage. An article in the *New York Times* (2000), for example, reads: "Cuban's Family Defies Reno; Court Issues a Stay." The sub-title of the article reads: "Crowd of Exiles Cheers as U.S. Backs Down From a Deadline." Interestingly, as televised throughout the world, while juveniles are being deported to their country of origin on a regular basis, the young celebrity was returned to Cuba (April 2000), but not until the end of a five-month international political and economic dance.

76.   Recall that the existing death penalty information on Latinos is aggregate data. The current death penalty literature has classified people of Spanish heritage "Hispanic" or "Latino." Thus, the exact ethnicity for Latino death sentence outcome cases is unknown.

77.   Some observers have noted that recent protests against the criminal justice system for prejudice and discrimination against Latinos/as and African Americans have emanated

almost entirely from African American associations and political and religious leaders (Goldberg, 1999; Russell, 1998; Weber, 1999).

78.   To this day, though, Mexicans play a small role in U.S. politics. Mexicans have had few connections to political or economic power. In 1995, Latinos made up one percent of all judges, three percent of all lawyers, nine percent of all police detectives, and five percent of all correctional officers. In addition, there was only one Latino federal U.S. Attorney and there has never been a U.S. Supreme Court Justice. Nationally, there was only 651 judicially elected Latino officials (Nixon, 1996). More recently, Latinos/as constitute approximately 12.5% of the U.S. population, but comprised less than 4% in the judiciary in 2002. According to the National Association of Latino Elected and Appointed Officials, nationally Latinos only hold 5,205 elected office in 2002.

79.   As noted earlier, based on 2000 census figures, Mexicans constitute the largest Latino/a group in California (followed by Puerto Ricans and Cubans, respectively) and Texas (followed by Puerto Ricans and Cubans, respectively), and Cubans constitute largest Latino/a group in Florida (followed by Puerto Ricans and Mexicans, respectively). Additionally, according to Immigration and Naturalization Service (1999), California, Florida, and Texas are three of the top states of preference for residence for Latinos.

80.   One problem with the commonly reported data is that prisons report individuals actually imprisoned on their death rows, not those who are actually under a death sentence. Several prisons probably still had many people on their death rows, even though the courts either had reversed their death sentences or were in the process of doing so. This problem continues until today, with the population of people imprisoned on death row not being the same as those under sentence of death (Streib, 1999). Thus, at times, the data that is being analyzed contains individuals whose sentence has been overturned, but still remain on death row. When this is the case, the sample of sentences overturned is actually larger than the one reported in official documents.

81.   By limiting the analysis to 1975-1995, 152 cases were lost: 86 in California, 44 in Florida, and 22 in Texas.

82.   The word clemency is derived from two Latin words: clemens, meaning merciful and clementia, meaning mildness.

83.   Please see Radelet and Zsembik (1993) and Vandiver (1999) for two recent qualitative analyses of commutations.

84.   Had the 3rd and 4th categories been retained in their original form, problems of zero cells would have plagued the analysis. And, since no cases fall under the 5th category, it is irrelevant.

85.   For a detailed discussion of logistic regression, see Menard (1995).

86.   Recall that in certain points in time in the past Mexicans have been identified as "white."

87.   Another factor to consider as a control variable is the structural context of the death sentence and death sentence outcomes. As mentioned earlier, most of the studies discussed herein focused on offender and victim characteristics and not on the structural context of the death sentence or the death sentence outcome.

88.   Sources include: Amnesty International, 1999; *Atlanta Journal and Constitution*, 1991; Bentele, 1993; *Courier-Journal*, 1993; Crocker, 1999; Dieter, 1997; Halperin, 1997; Hayes, 1999b; *Houston Chronicle*, 1992a; 1993b; League of Latin American Citizens, 1999; *Los Angeles Times*, 1994; Marquart et al., 1994; *New York Times,* 1985; 1993b; Office of the

Attorney General of Texas, 1999; Office of the Mexican Consulate, 1999; *Phoenix Gazette*, 1993; *Sacramento Bee*, 1994; *San Diego Union-Tribune*, 1985a; 1994; *San Francisco Chronicle*, 1993b; Snell, 1996; Texas Department of Corrections,1999; Texas Department of Criminal Justice,1999; *Washington Post*, 1994.

89.   The remaining executions by race and ethnicity in California, Florida, and Texas between 1975 and 1995 were identified as follows: 68 Caucasians, 46 African Americans, one "American Indian or Alaskan Native," one "Asian or Pacific Islander," and one "white" of unknown ethnicity and race (Snell, 1996).

90.   Like Cubans and Puerto Ricans, the nation's population of Dominican heritage is heavily concentrated in a single place. The majority of Dominicans (53%) resided in New York city in 2000.

91.   "The Yaquis are a famously fierce tribe, originally from northwestern Mexico, but now living partly in the U.S." (Shorris, 1992:420). Some of these individuals (or "Los Indios," as they call themselves) live in Arizona (Hayes, 1999b).

92.   Along these lines, it is important to point out that as of November 12, 1998, there were 73 foreign nationals from 24 different countries on death row in the United States (in 16 different states). (Total inmates includes four individuals of disputed nationality, four awaiting re-sentencing, and does not include one under jurisdiction of the federal government.) Almost 50% (35) came from Mexico, followed by Cuba, Canada, and Germany, each with four. Texas housed the highest number (20), followed by California (16), Arizona (9), and Florida with five (Amnesty International, 1999; *Los Angeles Times*, 1994; *National Law Journal*, 1998; *Phoenix Gazette*, 1993; *San Diego Union-Tribune*, 1994; *San Francisco Chronicle*, 1993a; 1993b; Warren, 1999).

93.   These southernmost islands in the West Indies, once under the British rule, now comprise a country named simply Trinidad and Tobago.

94.   After a 20-month international legal and political dance between Mexico and the United States, 23-year old Jose Luis del Toro was extradited to Florida for the November 7, 1997 murder of Sheila Bellush. Since the U.S. extradition treaty with Mexico requires states to waive the death penalty before Mexico sends a homicide defendant back for prosecution, Del Toro did not face the death penalty. Instead, prosecutors seek a life sentence. Del Toro, who was arrested in Mexico in November 1997 and returned on July 12, 1999, was convicted for first degree murder and burglary and was sentenced to life in prison on July 6, 2000.

95.   Except for military people, Mexico abolished the sentence of death in 1929. And, while on the books, it has not been used in the military.

96.   See Radelet and Zsembik (1993) and Vandiver (1999) for two recent qualitative analyses of commutations.

97.   During the early part of December 2002, one of the United States' leading literary publishers, Alfred A. Knopf, released a new book by Gabriel Garcia Marquez, the Colombian-born Nobel laureate many critiques consider the world's greatest living writer. The first printing of 50,000 was gone within a few weeks and the publisher ordered a second run–all without the usual commercial jump-start from author tours, morning television and radio shows or advertising. The book is considered the fastest-selling book in the history of Latin American publishing, out-placing the author's 1967 masterpiece, *One Hundred Years of Solitude*. By any conventional standard, the book is a bestseller and another victory for both the 75-year-old author and his distinguished American publisher. However, two months after the book was released, mainstream American is still not talking about it. So, why isn't

it on any of the bestseller lists? Why no reviews? Why no buss in all the usual literary places? The answer is that there are reviews by the ream and plenty of buss–though none of it is in the usual places, because *Vivir Para Contarla* (*Living to Tell the Tale*) is in Spanish. It is believed to be the first foreign-language book Knopf or any other major American imprint has ever distributed without an accompanying English translation. The point is that it appears that most non-Spanish speakers are not going out of their way to learn Spanish (or obtain a translated version) to read the masterpiece. Such action would go against ideological movements like "English Only."

98.   Logistic regression models were computed for the five dichotomous dependent variables mentioned in Chapter V. In addition, models were created for the third (capital sentence declared unconstitutional by State or U.S. Supreme Court) and fourth (conviction affirmed, sentence overturned by appellate court) dependent variables combined. Due to the small number of cases, though, the results presented here are for the latter. While these two dispositions are not identical, they are very similar (e.g., both focus on the sentence and not the conviction).

99.   Gender was excluded from the analysis because of the small number of cases.

100.   Logistic regressions models were also computed without the dummies for variables with missing values. And, as in the analysis presented herein, two sets of logistic regressions were computed: (1) Caucasians as the reference group, and (2) African Americans as the reference group. In both cases, Texas was used as reference.

101.   Ryan's decision to empty the entire state's death row was the culmination of an exhaustive review of Illinois death row cases that began three years ago when Ryan ordered a moratorium on executions after discovering that 13 death row inmates had been wrongly convicted. Ryan then came to the realization that the entire system was simply too error prone (Urbina, 2002b). As a safety precaution, Ryan noted, "They will be confined in a cell that is 5 feet by 12 feet ... in the summer months, the temperature gets as high as 100 degrees. It is a stark and dreary existence. Life without parole has even, at times, been described by prosecutors as a fate worse than death" (Pierre and Lydersen, 2003:14A).

102.   This cruel and sad situation was summed by Chicano poet and critique Luis Rodriguez (1993:250) in *Always Running*: "What to do with those whom society cannot accommodate? Criminalize them. Outlaw their actions and creations. Declare them the enemy, then wage war. Emphasize the differences–the shade of skin, the accent in the speech or manner of clothes. Like the scapegoat of the Bible, place society's ills on them, then 'stone them' in absolution. It's convenient. It's logical. It doesn't work."

References

Acker, J. (1999). Personal communication with author via e-mail. December 20, 1999.

Acosta-Belen, E. & Santiago, C.E. (1998). Merging borders: The remapping of America. In A. Darder & R. Torres (eds.), *The Latino studies reader: Culture, economy, and society*. Massachusetts: Blackwell Publishers.

Acuna, R. (1998). *Sometimes there is no other side: Chicanos and the myth of equality*. Notre Dame: University of Notre Dame Press.

Acuna, R. (1990). California commentary: Life behind bars is no way to build character. *Los Angeles Times*, February 12:B7.

Acuna, R. (1988). *Occupied America* (third edition). New York: Harper Collins.

Agresti, A. & Finlay, B. (1997). *Statistical methods for the social sciences* (third edition). New Jersey: Prentice Hall.

Aguirre, A. (1982). The political economy context of language in social service delivery for Hispanics. In W. Horne (ed.), *Ethnicity and public policy*. Madison: University of Wisconsin Press.

Aguirre, A. (1984). Language use in bilingual Mexican American households. *Social Science Quarterly*, 65:565-572.

Aguirre, A. & Baker, D. (2000). Latinos and the United States criminal justice system: Introduction. *The Justice Professional*, 13:3-6.

Aguirre, A. & Baker, D. (1999). Slave executions in the United States: A descriptive analysis of social and historical factors. *The Social Science Journal*, 36:1-31.

Aguirre, A. & Baker, D. (1997). A descriptive profile of Mexican American executions in the Southwest. *The Social Science Journal*, 34(3):389-402.

Aguirre, A. & Baker, D. (1990). Empirical research on racial discrimination in the imposition of the death penalty. *Criminal Justice Abstracts*, 22:135-153.

Aguirre, A. & Baker, D. (1989). The execution of Mexican American prisoners in the Southwest. *Social Justice*, 16(4):150-161.

Aguirre, A. & Baker, D. (1988). A descriptive profile of the Hispanic penal population: Conceptual and reliability limitations in public use data. *The Justice Professional*, 3:189-200.

Aguirre, A., Davin, R., Baker, D. & Lee, K. (1999). Sentencing outcomes, race, and victim impact evidence in California: A pre- and post-*Payne* comparison. *The Justice Professional*, 11:297-310.

Aldrich, J.H. & Nelson, F.D. (1986). *Linear probability, logit and probit modeling*. Beverly Hills: Sage.

Allman, T.D. (1987). *Miami: City of the future*. New York: Atlantic Monthly Press.

Allredge, E. (1942). Why the south leads the nation in murder and manslaughter. *The Quarterly Review*, 2:123.

Almaguer, T. (1994). *Racial fault lines: The historical origins of white supremacy in California*. Berkeley: University of California Press.

American Civil Liberties Union (2002). ACLU condemns Milwaukee police antibiotic raids on Latino businesses. Available at: http://www.aclu-wi.org/outrage/

Ammons, L. (1994). Discretionary justice: A legal and policy analysis of a governor's use of the clemency power in the cases of incarcerated battered women. *Journal of Law and Policy*, 3:1-79.

Amnesty International (1999). Execution of foreign nationals. Available at: http://www.amnesty-usa.org/abolish/fnnat.html.

Anaya, T. (1993). Statement by Toney Anaya on capital punishment. *University of Richmond Law Review*, 27(2):177-183.

Anderson, D. C. (1995a). *Crime and the politics of hysteria*. New York: Random House.

Anderson, E. (1995b). The police and the black male. In M.L. Andersen & P.H. Collins (eds.), *Race, class, and gender: An anthology* (second edition). Belmont: Wadsworth.

Anderson, J. & Hevenor, H. (1987). *Burning down the house*. New York: W.W. Norton and Company, Inc.

Arkin, S.D. (1980). Discrimination and arbitrariness in capital punishment: An analysis of post-*Furman* murder cases in Dade County, Florida, 1973-1976. *Stanford Law Review*, 33:75-101.

Atlanta Journal and Constitution (1991). Man executed for role in prison siege. May 23: A13.

Baldus, D. & Cole, J. (1980). *Statistical proof of discrimination*. Colorado Springs: Shepard's McGraw-Hill.

Baldus, D., Pulaski, C. & Woodworth, G. (1983). Comparative review of death sentences: An empirical study of the Georgia experience. *Journal of Criminal Law and Criminology*, 74(3):661-770.

Baldus, D., Pulaski, C., Woodworth, G. & Kyle, F. (1980). Identifying comparatively excessive sentences of death: A quantitative approach. *Stanford Law Review*, 33:1-74.

Baldus, D., Woodworth, G. & Pulaski, C. (1990). *Equal justice and the death penalty*. Boston: Northeastern University Press.

Baldus, D., Woodworth, G. & Pulaski, C. (1985). Monitoring and evaluating contemporary death sentencing systems: Lessons from Georgia. *University of California, Davis Law Review*, 18(4):1375-1407.

Baldus, D., Woodworth, G. & Pulaski, C. (1980). *McCleskey* v *Zant* and *McCleskey* v *Kemp*: A methodological critique. In D. Baldus & J. Cole (1980). *Statistical proof of discrimination* (1987 cumulative supplement). Colorado Springs: Shepard's McGraw-Hill.

Baldus, D., Woodworth, G., Zucherman, D., Weiner, N.A. & Broffitt, B. (1998). Symposium: Racial discrimination and the death penalty in the post-*Furman* era: An empirical and legal overview, with recent findings from Philadelphia. *Cornell Law Review*, 83(6):1638-1755.

Baltimore Sun (1995). Man with 65 IQ executed of Texas rape, killing. January 18:A9.

Barak, G. (1994). Between the waves: Mass-mediated themes of crime and justice. *Social Justice*, 21:133-147.

Barlett, D. L. & Steele, J.B. (1992). *America: What went wrong?* Kansas City: Andrews & McMeel.

Barnett, A. (1985). Some distribution patterns for the Georgia death sentence. *University of California, Davis Law Review*, 18:1327-74.

Barrios, G. (2001). Missing in action; Mexican-Americans are virtually absent from Tom

Brokaw's books on World War II. Where are our stories? A Latino war veteran asks. *San Antonio Press-News*, May 20.

Barth, E.A.T. & Noel, D.L. (1972). Conceptual frameworks for the analysis of race relations. *Social Forces*, 50:333-468.

Becklund, L. (1985). Immigrants may slow Latino achievements, study says. *Los Angeles Times*, December 10, 1985.

Bedau, H.A. (1965). Capital punishment in Oregon, 1903-1964. *Oregon Law Review*, 45(1):1-39.

Bedau, H.A. (1964). Death sentences in New Jersey, 1907-1960. *Rutgers Law Review*, 19(1):1-55.

Bell, D. (1992). *Faces at the bottom of the well: The permanence of racism.* New York: Basic Books.

Bell, D. (1980). *Brown v. Board of Education* and the interest-convergence dilemma. *Harvard Law Review*, 518:93.

Bensing, R.C. & Schroeder, O.J. (1960). *Homicide in an urban community.* Springfield, Illinois: Charles Thomas.

Bentele, U. (1993). Race and capital punishment in the United States and South Africa. *Brooklyn Journal of Internal Law*, 19(2):235-271.

Bentele, U. (1985). The death penalty in Georgia: Still arbitrary. *Washington University Law Quarterly*, 62(4):573-646.

Black, D. (1989). *Sociological justice.* New York: Oxford University Press.

Blalock, H. (1979). *Social statistics* (second edition). New York: McGraw-Hill.

Blalock, H. M. (1967). *Toward a theory of minority group relations.* New York: John Wiley & Sons.

Blumstein, A. (1982). On the disproportionality of the United States' prison populations. *The Journal of Criminal Law and Criminology*, 73:1259-1281.

Bohm, R. (1999). Personal communication with author via e-mail. December 19, 1999.

Bohm, R. (1989). Humanism and the death penalty, with special emphasis on the post-*Furman* experience. *Justice Quarterly*, 6:173-195.

Bohm, R.M. & Haley, K.N. (1997). *Introduction to criminal justice.* New York: Glencoe.

Bok, D. & Bowen, W. (1998). *The shape of the river: Long-term consequences of considering race in college and university admissions.* Princeton: Princeton University Press.

Bonacich, E. (1979). The past, present, and future of split labor market theory. *Research in Race and Ethnic Relations*, 1:17-64.

Bonacich, E. (1976). Advanced capitalism and black/white race relations in the United States: A split labor market interpretation. *American Sociological Review*, 41(1):34-51.

Bonacich, E. (1972). A theory of ethnic antagonism: The split labor market. *American Sociological Review*, 37:547-559.

Boris, S.B. (1979). Stereotypes and dispositions for criminal homicide. *Criminology*, 17(2):139-158.

Bourgois, P. (1995). *In search of respect: Selling crack in el barrio.* Cambridge: Cambridge University Press.

Bowers, W. (1984). *Legal homicide.* Boston: Northeastern University Press.

Bowers, W. (1983). The pervasiveness of arbitrariness and discrimination under post-*Furman* capital statutes. *Journal of Criminal Law and Criminology,* 74(3):1067-1100.

Bowers, W.J. (1974). *Executions in America.* Lexington: D.C. Heath.

Bowers, W. & Pierce, G. (1980). Arbitrariness and discrimination under post-*Furman* capital statutes. *Crime and Delinquency,* 74:563-635.

Box, S. & Hale, C. (1982). Economic crisis and the rising prison population in England and Wales. *Crime and Social Justice,* 12:20-35.

Braun, D. (1991). *The rich get richer: The rise of income inequality in the United States and the world.* Chicago: Nelson-Hall Publishers.

Brearley, H.C. (1930). The Negro and homicide. *Social Forces,* 9(2):247-253.

Bridge, F.M. & Mosure, J. (1961). *Capital punishment.* Columbus: Ohio Legislative Service Commission.

Bridges, G.S. & Crutchfield, R.D. (1988). Law, social standing, and racial disparities in imprisonment. *Social Forces,* 66(3):699-724.

Briere, E. (1978). Limited English speakers and the Miranda rights. *TESOL Quarterly,* 12:235-245.

Brigham, W. (1996). Whatup in the 'hood?: The rage of African American film makers. In R.Curry & T. Allison (eds.), *States of rage: Emotional eruption, violence, and social change.* New York: New York University Press.

Brokaw, T. (1998). *The greatest generation.* New York: Random House.

Brown, D. L. & Fuguitt, G.V. (1972). Percent nonwhite and racial disparity in non-metropolitan cities in the South. *Social Science Quarterly,* 53:573-582.

Camarillo, A. (1984). Chicanos in the American city. In E. Garcia, F. Lomeli & I. Ortiz (eds.), *Chicano studies: A multidisciplinary approach.* New York: Teachers College Press.

Cardenas, J. (2002). History of WWII gets the Latino perspective. Available at: http://www.pbs.org/now/society/scrapbook2.html.

Carroll, L. & Mondrick, M.E. (1976). Racial bias in the decision to grant parole. *Law and Society Review,* 11:93-107.

Carter, R. & Smith, L. (1969). The death penalty in California: A statistical composite portrait. *Crime and Delinquency,* 15(1):63-76.

Chambliss, W. & Seidman, R. (1971). *Law, order, and power.* Mass.: Addison-Wesley.

Chicago Daily Law Bulletin (1992). Drano killer' executed in Utah. July 30:1.

Chang, W. & Araujo, M. (1975). Interpreters for the defense: Due process for the non-English-speaking defendants. *California Law Review,* 63:801-823.

Chiricos, T. (1996). Moral panic as ideology: Race, drugs, violence, and punishment in America. In M. Lynch & E.B. Patterson (eds.), *Race with prejudice: Race and justice in America.* New York: Harrow & Heston Publishers.

Chiricos, T. & Delone, M. (1992). Labor surplus and punishment: A review and assessment of theory and evidence. *Social Problems,* 39 (4):421-446.

Christianson, S. (1980a). Legal implications of racially disproportionate incarceration rates. *Criminal Law Bulletin,* January-February:59-63.

Christianson, S. (1980b). Racial discrimination and prison confinement. *Criminal Law Bulletin*, November-December:616-621.

Clair, J. (2000). Hunting down Mexicans like dogs. Available at: http://www.counterpunch.org/pipermail/counterpunch-list/2000-May/000341.html.

Clarke, A. (1999). Personal communication with author via telephone. December 14, 1999.

Cockcroft, J. (1982). Mexican migration, economic crisis, and the international labor struggle. In M. Dixon & S. Jonas (eds), *The new nomads: From immigrant labor to transnational working class*. San Francisco: Synthesis Publications.

Cole, S. & Barber, E. (2003). *Increasing faculty diversity: The occupational choices of high-achieving minority students*. Cambridge: Harvard University Press.

Colon, V. (1999). Low Hispanic jobless rate sets record. Available at: http://latinolink.com/opinion/opinion99/0418hi3e.htm.

Comment (1978). Trying non-English conversant defendants: The use of an interpreter. *Oregan Law Review*, 57:549-565.

Conciatore, J. & Rodriguez, R. (1998). Black and Hispanics: A fragile alliance. In P.S. Rothenberg (ed.), *Race, class, and gender in the United States: An integrated study* (forth edition). New York: St. Martin's Press.

Contreras, R. (2001). Hunting Mexicans again. Available at: http://www.nctimes.com/news/2001/20010127/g.html.

Cooper, A.J. (1988). *A voice from the South*. New York: Oxford University Press.

Courier-Journal (1993). Mexican executed for Texas slaying. March 26:A4.

Crawford, C., Chiricos, T. & Kleck, G. (1998). Race, racial threat, and sentencing of habitual offenders. *Criminology*, 36(3):481-512.

Crocker, P.L. (1999). Personal communication with author via e-mail. May 3, 1999.

Cronheim, A. and Schwartz, A (1976). Non-English-speaking persons in the criminal justice system: Current state of the law. *Cornell Law Review*, 61:289-311.

Culver, J.H. (1992). Capital punishment, 1977-1990: Characteristics of the 143 executed. *Sociology and Social Research*, 76(2):59-61.

Curran, D. J. and Renzetti, C. M. (1994). *Theories of crime*. Boston: Allyn & Bacon.

Currie, E. (1993). *Reckoning: Drugs, the cities, and the American future*. New York: Hill & Wang.

Darder, A. & Torres, R., eds. (1998). *The Latino studies reader: Culture, economy, and society*. Massachusetts: Blackwell Publishers.

Davis, K.C. (1969). *Discretionary justice*. Chicago: University of Chicago Press.

de la Garza, R.O. & DeSipio, L., eds. (1999). *Awash in the mainstream: Latino politics in the 1996 elections*. Boulder: Westview Press.

de la Garza, R.O. & DeSipio, L., eds. (1996). *Ethnic ironies: Latino politics in the 1992 elections*. Boulder: Westview Press.

de la Garza, R.O. & DeSipio, L., eds. (1992). *From rhetoric to reality: Latino politics in the 1988 elections*. Boulder: Westview Press.

Delgado, R., ed. (1995). *Critical race theory: The cutting edge*. Philadelphia: Temple University Press.

Diaz-Cotto, J. (1996). *Gender, ethnicity, and the state: Latina and Latino prison politics*. Albany NY: State University of New York Press.

Dieter, R. (1997). Innocence and the death penalty: The increasing danger of executing the innocent. Death penalty information center, available at: http://www.essential.org/dpic/inn.html.

Dike, S. (1982). *Capital punishment in the United States*. Hackensack: National Council on Crime and Delinquency.

Drummond, W.J. (1990). About face: Blacks and the news media. *The American Enterprise,* July/August: 23-29.

Durkheim, E. (1973). Two laws of penal evolution. (Translated by T. Anthony & A. Scull.) *Economy and Society,* 2:285-308.

Durkheim, E. (1964). *The Division of labor in society*. New York: Free Press.

Edwards, D. (1993). Innocence and the death penalty: Assessing the danger of mistaken execution. Available at: http://www.essential.org/dpic/dpic.r06.html.

Ehrmann, H. (1952). The death penalty and the administration of justice. *Annals of the American Academy of Political and Social Research*, 284:73-84.

Ekland-Olson, S. (1988). Structured discretion, racial bias, and the death penalty: The first decade after *Furman* in Texas. *Social Science Quarterly,* 69:853-873.

Elias, P. & Fried, R. (1999). A failure to execute. Available at: http://www.law/newsnetwork.com/stories/death/

Ezekiel, R.S. (1995). *The racist mind: Portraits of American neo-Nazis and Klansmen*. New York: Viking.

Faria, M. (2000). The Cuban-American vote in Florida: 'Elian's revenge.' *Sierra Times*. Available at: http://www.sierratimes.com/archive/guesteds/gedmf122800.htm.

Farrell, R. & Swigert, V. (1978). Prior offense record as a self-fulfilling prophecy. *Law and Society*, 12:437-453.

Farrell, W. (1993). *The myth of male power*. New York: Simon & Schuster.

Feagin, J.R. & Vera, H. (1995). *White racism: The basics*. New York: Routledge.

Fernandez, R. (1994). *Prisoners of colonialism: The struggle for justice in Puerto Rico*. Monroe: Common Courage Press.

Florida Civil Liberties Union (1964). *Rape: Selective electrocution based on race*. Miami, Florida: Florida Civil Liberties Union.

Foley, L. (1987). Florida after the *Furman* decision: The effect of extralegal factors on the processing of capital cases. *Behavioral Sciences & the Law*, 5(4):457-465.

Foley, L. & Powell, R. (1982). The discretion of prosecution, judges, and juries in capital cases. *Criminal Justice Review*, 7:16-22.

Foner, E. (1998). Who is an American? In P.S. Rothenberg (ed.), *Race, class, and gender in the United States: An integrated study* (forth edition). New York: St. Martin's Press.

Franklin, J.H. & Moss, A.A. (1988). *From slavery to freedom: A history of Negro Americans* (sixth edition). New York: Alfred A. Knopf.

Fredrickson, G.M. (1981). *White supremacy: A comparative study in American and South African history*. Oxford: Oxford University Press.

Frisbie, W.P. & Neidert, L. (1976). Inequality and the relative size of minority populations: A comparative analysis. *American Journal of Sociology*, 82:1007-1030.

Gans, H. (1995). *The war against the poor*. New York: Basic Books.

Garcia, M.T. (1997). La frontera: The border as symbol and reality in Mexican-American thought. In D. Gutierrez (ed.), *Between two worlds: Mexican immigrants in the United States*. Wilmington, Delaware: Jaguar Books.

Garcia, R. (1994). Crime & justice: Latinos and criminal justice. *Chicano-Latino Law Review*, 14(6):6-19.

Garcia y Griego, M. (1997). The importation of Mexican contract laborers to the United States, 1942-1964. In D. Gutierrez (ed.), *Between two worlds: Mexican immigrants in the United States*. Wilmington, Delaware: Jaguar Books.

Garfinkel, H. (1949). Research note on inter- and intra-racial homicides. *Social Forces*, 27:369-381.

Gates, H. & West, C. (1997). *The future of the race*. New York: Vintage Books.

Giardini, G.I. & Farrow, R.G. (1952). The paroling of capital offenders. *The Annals of the American Academy of Political and Social sciences*, 284:85-94.

Gibbons, D.C. (1994). *Talking about crime and criminals: Problems and issues in theory development in criminology*. Englewood Cliffs: Prentice Hall.

Gillespie, L.K. (2000). *Dancehall Ladies*. Lanham: University of America.

Goldberg, D. (1996). City found liable in attack on MOVE. *The Washington Post*, June 25:A03.

Goldberg, J. (1999). The color of suspicion. *New York Times Magazine*, 20:5-15.

Gonzalez, G.G. & Fernandez, R. (1998). Chicano history: Transcending cultural models. In A. Darder & R. Torres (eds.), *The Latino studies reader: Culture, economy, and society*. Malden Massachusetts: Blackwell Publishers.

Gordon, M. (1964). *Assimilation in American life: The role of race, religion, and national origins*. New York: Oxford University Press.

Governor Young's Report (1930). *Mexicans in California: Report of Governor C.C. Young's committee*. Sacramento, California.

Gray, D. (2001). Journalist looking for Latino voices of World War II. *Albuquerque Journal*, July 7.

Greene, J. & Winters, M. (2002). Public school graduation rates in the United States. Available at: http://www.manhattan-institute.org/html/cr_31.htm.

Griffin, J.H. (1961). *Black like me*. New York: The New American Liberty.

Grogger, J. & Trejo, S. (2002). Falling behind or moving up? The intergenerational progress of Mexican Americans. Available at: http://www.ppic.org/publications/PPIC160/ppic160.abstract.html.

Gross, H. (1981). Proportional punishment and justifiable sentences. In H. Gross & A. von Hirsch (eds.), *Sentencing*. New York/Oxford: Oxford University Press.

Gross, S. (1985). Race and death: The judicial evaluation of evidence of discrimination in capital sentencing. *University of California, Davis Law Review*, 18:1275-1325.

Gross, S. & Mauro, R. (1989). *Death and discrimination: Racial disparities in capital sentencing*. Boston: Northeastern University Press.

Gross, S. & Mauro, R. (1984). Patterns of death: An analysis of racial disparities in capital sentencing and homicide victimization. *Sanford Law Review*, 37:27-153.

Groves, C. (1991). Us and them: Reflections on the dialectics of moral hate. In B.D.

MacLean & D. Milovanovic, *New directions in critical criminology*. Vancouver: Collective Press.

Gutierrez, D., ed. (1997). *Between two worlds: Mexican immigrants in the United States*. Wilmington, Delaware: Jaguar Books.

Hagan, J. (1974). Extra-legal attributes and criminal sentencing: An assessment of a sociological viewpoint. *Law and Society Review,* 8:357-383.

Halperin, R. (1997). Death penalty news. Available at: http://venus.soci.niu.edu/~archives/ABOLISH/sep97/0226.html.

Hamm, M. (1995). *Abandoned ones: The imprisonment and uprising of the mariel boat people*. Boston: Northeastern University Press.

Harrington, M. (1971). *The other America: Poverty in the United States*. Baltimore: Penguin Books.

Hawkins, D. (1995). Ethnicity, race and crime: A review of selected studies. In D. Hawkins (ed.), *Ethnicity, race and crime: Perspectives across time and place*. Albany, New York: SUNY Press.

Hawkins, D. (1994). Ethnicity: The forgotten dimension of American social control. In G. Bridges & M. Myers (eds.), *Inequality, crime, and social control*. Boulder: Westview Press.

Hayes, K.W. (1999a). Personal communication with author via e-mail. May 27, 1999.

Hayes, K.W. (1999b). Personal communication with author via e-mail. May 7, 1999.

Healey, J. (1995). *Race, ethnicity, gender, and class*. Thousand Oaks: Fine Forge Press.

Hebert, C.G. (1997). Sentencing outcomes of black, Hispanic, and white males convicted under federal sentencing guidelines. *Criminal Justice Review,* 22(2):133-156.

Heilburn, A., Foster, A. & Golden, J. (1989). The death penalty sentence in Georgia, 1974-1987. Criminal justice or racial injustice? *Criminal Justice and Behavior,* 16(2):139-154.

Herrnstein, R. & Murray, C. (1994). *The bell curve: Intelligence and class structure in American life*. New York: Free Press.

Hess, B.B., Markson, E.W. & Stein, P.J. (1998). Racial and ethnic minorities: An overview. In P.S. Rothenberg (ed.), *Race, class, and gender in the United States: An integrated study* (forth edition). New York: St. Martin's Press.

Hindelang, M.J. (1978). Race and involvement in common law personal crimes. *American Sociological Review,* 43:993-1009.

Hobbes, T. (1950). *Leviathan*. New York: E.P. Dutton.

Hochstetler, A. & Shover, N. (1997). Street crime, labor surplus, and criminal punishment, 1980-1990. *Social Problems,* 44(3):358-368.

Holmes, M. & Daudistel, H. (1984). Ethnicity and justice in the Southwest: The sentencing of Anglo, black, and Mexican American defendants. *Social Justice Quarterly,* 65:265-277.

Hooks, b. (1995). *Killing rage: Ending racism*. New York: H. Holt & Company.

Houston Chronicle (1995). Execution cleared; no stay given retarded child-killer. January 17:A13.

Houston Chronicle (1993a). No stars for Ruben Cantu. September 4:A37.

Houston Chronicle (1993b). I am innocent, innocent. May 12:A1.

Houston Chronicle (1993c). Mexican national's execution draws angry remarks, protests. March 26:A34.

Houston Chronicle (1992a). Ex-migrant worker executed in teen's rape-murder. May 20:A18.

Houston Chronicle (1992b). Three-time loser is put to death. January 22:A13.

Hubbard, F. (1985). 'Reasonable levels of arbitrariness' in death sentencing patterns: A tragic perspective on capital punishment. *University of California, Davis Law Review*, 18:1113-1164.

Hudson, B. (1987). *Justice through punishment: A critique of the 'justice model' of corrections*. New York: St. Martin's Press.

Humphries, D. (1999). *Crack mothers: Pregnancy, drugs, and the media*. Columbus: Ohio State University.

Humphries, D. & Greenberg, D. (1981). The dialectics of crime control. In Greenberg (ed.), *Crime and capitalism*, 209-255. Palo Alto: Mayfield Press.

Immigration and Naturalization Service (1999). Available at: http://www.ins.usdoj.gov/graphics/publicaffairs/newsrels/Legal.htm

Independent, London (1995). Man with IQ of 65 is executed. January 18:13.

Inter-American Commission on Human Rights (2001). Los Marielitos, summary report. Available at: http://www.cidh.org/annualrep/2000eng/ChapterIII/Merits/USA9903.htm

Irwin, J. & Austin, J. (1997). *It's about time: America's imprisonment Binge* (second edition). Belmont: Wadsworth Publishing Company.

Jacobs, D. (1978). Inequality and the legal order: An ecological test of the conflict model. *Social Problems*, 25:515-225.

Jacoby, J. & Paternoster, R. (1982). Sentencing disparity and jury packing: Further challenges to the death penalty. *Journal of Criminal Law and Criminology*, 73(1):379-387.

Jensen, A. (1998). *G factor: The science of mental ability*. West Port: Praeger.

Johnson, E.H. (1957). Selective factors in capital punishment. *Social Forces*, 36:165-169.

Johnson, G.B. (1941). The Negro and crime. *The Annals*, 217:93-104.

Johnson, J. & Secret, P. (1990). Race and juvenile court decision making revisited. *Criminal Justice Policy Review*, 4(2):159-187.

Johnson, O.C. (1970). Is the punishment of rape equally administered to Negroes and whites in the state of Louisiana? In W.L. Patterson (ed.), *We charge genocide*. New York: International Publishers Company.

Johnson, R. (1990). *Death work: A study of the modern execution process*. Pacific Grove:Brooks/Cole Publishing Company.

Judson, C.J., Pandell, J.J., Owens, J.B., McIntosh, J.L. & Matschullat, D.L. (1969). A study of the California penalty jury in first degree murder cases. *Stanford Law Review*, 21:1297-1497.

Kalven, H. (1969). A study of the California penalty jury in first-degree murder cases. *Stanford Law Review*, 21:1297-1301.

Kappeler, V.E., Blumberg, M. & Potter, G.W. (1996). *The mythology of crime and criminal justice* (second edition). Prospect Heights, Illinois: Waveland Press.

Karns, J. & Weinberg, L. (1991). The death sentence in Pennsylvania–1978-1990: A preliminary analysis of statutory and non-statutory factors. *Dickinson Law Review*, 95:691-738.

Keil, T. & Vito, G. (1995). Race and the death penalty in Kentucky murder trials: 1976-1991. *American Journal of Criminal Justice*, 10:17-36.

Keil, T. & Vito, G. (1990). Race and the death penalty in Kentucky murder trials: An analysis of post-*Gregg* outcomes. *Justice Quarterly*, 7:189-207.

Keil, T. & Vito, G. (1989). Race, homicide severity, and application of the death penalty: A consideration of the Barnett scale. *Criminology*, 27:511-531.

Kelly, H.E. (1976). Comparison of defense strategy and race as influences in differential sentencing. *Criminology*, 14:241-249.

Kertscher, T. (2002). Police accused of racial profiling: Sauk Prairie targets Mexicans, ACLU and Hispanic leaders say. *Milwaukee Journal Sentinel*, July 11.

Keyes, D., Edwards, W. & Perske, R. (1999). Defendants with mental retardation executed in the United States since the death penalty was reinstated in 1976. Available at: http://www.essential.org/dpic/dpicmr.html.

Kinder, K. (1982). *Victim: The other side of murder*. New York: Delacorte Press.

King, J. (1981). *The biology of race*. Berkeley: University of California Press.

Kleck, G. (1981). Racial discrimination in criminal sentencing: A critical evaluation of the evidence with additional evidence on the death penalty. *American Sociological Review*, 46:783-805.

Klein, S.P. & Rolph, J.E. (1991). Relationship of offender and victim race to death penalty sentences in California. *Jurimetrics*, 32:33-48.

Klein, S.P. & colleagues (1987). Racial equity in prosecutor requests for the death penalty. Cited in D. Baldus, G. Woodworth, D. Zucherman, N. Weiner & B. Broffitt (1998), Symposium: Racial discrimination and the death penalty in the post-*Furman* era: An empirical and legal overview, with recent findings from Philadelphia. *Cornell Law Review*, 83(6):1638-1755.

Klepper, S., Nagin, D. & Tierney, L. (1983). Discrimination in the criminal justice system: A critical appraisal of the literature. In A. Blumstein, J. Cohen, S. Martin & M. Tonry (eds.), *Research on sentencing: The search for reform, Volume 2* (pp. 55-128). Washington, DC: National Academy Press.

Koeninger, R. (1969). Capital punishment in Texas, 1924-1968. *Crime and Delinquency*, 15(1):132-141.

Kramer, M. (1994). Frying them isn't the answer. *Time*, March 14:32.

Kuhn, T. (1996). *The structure of scientific revolutions* (third edition). Chicago: University of Chicago Press.

LaFree, G.D. (1985). Official reactions to Hispanic defendants in the Southwest. *Journal of Research in Crime and Delinquency*, 22:213-237.

Langan, P. (1985). Racism on trial: New evidence to explain the racial composition of prisons in the United States. *The Journal of Criminal Law and Criminology*, 76:666-683.

LatinoLink (1999). Number of young Hispanics in U.S. exceeds young blacks. Available at: http://www.latinolink.com/news/news98/0715nkid.htm.

La Voz de Aztlan (2000). Mexican migrant workers savagely attacked by racists in San Diego, California. Available at: http://aztlan.net/lynched.html.

League of Latin American Citizens (1999). Personal communication with author via telephone, Washington D.C. office. May 20, 1999.

Ledewitz, B. & Staples, S. (1993). The role of executive clemency in modern death penalty cases. *University of Richmond Law Review*, 27:227-239.

Lester, W. (2002). Democrats see Hispanic voters as a key to success in House elections. Available at:
http://www.hannibal.net/stories/041002/opi_0410020003.shtml.

Levin, J. (1999). *Seeing social structure and change in everyday life*. Thousand Oaks: Pine Forge Press.

Levin, J. & McDevitt, J. (1993). *Hate crimes: The rising tide of bigotry and bloodshed*. New York: Plenum Press.

Levin, M. (1997). *Why race matters: Race differences and what they mean*. Westport: Praeger.

Levine, A. (2003). American education: Still separate, still unequal. *Los Angeles Times*, February 2. Available at: http://www.latimes.com/news/opinion/comentary/la-op-levine2feb02,0,1751431.story?coll=la%2Dnews%2Dcomment%2 Dopinions

Lewis, P. & Peoples, K. (1978). Life on death row: A post-*Furman* profile of Florida's condemned. In P.W. Lewis & K.D. Peoples (eds.), *The Supreme Court and the criminal process–cases and comments* (pp.969-951). Philadelphia: Saunders.

Liebman, E. (1985). Appellate review of death sentences: A critique of proportionality review. *University of California, Davis Law Review*, 18:1433-1480.

Lind, M. (1995). To have and to have not: Notes on the progress of the American class war. *Harpers Magazine*, June:35-47.

Liska, A.E. (1992). *Social threat and social control*. Albany: SUNY Press.

Lizotte, A. (1978). Extra-legal factors in Chicago's criminal courts: Testing the conflict model of criminal justice. *Social Problems*, 25:564-580.

Los Angeles Times (1994). Unexpected friend on death row. January 2:A1.

Los Angeles Times (1985a). Texan executed after assailing society as 'a bunch of cold-blooded murderers.' July 10:11.

Los Angeles Times (1985b). Texas executes man who killed policeman. July 9:A19.

Los Angeles Times (1985c). May 7.

Lynch, M.J. & Groves, W.B. (1986). *A primer in radical criminology*. New York: Harrow & Heston.

Mangum, C.S. (1940). *The legal status of the Negro*. Chapel Hill: University of North Carolina Press.

Mann, C.R. (1993). *Unequal justice: A question of color*. Bloomington: Indiana University Press.

Marin, M. (1991). *Social protest in an urban barrio: A study of the Chicano movement, 1966-1974*. Lanham: University Press of America.

Marquart, J., Ekland-Olson, S. & Sorensen, J. (1994). *The rope, the chair, and the needle: Capital punishment in Texas, 1923-1990.* Austin: University of Texas Press.

Marx, K. (1967). *Capital* (Volume 1). New York: International.

Massey, D.S. & Denton, N.A. (1993). *American apartheid: Segregation and the making of the underclass.* Cambridge: Harvard University Press.

Massey, D. (1990). American apartheid: Segregation and the making of the underclass. *American Journal of Sociology,* 96:329-359.

Mauer, M. (1990). *Young black men and the criminal justice system: A growing national problem.* Washington, D.C.: The Sentencing Project.

Maxon, T. (1985). Hart angers Hispanics with letter on aliens. *Dallas Morning News,* February 5, 1985.

McCafferty, J.A. (1962). Prisoners sentenced to death in Maryland, 1936-1961. In *Report of the Legislative Council Committee on Capital Punishment,* October 3, 1962. Baltimore, Maryland.

McCleskey v. Kemp, 481 U.S. 279 (1987).

McGehee, E.G. & Hildebrand, W.H., eds (1964). *The death penalty: A literary and historical approach.* Boston: D.C. Heath.

Melossi, D. (1989). An introduction: Fifty years later, punishment and social structure in comparative analysis. *Contemporary Crises,* 13:311-326.

Melossi, D. (1985). Punishment and social action: Changing vocabularies of punitive motive within a political business cycle. *Current Perspectives in Social Theory,* 6:169-197.

Menard, S. (1995). *Applied logistic regression analysis.* Thousand Oaks: Sage Publications.

Mendoza Report (1978). Access of non or limited English speaking persons of Hispanic origin to the New York City Department of Social Services. Washington, D.C.: Office of Civil Rights.

Meyer, M. & Sherman, W. (1995). *The course of Mexican history* (fifth edition). New York: Oxford University Press.

Migration News (1994). English-only rule upheld by Supreme Court. Available at: http://migration.ucdavis.edu/mn/archive_mn/oct.1994-10mn.html.

Moore, J. & Pinderhughes, R. (1995). The Latino population: The importance of economic restructuring. In M. Andersen & P. Collins (eds.), *Race, class, and gender: An anthology* (second edition). Belmont: Wadsworth Publishing Company.

Moore, J. & Pinderhughes, R., eds. (1993). *In the barrios: Latinos and the underclass debate.* New York: Russell Sage Foundation.

Morin, R. (1966). *Among the valiant.* Alhambra: Borden.

Morris, N. (1981). Punishment, dessert and rehabilitation. In H. Gross & A. von Hirsch (eds.), *Sentencing.* New York/Oxford: Oxford University Press.

Mowry, G. & Brownell, B.A. (1981). *The urban nation 1920-1980.* New York: Hill & Wang.

Myrdal, G. (1944). *An American dilemma.* New York: Harper & Row.

NAACP Legal Defense Fund and Death Penalty Information Center (1999). Available at: http://www.essential.org/dpic/exec76-90 [and 91-95].gif.

Naples Daily News (1999). English-only resolution enrages Hispanics. April 18. Available at: http://www.naplesnews.com/today/florida/a153171b.htm.

National Law Journal (1998). Are 65 illegally on death row in U.S.? April 27:A16.

Nebbia, G. & McLaughlin, M. (1999). Puerto Rican nationalists to be released after two decades in prison. Available at:
http://www.wsws.org/articles/1999/sep1999/faln-s09.shtm.

Nelson, J. & Maddox, G.K. (996). A rhetorical study of the MOVE diatribe in contemporary America. *The Pennsylvania Speech Communication Annual*, 1-3.

Newman, G. (1985). *The punishment response*. Albany: Harrow & Heston.

New York Times (2000). Cuban's family defies Reno; Court issues a stay. April: 14:A1,24.

New York Times (1996). *Downsizing America*. New York: Random House.

New York Times (1995a). Ghoulish murderer is executed in Texas. December 12:A24.

New York Times (1995b). Texan who killed ex-wife and her niece is executed. January 18:A16.

New York Times (1993a). Texas executes a Mexican killer, raising a furor across the border. March 26:A15.

New York Times (1993b). Mexico fights to stop U.S. execution. January 26:A19.

New York Times (1987). Texan who killed 6 in 1983 is executed by lethal injection. March 5:A9.

New York Times (1986). Texan executed by injection for killing of a drug agent. June 9:A19.

New York Times (1985). Killer put to death in Texas. July 10:A11.

Nixon, R. (1996). Crime & punishment: How the criminal justice system fails Hispanics. *Hispanic*, September:26-32.

Oboler, S. (1995). *Ethnic labels, Latino lives: Identity and the politics of (re)presentation in the United States*. Minneapolis: University of Minnesota Press.

Office of the Attorney General of Texas (1999). Defendants' information was provided to the author by Douglas Danzeiser, Assistant Attorney General. May 2, 1999.

Office of the Mexican Consulate (1999). Personal communication with author via telephone, Houston, Texas office. May 17, 1999.

Page, C. (1995). The murky line between who gets life or death. *Chicago Tribune*, August 2:section 1:15.

Palacios, V. (1996). Faith in fantasy: The Supreme Court's reliance on commutation to ensure justice in death penalty cases. *Vanderbilt University*, 49:311-372.

Park, R.E. (1950). *Race and culture*. Glencoe: The Free Press.

Partington, D. (1965). The incidence of the death penalty for rape in Virginia. *Washington and Lee Law Review*, 22:43-75.

Partington, K. (1999). Lee elections supervisor decides Bonita ballots to be printed in English only. *Naples Daily News*, December 2. Available at:
http://www.naplesnews.com/today/bonita/d396246a.htm.

Paternoster, R. (1984). Prosecutorial discretion in requesting the death penalty: A case of victim-based racial discrimination. *Law & Society Review*, 18:437-78.

Paternoster, R. (1983). Race of victim and location of crime: The decision to seek the death penalty in South Carolina. *Journal of Criminal Law and Criminology*, 74(3):754-785.

Paternoster, R. & Kazyaka, A. (1988). Racial considerations in capital punishment. In K.C. Haas & J.A. Inciardi (eds.), *Challenging capital punishment: Legal and social sciences approaches* (pp. 113-148). Newbury Park: Sage.

Perales, A. (1974). *Are we good neighbors?* New York: Arno Press.

Perea, J. (1997). The black/white binary paradigm of race: The 'normal science' of

American racial thought. *California Law Review*, 85:1213-1258.

Perez, W. (1969). Constitutional law–translators: Mandatory for due process. *Connecticut Law Review*, 2:163-170.

Petersilia, J. (1983). *Racial disparities in the criminal justice system*. Rand Corporation.

Peterson, R. & Hagan, J. (1984). Changing conceptions of race: Towards an account of anomalous findings of sentencing research. *American Sociological Review*, 49:56-70.

Phelps, N. (2002). Action delayed on English-only plan. *Green Bay Press-Gazette*, June 20. Available at:
http://www.greenbaypressgazette.com/news/archieve/local_4638471.shtm.

Phoenix Gazette (1995). Inmate with low IQ is executed in Texas. January 17:A9.

Phoenix Gazette (1993). Execution of Mexican in Texas spurs protests. March 26:B5.

Pierre, R. & Lydersen, K. (2003). Illinois' Ryan empties state's death row. *Milwaukee Journal Sentinel*, January 12:1A, 14A.

Pitt, L. (1970). *The decline of the Californios: A social history of the Spanish-speaking Californians, 1846-1890*. Berkeley: University of California Press.

Pollock-Byrne, J.M. (1989). *Ethics in crime and justice: Dilemmas and decisions*. Pacific Grove: Brooks/Cole Publishing Company.

Pridemore, W.A. (2000). An empirical examination of commutations and executions in post-*Furman* capital cases. *Justice Quarterly*, 17(1):159-183.

Pruitt, C.R. & Wilson, J.Q. (1983). A longitudinal study of the effect of race on sentencing. *Law and Society Review*, 17:613-635.

Pumpelly, R. (1870). *Across America and Asia* (fourth edition). New York: Leypodt & Holt.

Quinney, R. (1977). *Class state and crime*. New York: David McKay Company.

Quinney, R. (1974). *Critique of the legal order*. Boston: Little, Brown.

Quinney, R. (1970a). *The social reality of crime*. Boston: Little, Brown

Quinney, R. (1970b). *The problem of crime*. New York: Dodd, Mead.

Radelet, M. (1981). Racial characteristics and the imposition of the death penalty. *American Sociological Review*, 46:918-27.

Radelet, M., Lofquist, W.S. & Bedau, H.A. (1996). Death penalty symposium: Prisoners released from death row since 1970 because of doubts about their guilt. *Thomas and Cooley Law Review*, 13:907-966.

Radelet, M. & Pierce, G. (1991). Choosing those who will die: Race and the death penalty in Florida. *Florida Law Review*, 43(1):1-34.

Radelet, M. & Pierce, G. (1985). Race and prosecutorial discretion in homicide cases. *Law & Society Review*, 19:587-621.

Radelet, M. & Vandiver, M. (1983). The Florida Supreme Court and death penalty appeals. *Journal of Criminal Law and Criminology*, 73:913-926.

Radalet, M.L. & Zsembik, B.A. (1993). Executive clemency in post-*Furman* capital cases. *University of Richmond Law Review*, 27:289-314.

Randall, K. (1999). Two Cuban detainees surrender in Louisiana jail standoff. Available at: http://www.wsws.org/articles/1999/dec1999/cuba-d18.shtml.

Reid, D. (1973). *Eyewitness: I saw 189 men die in the electric chair*. Houston: Cordovan Press.

Reggio, M.H. (1997). History of the death penalty. In L.E. Randa (ed.), *Society's final solution: A history and discussion of the death penalty*. Lanham: University Press of America.

Reiman, J. (1995). *The rich get richer and the poor get prison: Ideology, class, and criminal justice* (fourth edition). Boston: Allyn & Bacon.

Reisler, M. (1997). Always the laborer, never the citizen: Anglo perceptions of the Mexican immigrant during the 1920s. In G. Gutierrez (ed.), *Between two worlds: Mexican immigrants in the United States*. Wilmington, Delaware: Jaguar Books.

Rentschler, W. (1994). The death penalty–a pivotal issue. *Chicago Tribune*, November 29:19.

Rex, J. (1983). *Race relations in sociological theory* (second edition). Boston: Routledge & Kegan Paul.

Reyes, M. & Halcon, J. (1988). Racism in academia: The old wolf revisited. *Harvard Educational Review*, 58:299-314.

Riedel, M. (1976). Discrimination in the imposition of the death penalty: A comparison of the characteristics of offenders sentenced pre-*Furman* and post-*Furman*. *Temple Law Quarterly*, 49:261-287.

Rodriguez, C. (1999). INS law means lengthy sentences for convicted immigrants. Available at: http://www.latino.com/news/ news99/0414nlaw.htm.

Rodriguez, C. & Cordero-Gusman, H. (1992). Placing race in context. *Ethnic and Racial Studies*, 15:523-542.

Rodriguez, L. (1993). *Always running: La vida loca, gang days in L.A.* New York: Simon and Schuster.

Rohrlich, T. & Tulsky, F.N. (1996). Not all L.A. murder cases are equal. *Los Angeles Times*, A1: December 3, 1996.

Romero, L. & Stelzner, L. (1985). Hispanics and the criminal justice system. In P. Cafferty & W. McCready (eds.), *Hispanics in the United States*. New Brunswick: Transaction Books.

Rowan, C. (1993). *Dream makers, dream breakers, the world of Justice Thurgood Marshall*. Boston: Little, Brown & Company.

Ruiz, V.L. (1997). Star struck: Acculturation, adolescence, and the Mexican-American woman, 1920-1950. In D. Gutierrez (ed.), *Between two worlds: Mexican immigrants in the United States*. Wilmington, Delaware: Jaguar Books.

Rusche, G. & Kirchheimer, O. (1968). *Punishment and social structure*. Russell & Russell.

Rushton, J. P. (1999). *Race, evolution and behavior*. New Brunswick: Transaction Publishers.

Russell, K. (1998). *The color of crime: Racial hoaxes, white fear, black protectionism, police harassment, and other macro aggressions*. New York: New York University Press.

Sacramento Bee (1994). Foes of death penalty have a friend: Mexico. June 26:A1.

Safford, J. (1977). No comprendo: The non-English-speaking defendant and the criminal process. *The Journal of Criminal Law and Criminology*, 68:15-30.

Saldana, A. (2002). Antonia Saldana column: English-only measure and act of apartheid. *Green Bay Press-Gazette*, June 15. Available at: http://www.greenbaypressgazette.com/news/archive/opinion_4503499.shtml.

Sampson, R.J. & Laub, J.H. (1993). Structural variations in juvenile court processing: Inequality, the underclass and social control. *Law and Society Review*, 27:285-311.

Sanchez, R. (1998). Mapping the Spanish language along a multiethnic and multilingual border. In A. Darder & R. Torres (eds.), *The Latino studies reader: Culture, economy, and society*. Massachusetts: Blackwell Publishers.

San Antonio Express News (1999). Death row: Death row history. Available at: http://express-news.com/news/deathrow/history.shtml.

San Diego Union-Tribune (1994). A binational dance with death Mexicans on U.S. death row stir a growing furor. August 18:B11,13,15.

San Diego Union-Tribune (1993). Mexico's influence growing in U.S. political, fiscal clout now felt. August 22:A1.

San Diego Union-Tribune (1987). Texas executes murderer called jail-house lawyer. January 30:A20.

San Diego Union-Tribune (1986). Killer-rapist is executed by injection; 10th put to death in Texas this year. December 18:A14.

San Diego Union-Tribune (1985a). Texas man put to death for slaying. July 9:A4, 8.

San Diego Union-Tribune (1985b). Texas executes man for 1979 six-pack' murder. May 15:A3.

San Francisco Chronicle (1993a). Mexican officials visit San Quentin death row. August 7:B4.

San Francisco Chronicle (1993b). Mexico to fight California executions. August 5:A15.

San Francisco Chronicle (1985). March 8.

Savitz, L. (1973). Black crime. In K. Miller & R. Dreger (eds.), *Comparative studies of blacks and whites in the United States*. New York: Seminar Press.

Sellin, T. (1980). *The penalty of death*. Beverly Hills: Sage Publications.

Sellin, T. (1959). *The death penalty*. Philadelphia: American Law Institute.

Shorris, E. (1992). *Latinos: A biography of the people*. New York: W W Norton & Company.

Silko, L.M. (1994). America's iron curtain: The border patrol states. *Nation*, 259(12):412.

Silva, M. (2000). Seniors, Cuban exiles key forces. *The Miami Herald*, November 9. Available at: http://www.rose-hulman.edu/~delacova/exile/exile-vote.htm.

Simon, R. (1990). Virulent foot-in-mouth disease strikes again. *Los Angeles Times*, April 1:E7.

Smith, M. (1987). Patterns of discrimination in assessment of the death penalty: The Case of Louisiana. *Journal of Criminal Justice*, 15:179-286.

Snell, T.L. (1996). Capital punishment 1995. U.S. Department of Justice, Bureau of Justice Statistics.

Sorensen, J.R. & Wallace, D.H. (1995). Capital punishment in Missouri: Examining the issue of racial disparity. *Behavioral Sciences and the Law*, 13:61-80.

Spitzer, S. (1975). Toward a Marxian theory of deviance. *Social Problems*, 22:638-651.

Spohn, C. & Holleran, D. (2000). The imprisonment penalty paid by youth, unemployed black and Hispanic male offenders. *Criminology*, 38(1):281-306.

Stein, N. (1995). Questions and answers about affirmative action. *Social Justice: A Journal of Crime, Conflict, and World Order*, 22(3):45-52.

St. Petersburg Times (1989a). Santeria dust fails defendants. May 2:B2.

St. Petersburg Times (1989b). Three executions scheduled. April 19:B2.

Streib, V. (1999). Personal communication with author via e-mail. December 20, 1999.

Swigert, V.L. & Farrell, R.A. (1977). Normal homicides and the law. *American Sociological Review*, 42:16-32.

Tabb, W. (1970). *The political economy of the black ghetto*. New York: W W Norton & Company.

Terman, L. (1906). Genius and stupidity: A study of some of the intellectual processes of seven 'bright' and seven 'stupid' boys. *Pedagogical Seminary*, 13:307-373.

Texas Department of Corrections (1999). Personal communication with author via e-mail. June 20, 1999.

Texas Department of Criminal Justice (1999). Defendant's information was provided to the author by Christina Wooderson, administrative assistant for public information. June 10, 1999.

Texnews (1999). Report: U.S. operates double standard when Mexicans are arrested for murder. Available at: http://texnews.com/texas97/execute 092997.html (September 29, 1997 page 1-2).

Thomson, E. (1997). Discrimination and the death penalty in Arizona. *Criminal Justice Review*, 22(1):65-76.

Thomson, R. & Zimgraff, M. (1981). Detecting sentencing disparity: Some problems and evidence. *American Journal of Sociology*, 86:869-880.

Thorsen, L. (2002). Brown County leader vetoes making English official language. *Milwaukee Journal Sentinel*, August 20. Available at: http://www.jsonline.com/news/metro/aug02/67935.asp.

Thurow, L. (1995). Falling wages are America's major economic problem. *St. Petersburg Times*, September 11.

Tierney, C. (1992). Mexicans view U.S. death penalty as barbaric. *Reuters*, September 23: available in LEXIS.

Time (1970). J. Edgar Hoover speaks out with vigor. December 14, 16-17.

Tonry, M. (1995). *Malign neglect: Race, crime, and punishment in America.* New York: Oxford University Press.

Tonry, M. (1992). Proportionality, interchangeability, and intermediate punishments. In R. Dobash, R.A. Duff & S. Marshall (eds.), *Penal theory and penal practice.* Manchester: University of Stirling.

Toosi, N. (2002). English-only measured approved. *Milwaukee Journal Sentinel*, July 17. Available at: http://www.jsonline.com/news/state/jul02/59757.asp.

Torres, M. (1998). Encuentros y encontronazos: Homeland in the politics and identity of the Cuban diaspora. In A. Darder & R. Torres (eds.), *The Latino studies reader: Culture, economy, and society.* Massachusetts: Blackwell Publishers.

Trujillo, L. (1974). La evolucion del bandido 'Al Pachuco': A critical examination of criminological literature on Chicanos. *Issues in Criminology*, 9:43-67.

Turk, A. (1969). *Criminality and legal order.* Chicago: Rand McNally.

University of California, Office of the President (2003). Mexican-origin population in California: Health fact sheet. Available at: http://www.ucop.edu/cprc/mexoriginfacts.pdf.

Urbina, M.G. (2002a). Death sentence outcomes. In D. Levinson (ed.), *Encyclopedia of Crime and Punishment*, 2:482-485. Thousand Oaks: Sage.

Urbina, M.G. (2002b). *Furman* and *Gregg* exit death row?: Un-weaving an old controversy. *The Justice Professional*, 15(2):105-125.

U.S. Department of Justice (1994). An analysis of non-violent drug offenders with minimal criminal histories. February 4.

U.S. Department of Justice, Bureau of Justice Statistics (1997). Capital punishment in the United States, 1973-1995, [computer file]. Compiled by the U.S. Department of Commerce, Bureau of the Census. ICPSR (ed.), Ann Arbor, Michigan: *Inter-university Consortium for Political and Social Research* [producer and distributor].

Vandiver, M. (1999). An apology does not assist the accused: Foreign nationals and the death penalty in the United States. *The Justice Professional,* 12:223-245.

Vandiver, M. (1993). The quality of mercy: Race and clemency in Florida death penalty cases, 1924-1966. *University of Richmond Law Review,* 27(2):315-343.

Vick, D. (1995). Poorhouse justice: Underfunded indigent defense services and arbitrary death sentences. *Buffalo Law Review,* 43(2):329-460.

Vito, G. & Keil, T. (1988). Capital sentencing in Kentucky: An analysis of the factors influencing decision making in the post-*Gregg* period. *Journal of Criminal Law and Criminology,* 79(2):483-503.

von Hirsch, A. (1993). *Censure and sanctions.* New York: Oxford/Clarendon Press.

von Hirsch, A. (1981). Doing justice: The principle of commensurate desserts. In H. Gross & A. von Hirsch (eds.), *Sentencing.* New York: Oxford University Press.

Wagner-Pacifici, R. (1994). *Discourse and destruction.* Chicago: The University of Chicago Press.

Walker, S. (1994). *Sense and nonsense about crime and drugs: A policy guide* (third edition). Belmont: Wadsworth Publishing Company.

Walker, S. (1980). *Popular justice: A history of American criminal justice.* New York: Oxford University Press.

Wallace, D. & Humphries, D. (1981). Urban crime and capitalist accumulation: 1950-1971. In D. Greenberg (ed.), *Crime and capitalism,* 140-157. Palo Alto: Mayfield Publishing Company.

Warren, M. (1999). Foreign nationals and the death penalty in the United States. Available at: http://www.essential.org/dpic/foreignnatl.html.

Washington Post (1994). For the road. July 8:A22.

Washington Post (1993). Texas, California executions. August 25:A9.

Weber, D. (1999). N.A.A.C.P. Chief to urge study of racial 'profiling' by cops. *Boston Herald,* April 12, A5.

Weekly Arizonian. June 30, 1859.

Weekly Alta Californian. May 28, 1859.

Weinberg, M. (1977). *Minority students: Research appraisal.* Washington, D.C.: U.S. Department of Health, Education and Welfare.

Wilbanks, W. (1987). *The myth of a racist criminal justice system.* Belmont: Wadsworth.

Wilbanks, W. (1986). Are female felons treated more leniently by the criminal justice system? *Justice Quarterly,* 3(4):517-529.

Williams, P. (1997). *Seeing a color-blind future: The paradox of race.* New York: The Noonday Press.

Wilson, W.J. (1987). *The truly disadvantaged.* Chicago: University of Chicago Press.

Winfree, L.T. & Abadinsky, H. (1996). *Understanding crime: Theory and practice.* Chicago: Nelson-Hall Publishers.

Wolf, E.D. (1964). Abstract analysis of jury sentencing in capital cases: New Jersey: 1937-1961. *Rutgers Law Review,* 19:56-64.

Wolfgang, M. (1978). The death penalty: Social philosophy and social science research. *Criminal Law Bulletin,* 14(1):18-33.

Wolfgang, M. (1974). Racial discrimination in the death sentence for rape. In W. Bowers (ed.), *Executions in America* (pp. 109-120). Lexington: D.C. Heath and Company.

Wolfgang, M., Kelly, A. & Nodle, H. (1962). Comparison of the executed and the commuted among admissions to death row. *Journal of Criminal Law, Criminology and Police Science*, 53(3):301-311.

Wolfgang, M.& Riedel, M. (1976). Rape, racial discrimination, and the death penalty. In H. Bedau & C. Pierce, *Capital Punishment in the United States* (pp. 99-121).

Wolfgang, M.& Riedel, M. (1975). Rape, race, and the death penalty in Georgia. *American Journal of Orthopsychiatry*, 45:658-668.

Wolfgang, M.& Riedel, M. (1973). Race, judicial discretion, and the death penalty. *The Annals*, 407:119-133.

Zatz, M. S. (1984). Race, ethnicity, and determinate sentencing: A new dimension to an old controversy. *Criminology*, 22(2):147-171.

Zatz, M. & Portillos, E. (2000). Voices from the barrio: Chicano/a gangs, families, and communities. *Criminology*, 38:369-402.

Zeisel, H. (1981). Race bias in the administration of the death penalty: The Florida experience. *Harvard Law Review*, 95:456-468.

Zimring, F., Eigen, J. & O'Malley, S. (1976). Punishing homicide in Philadelphia: Perspectives on the death penalty. *University of Chicago Law* Review, 43:227-252

Zuniga, J.A. (1993). The Wrong Man? *Houston Chronicle*, January 10:A1.

Index